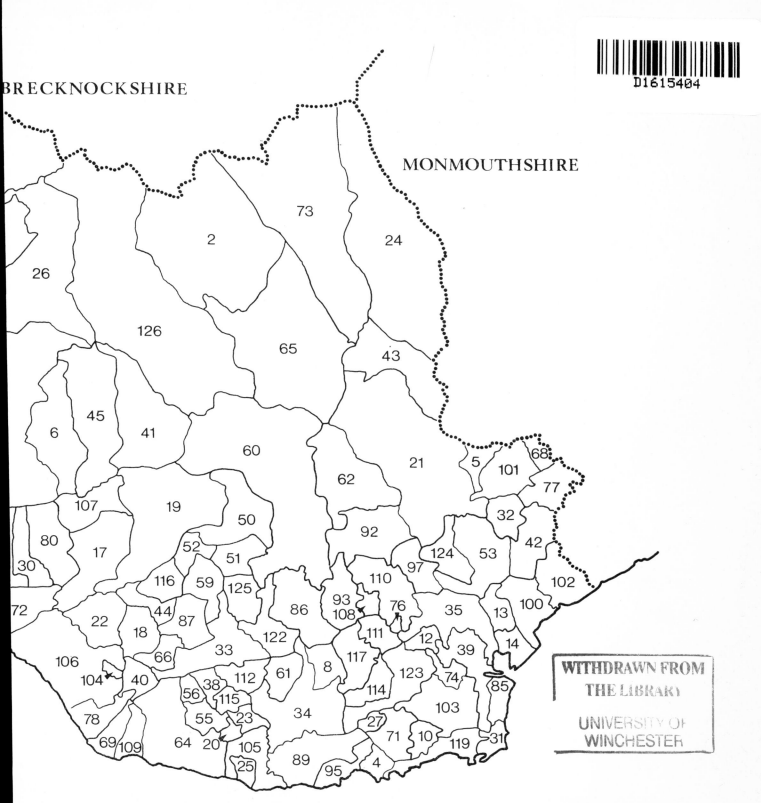

BRECKNOCKSHIRE

MONMOUTHSHIRE

The numbering of parishes on this map corresponds to that in the List of Ecclesiastical Parishes on p. xvii.

Llandough, pillar-cross (938), W. side; late 10th–early 11th century.

THE ROYAL COMMISSION
ON ANCIENT AND HISTORICAL MONUMENTS
IN WALES

AN INVENTORY OF THE ANCIENT MONUMENTS IN

GLAMORGAN

VOLUME I: PRE-NORMAN

PART III
THE EARLY CHRISTIAN PERIOD

CARDIFF
HER MAJESTY'S STATIONERY OFFICE

© Crown copyright 1976

First published 1976

ISBN 0 11 7005 90 8

TABLE OF CONTENTS

SUMMARY OF CONTENTS OF PARTS i AND ii OF VOLUME I

Introductory material, lists and indexes are similar in all three parts.

LIST OF PLATES

v

Plate 14, No. 922 is reproduced by permission of the National Museum of Wales.

LIST OF FIGURES

Figs. 10, 15 and 17 are reproduced by permission of the British Museum, and Fig. 9 by permission of the National Library of Wales. Figs. 1–5 and the end-papers are based on Ordnance Survey maps, with additions.

vii

CHAIRMAN'S PREFACE

IN this volume, the first of those for Glamorgan, the Commission has dealt with the pre-Norman remains of the county; the accepted monuments total some 800, and the staff concerned have examined 1030 sites during the course of the work. At the same time, the investigation of later remains has proceeded.

There are three major changes in this Inventory as compared with those for Caernarvonshire and Anglesey. The first is the arrangement of entries according to types of monument instead of by parishes. It is recognised that the user who is interested in the complete history of a limited area will find this a disadvantage, but the older system was excessively inconvenient for the growing number of students who are concerned with the study of particular periods. The new arrangement also makes it possible to place the entries for individual monuments in close conjunction with the relevant general discussion. Further, since the division of material by volumes corresponds roughly to the division of expert knowledge among the investigating staff, publication of one section does not need to await completion of another.

This arrangement makes a second change possible. The Commissioners have long been concerned that the high and increasing cost of printing has made the price of the Inventories almost prohibitive for many people. They have therefore arranged, with the co-operation of Her Majesty's Stationery Office, to publish the material in separate sections. The details of the arrangements which result are described in the note on the Presentation of Material.

The third major change is the omission of the lists of 'finds'. The grounds for this decision, which was reached with considerable regret, were three-fold. First, this branch of the work for Caernarvonshire absorbed a disproportionately large part of the time of the investigating staff especially of those concerned with the earlier monuments. Secondly, by the nature of the problem, the results could not even approach finality, for portable objects are continually being recovered from the soil, as demonstrated by the five pages of addenda given in the last volume of the Caernarvonshire Inventory; by contrast the list of surviving monuments can be completed at least in principle, although in practice a few escape record. Finally, it seems questionable whether small portable objects can be defined as 'monuments and constructions', and the preparation of such lists might therefore be regarded as outside the scope of the Commission's Warrant. Taking into consideration the great number of monuments requiring record, the rapidity with which specimens of many classes are destroyed, and the very limited number of staff available for the work it seems right in future to omit lists of finds.

Nevertheless there can be no question that such work is a very necessary contribution to archaeology, especially the accurate description of objects in private hands and the maintenance of a continuous record of new discoveries, and it is highly desirable that some organisation should be set up to continue it, whether by an extension of the field covered by the Commission or by some other means.

In view of some recent misunderstanding it seems desirable to explain that inclusion of a monument in the list of those recommended as 'most worthy of preservation' indicates that in the view of the Commissioners it is of quite exceptional importance. There are many other monuments which are of considerable interest and which should be preserved if at all possible.

Corrections or criticisms of the contents of this volume will be welcomed with a view to their possible inclusion in some future edition; they should be sent to the Secretary. Properly accredited persons may consult the records of the Commission at the headquarters at Edleston House, Queen's Road, Aberystwyth, Dyfed.

The contents of the volume are Crown Copyright, including most of the illustrations. Copies of these can be purchased through the Secretary of the Commission.

August 1973   W. F. GRIMES

REPORT

TO THE QUEEN'S MOST EXCELLENT MAJESTY

MAY IT PLEASE YOUR MAJESTY

We, the undersigned Commissioners, appointed to make an *Inventory of the Ancient and Historical Monuments and constructions connected with or illustrative of the contemporary culture, civilisation and conditions of life of the people in Wales from the earliest times, and to specify those which seem most worthy of preservation*, humbly submit to Your Majesty the following Report, being the fourteenth on the work of the Commission since its first appointment. This Report will accompany the first volume of the Inventory of Monuments in the County of Glamorgan.

2. It is with deep regret that we record the deaths of our former Commissioners Sir Cyril Fox and Sir Ifor Williams.

3. We have also to record the loss by retirement, on expiry of term of office, of our former Chairman Sir John Goronwy Edwards and of Professor Arthur Herbert Dodd.

4. We have to thank Your Majesty for the issue of a Commission under Your Majesty's Royal Sign Manual dated 28 September, 1963, revoking former Warrants but repeating the terms of reference given therein, and further empowering us to assume the general control and management of that part of the collection of the National Buildings Record which relates to Wales, and to make arrangements for the creation of a wider record concerning important sites and buildings throughout Wales.

5. We have to thank Your Majesty for the appointment of Professor William Francis Grimes to be Chairman of this Commission in succession to Sir John Goronwy Edwards for a period of ten years from January 1967, under Your Majesty's Royal Sign Manual dated 31 March, 1967.

6. We have also to thank Your Majesty for the appointment or re-appointment under Your Majesty's Royal Sign Manual of the following Commissioners: on 28 September, 1963, Professor Richard John Copland Atkinson, Professor Glanmor Williams and Dr. Raymond Bernard Wood-Jones, for nine years from 1963; on 31 March, 1967, Dr. John Davies Knatchbull Lloyd for seven years from 1967 and Professor John Gwynn Williams for ten years from 1967; and on 15 June, 1970, Professor Idris Llewelyn Foster, Professor Edward Martyn Jope, Dr. Arnold Joseph Taylor, Professor Dewi-Prys Thomas, and Dr. Hubert Newman Savory, for ten years from 1970, the first three being re-appointments. Tenure in each case is from 1 January.

7. We have pleasure in reporting the completion of our enquiries into the pre-Norman remains of the County of Glamorgan, in which we have recorded 803 Monuments. Rather more than 1000 sites were visited.

8. We have prepared a full Inventory of these Monuments, which will be issued as a non-Parliamentary publication.

9. We have considered the arrangement of the Inventory, and have concluded that for most users it will be more convenient to group the monuments by types rather than according to parishes. We are therefore adopting this system. We have also concluded that it will be an advantage to reduce the size of individual publications, and we have therefore arranged for this volume to be issued as three parts.

10. We desire to record our special thanks for valuable assistance from the owners and occupants of land where monuments exist; also from Professor L. Alcock, M.A., F.S.A.; Mr. G. C. Boon, B.A., F.S.A.; Mr. D. Q. Bowen, B.Sc., Ph.D.; Mr. J. B. Campbell, B.A.; Mr. C. B. Crampton, M.A., Ph.D.; Mr. J. L. Davies, B.A., F.S.A.; Mrs. B. Heywood, B.A., Ph.D., F.S.A.; Mr. M. G. Jarrett, B.A., Ph.D., F.S.A.; Mr. J. M. Lewis, M.A., F.S.A.; Mr. C. B. M. McBurney, M.A., Ph.D., F.B.A., F.S.A.; Mr. T. K. Penniman, M.A., F.S.A.; Professor J. K. S. St. Joseph, O.B.E., M.A., Ph.D., F.S.A.; Mr. G. de G. Sieveking, M.A., F.S.A.; Mrs. V. G. Swan, B.A.; Mr. R. J. Thomas, M.A.; Mr. D. P. Webley, B.Sc., D.I.C.; Sir Mortimer Wheeler, C.H.; Mr. D. R. Wilson, M.A., F.S.A.

11. We desire to express our acknowledgement of the good work of our executive staff; their names, and indications of their particular contributions, are included in the Inventory volumes.

12. We humbly recommend to Your Majesty's notice the following Monuments as most worthy of preservation:

CAVES
5. Goat's Hole.
8. Long Hole.
12. Minchin Hole.
16. Tooth Cave.
17. Cat Hole.

MESOLITHIC OPEN SITES
26. Burry Holms.

MEGALITHIC CHAMBERED TOMBS
33. Maen Ceti (Arthur's Stone).
36. Long Cairn, Parc Cwm.
40. Long Cairn, Tinkinswood.
42. Long Cairn, Maesyfelin.

CUP-MARKED STONES
49. Maen Catwg.

ROUND CAIRNS
57. Ring near Graig Fawr.
60. Ring on Tor Clawdd.
66. Carn Llechart.
111. Ring-cairn on Carn Caca.
153. Ring-cairn S.W. of Pen Garnbugail.
156. Carn Bugail.
173. Cairn on Rhosili Down.
262. Cairn S.E. of Mynyddherbert.
290. Cairn near Llyndwr Fawr.
348. Pebyll.
349. Crug yr Afan.
378-9. The Beacons.

GROUPS OF SMALL CAIRNS
482. Group on Mynydd Carnllechart.
484. Group on Mynydd y Capel.
490. Group near Tir-lan.

STANDING STONES
543. Stone N. of Knelston.
548. Mansel Jack (Sampson's Jack).
553. Carreg Bica.
554. Carreg Hir.

COOKING MOUNDS
586. Mound on Druids Moor.

HILL-FORTS AND RELATED STRUCTURES
In all these it is important that the interior should be protected as well as the ramparts.
613. Mynydd y Castell.
615. Castle Ditches, Llancarfan.
619. Gwersyll.
637. Coedcae Gaer.
646. Hardings Down, N. enclosure.
657. Caer Blaen-y-cwm.
665. Cil Ifor Top.
666. Dunraven.
667. Nash Point.
668. Castle Ditches, Llantwit Major.
669. Summerhouse Camp.
670. Caer Dynnaf.
671. Porthkerry Bulwarks.
673. Caerau, Ely.
678. Fort at Craig Tŷ-isaf.
681. Fort on Mynydd Bychan.
687–8. Hardings Down, W. and E. enclosures.
689. The Bulwark, Llanmadog.
690. Gaer Fawr.
693. Y Bwlwarcau.
698. Fort on Thurba Head.
699. Fort on The Knave.
700. Fort on Yellow Top.
705. Burry Holms Church site.

UNENCLOSED HUT SETTLEMENTS
711. Huts and enclosures above Garreg Lwyd.
715. Huts and enclosures, Buarth Maen.

ROMAN FORTS
731. Fort at Coelbren.
735. Fort at Cardiff.
737. Forts and annexe at Gelli-gaer.

OTHER ROMAN MILITARY WORKS
739. Marching camp, Blaen-cwm Bach.
741. Marching camp, Twyn y Briddallt.
743. W. Practice camp, Mynydd Carn-goch.
747 and 749. Practice camps, Fforest Gwladys.
751. Signal station on Hirfynydd.

ROMAN CIVIL SITES
758. Villa at Cae'r-mead.
762. Villa at Ely.

EARLY CHRISTIAN MONUMENTS
In most cases these are already in museums or churches.
841. Vicuritinus stone, Clwydi Banwen.
843. Tegernacus stone, Gelli-gaer.
844. Inscribed stone, Llanmadog.
846. Cantusus stone, Port Talbot.
847. Paulus stone, Merthyr Mawr.
848. Bodvocus stone, Mynydd Margam.
849. Pumpeius stone, Eglwys Nynnid.
850. Vendumaglus stone, Capel Llanilltern.
902. Carved slab, Nash.
907. Conbelin stone, Margam.
908. Enniaun stone, Margam.
911. Houelt stone, Llantwit Major.
912. Samson stone, Llantwit Major.
933. Ithel stone, Llantwit Major.
938. Irbicus stone, Llandough.
951. Carved slab, Llanrhidian.

The Monuments in this list have been selected solely with regard to their archaeological or historical importance. We consider that these are outstanding from that point of view; there are many other Monuments which are of considerable interest and which deserve protection.

All! of which we submit with our humble duty to Your Majesty.

(Signed) W. F. GRIMES *(Chairman)*
R. J. C. ATKINSON
I. LL. FOSTER
E. M. JOPE
J. D. K. LLOYD
H. N. SAVORY
A. J. TAYLOR
D.-P. THOMAS
G. WILLIAMS
J. G. WILLIAMS
R. B. WOOD-JONES
A. H. A. HOGG *(Secretary)*

COMMISSIONERS AND STAFF

During the preparation of this volume (1963–1972), the following Members, appointed by Royal Warrant, have served on the Commission:

Sir (John) Goronwy Edwards, M.A., D.Litt.(Oxon), F.B.A., F.S.A., Emeritus Professor of History in the University of London. (Chairman, retired 1967.)

William Francis Grimes, C.B.E., M.A., D.Litt., F.S.A., F.M.A., Professor of Archaeology in the University of London and Director of the Institute of Archaeology. (Appointed Chairman 1967 for ten years.)

Richard John Copland Atkinson, M.A., F.S.A., Professor of Archaeology in the University College of South Wales and Monmouthshire. (Appointed 1963 for nine years.)

Arthur Herbert Dodd, M.A., D.Litt., F.R.Hist.S., Emeritus Professor of History in the University College of North Wales. (Re-appointed 1963, retired 1966.)

Idris Llewelyn Foster, M.A., F.S.A., Jesus Professor of Celtic in the University of Oxford. (Re-appointed 1970 for ten years.)

Edward Martyn Jope, M.A., B.Sc., F.B.A., F.S.A., Professor of Archaeology in The Queen's University, Belfast. (Re-appointed 1970 for ten years.)

John Davies Knatchbull Lloyd, O.B.E., D.L., J.P., M.A., LL.D., F.S.A., Chairman of the Ancient Monuments Board for Wales. (Appointed 1967 for seven years.)

Hubert Newman Savory, M.A., D.Phil., F.S.A., Keeper of Archaeology in the National Museum of Wales. (Appointed 1970 for ten years.)

Arnold Joseph Taylor, C.B.E., M.A., D.Litt., F.B.A., Dir.S.A., F.R.Hist.S., Chief Inspector of Ancient Monuments and Historic Buildings. (Re-appointed 1970 for ten years.)

Dewi-Prys Thomas, B.Arch., F.R.I.B.A., M.R.T.P.I., Professor of Architecture and Head of the Welsh School of Architecture. (Appointed 1970 for ten years.)

Glanmor Williams, M.A., D.Litt., F.R.Hist.S., Professor of History in the University College of Swansea. (Appointed 1963 for nine years.)

John Gwynn Williams, M.A., Professor of Welsh History in the University College of North Wales. (Appointed 1967 for ten years.)

Raymond Bernard Wood-Jones, M.A., B.Arch., Ph.D., F.S.A., A.R.I.B.A., Architect, and Senior Lecturer in the School of Architecture of the University of Manchester. (Appointed 1963 for nine years.)

STAFF

During the preparation of this volume (1963–1972), the following have served as Staff of the Commission.

Investigating Staff
Secretary	Mr. A. H. A. Hogg, C.B.E., M.A., F.S.A.
Investigators	Mr. H. Brooksby (from 1969).
	Mr. L. A. S. Butler, Ph.D., F.S.A. (to 1965).
	Mr. W. E. Griffiths, M.A., F.S.A.
	Mr. D. B. Hague, A.R.I.B.A., F.S.A.
	Mr. C. H. Houlder, M.A., F.S.A.
	Mr. C. N. Johns, M.A., F.S.A. (to 1969).
	Mrs. B. A. Morris, B.A. (1966 to 1967).
	Mr. A. J. Parkinson, B.A. (from 1970).
	Mr. P. Smith, B.A., F.S.A.
	Mr. C. J. Spurgeon, B.A., F.S.A.
	Mr. H. J. Thomas, B.A. (from 1969).
	Mr. W. G. Thomas, M.A., F.S.A.

Ancillary Staff
Executive Officer	Mr. E. Whatmore (from 1965).
Research Assistants	Mrs. E. T. Richards, B.Sc. (from 1970).
	Mr. J. F. O'N. Russell, M.A. (1968 to 1970).
Illustrating Staff	Mr. C. Baker (from 1971).
	Mr. D. J. Roberts (from 1966).
Photographic Staff	Mr. H. Brooksby (to 1969).
	Mr. R. G. Nicol (from 1970).
	Mr. C. J. Parrott (from 1970).
	Miss J. R. Rogers (1968 to 1970).
Audio Typist	Miss D. M. Ward.
Clerical Staff	Miss B. M. Davies (from 1970).
	Miss G. M. Davies (1966 to 1967).
	Miss C. A. Griffiths (from 1969).
	Miss P. A. Lawden (to 1966).
	Miss A. R. Williams (1967 to 1969).

Authorship and compilation of sections of this Volume were allocated as follows:

Part i.	Caves; Neolithic Burial and Ritual Structures—C. H. Houlder.
	Bronze Age Burial and Ritual Structures; Cooking Mounds—W. E. Griffiths.
Part ii.	Hill-forts and Related structures; Hut Settlements—A. H. A. Hogg.
	Roman Remains—W. E. Griffiths.
Part iii.	Dykes—A. H. A. Hogg.
	Monastic Sites—D. B. Hague and W. G. Thomas.
	Inscribed and Sculptured Stones—W. G. Thomas.
All Parts.	Physical Background—C. H. Houlder.
	Communications—A. H. A. Hogg.

LIST OF ECCLESIASTICAL PARISHES

WITH INCIDENCE OF MONUMENTS

THIS list corresponds with the map forming the end-paper at the front of the book, and indicates the ecclesiastical subdivision of Glamorgan into parishes as it stood *ca.* 1850, before any of the changes of names and boundaries which have taken place for administrative purposes (*cf.* back end-paper and list on p. xxi).

Ecclesiastical parishes are noted at the end of Inventory entries, distinguished by the letter (E) when the monument concerned stands in a civil parish of a different name (C). Spellings used are as shown on the left, generally agreeing with those used on O.S. maps current in 1970. The only departures from this practice (other than cases simply involving hyphens or capitals) are indicated by the addition of the map spellings in square brackets. The Welsh forms, which follow the recommendations of the Board of Celtic Studies, are given on the right only when they differ from those already adopted for use in this Inventory.

Nos. 5, 68 and 77 are parts of parishes which straddle the Monmouthshire border. No. 102 is included as a result of the expansion of Cardiff.

No.	Parish name used	Correct Welsh form	Monument Nos.
1	Aberavon	Aberafan	884 887
2	Aberdâr [Aberdare]		803 810
3	Baglan		886 923 961
4	Barry	Y Barri	————
5	Bedwas (Van hamlet)		————
6	Betws [Bettws]		————
7	Bishopston	Llandeilo Ferwallt	822
8	Bonvilston	Tresimwn	————
9	Briton Ferry	Llansawel	————
10	Cadoxton-juxta-Barry	Tregatwg	————
11	Cadoxton-juxta-Neath	Llangatwg Nedd	841 869 871 904
12	Caerau		————
13	Cardiff St. John	Caerdydd ————	————
14	Cardiff St. Mary	Caerdydd ————	830 893
15	Cheriton	————	————
16	Cilybebyll		————
17	Coety [Coity]		807 936 939 1003
18	Colwinston	Tregolwyn	————
19	Coychurch	Llangrallo	934 935
20	Eglwys Brewys [Eglwysbrewis]		————
21	Eglwysilan		812 891
22	Ewenni [Ewenny]		924 955 975–981
23	Flemingston	Trefflemin	
24	Gelli-gaer		804 805 842 843 881 892

No.	Parish name used	Correct Welsh form	Monument Nos.
25	Gileston	Silstwn	———
26	Glyncorrwg		———
27	Highlight	Uchelola	———
28	Ilston	Llanilltud Gŵyr	———
29	Knelston	Llan-y-tair-mair	———
30	Laleston	Trelales	963 972
31	Lavernock	Larnog	———
32	Lisvane	Llys-faen	———
33	Llanblethian	Llanfleiddan	902
34	Llancarfan		827 940
35	Llandaf [Llandaff]		829 937 985
36	Llanddewi		———
37	Llandeilo Tal-y-bont		———
38	Llandough (near Cowbridge)	Llandochau	———
39	Llandough, Cogan and Leckwith	Llandochau, Cogan a Lecwydd	828 938
40	Llandŵ [Llandow]		———
41	Llandyfodwg		811
42	Llanedern [Llanedeyrn]		———
43	Llanfabon		———
44	Llan-gan		913 925 982
45	Llangeinwyr [Llangeinor]		809
46	Llangennith	Llangynydd	821 905
47	Llanguicke	Llan-giwg	986
48	Llangyfelach		801 823 882 883 903 931 933
49	Llangynwyd		808 988
50	Llanharan		———
51	Llanhari [Llanharry]		———
52	Llanilid		———
53	Llanisien [Llanishen]		———
54	Llanmadog [Llanmadoc]		844 865 866
55	Llanmaes	Llan-faes	———
56	Llanmihangel	Llanfihangel y Bont-faen	———
57	Llanrhidian		951
58	Llansamlet		———
59	Llansanwyr [Llansannor]		———
60	Llantrisant		888 992
61	Llantrithyd	Llantriddyd	———
62	Llantwit Fardre	Llanilltud Faerdref	———
63	Llantwit-juxta-Neath	Llanilltud Nedd	806 861 915
64	Llantwit Major	Llanilltud Fawr	826 911 912 932 953 954 974
65	Llanwynno [Llanwonno]		863 889 890
66	Llyswyrny [Llysworney]		956
67	Loughor	Casllwchwr	845
68	Machen (Rhyd-y-gwern hamlet)		———
69	Marcroes [Marcross]		———

No.	Parish name used	Correct Welsh form	Monument Nos.
70	Margam		825 846 848 849 868 870 885 901 906–910 914 919–921 929 973 991
71	Merthyr Dyfan		————
72	Merthyr Mawr		824 847 917 918 927 928 952 964–970 987
73	Merthyr Tudful [Merthyr Tydfil]		862
74	Michaelston-le-Pit	Llanfihangel-y-pwll	————
75	Michaelston-super-Avon	Llanfihangel-ynys-Afan	————
76	Michaelston-super-Ely	Llanfihangel-ar-Elái	————
77	Michaelston-y-Vedw (Llanfedw hamlet)	Llanfihangel-y-fedw	————
78	Monknash	Yr As Fawr	————
79	Neath	Castell-nedd	————
80	Newcastle	Y Castellnewydd	922 983 984
81	Newton Nottage	Drenewydd yn Notais	————
82	Nicholaston	————	————
83	Oxwich	————	————
84	Oystermouth	Ystumllwynarth	1001
85	Penarth		————
86	Pendeulwyn [Pendoylan]		————
87	Pen-llin [Penllyn]		————
88	Pen-maen		————
89	Pen-marc [Penmark]		————
90	Pennard		————
91	Penrice	Pen-rhys	————
92	Pen-tyrch		————
93	Peterston-super-Ely	Llanbedr-y-fro	————
94	Port Einon [Porteynon]		————
95	Porthkerry	Porthceri	————
96	Pyle and Kenfig	Y Pîl a Cynffig	971
97	Radur [Radyr]		————
98	Reynoldston	————	864
99	Rhosili		————
100	Roath	Y Rhath	————
101	Rudry	Rhydri	————
102	Rumney (formerly in Monmouthshire)	Tredelerch	————
103	St. Andrews	Saint Andras	————
104	St. Andrews Minor	————	————
105	St. Athan	Sain Tathan	————
106	St. Brides Major and Wick	Saint-y-brid ac Y Wig	926 1002
107	St. Brides Minor	Llansanffraid-ar-Ogwr	————
108	St. Brides-super-Ely	Llansanffraid-ar-Elái	————
109	St. Donats	Sain Dynwyd	————
110	St. Fagans with Llanilterne	Sain Ffagan gyda Llanilltern	850
111	St. George	Sain Siorys	941

No.	Parish name used	Correct Welsh form	Monument Nos.
112	St. Hilary	Saint Hilari	———
113	St. John-juxta-Swansea	———	———
114	St. Lythans	Llwyneliddon	———
115	St. Mary Church	Llan-fair	———
116	St. Mary Hill	Eglwys Fair y Mynydd	———
117	St. Nicholas	Sain Nicolas	———
118	Sker (extra-parochial)	Y Sgêr	———
119	Sully	Sili	———
120	Swansea	Abertawe	———
121	Tythegston	Llandudwg	916 962
122	Welsh St. Donats	Llanddunwyd	———
123	Wenvoe	Gwenfô	———
124	Whitchurch	Yr Eglwys Newydd	———
125	Ystradowen		———
126	Ystradyfodwg		802 803 811
127	Land common to five parishes: Llanrhidian, Nicholaston, Pen-maen, Penrice, Reynoldston		———

LIST OF CIVIL PARISHES

WITH INCIDENCE OF MONUMENTS

THIS list corresponds with the map forming the end-paper at the back of the book, and indicates the civil subdivision of Glamorgan into parishes as it stood at the end of 1970. The boundaries and the names have undergone many changes since the original adoption of the ecclesiastical pattern for secular administrative purposes (*cf.* front end-paper and list on p. xvii), and modifications will continue to be made.

Civil parishes are noted at the end of Inventory entries, distinguished by the letter (C) when the monument concerned stands in an ecclesiastical parish of a different name (E). Spellings used are as shown on the left, in general agreeing with those used on the O.S. 1:100,000 Administrative Areas map, 1970. The only departures from this practice (other than cases simply involving hyphens or capitals) are indicated by the addition of the O.S. spelling in square brackets. The Welsh forms, which follow the recommendations of the Board of Celtic Studies, are given on the right only when they differ from those already adopted for use in this Inventory.

No.	Parish name used	Correct Welsh form	Monument Nos.
1	Aberdâr [Aberdare]		803 810
2	Baglan Higher		923
3	Barry	Y Barri	————
4	Betws [Bettws]		————
5	Bishopston	Llandeilo Ferwallt	822
6	Blaen-gwrach		————
7	Blaenhonddan		869
8	Bonvilston	Tresimwn	————
9	Bridgend	Pen-y-bont ar Ogwr	983 984
10	Cardiff	Caerdydd	829 830 893 937 985
11	Cheriton	————	
12	Cilybebyll		————
13	Clyne	Y Clun	861
14	Coed-ffranc		————
15	Coety Higher [Coity H.]	Coety Uchaf	936 939 1003
16	Colwinston	Tregolwyn	————
17	Cowbridge	Y Bont-faen	————
18	Coychurch Higher	Llangrallo Uchaf	————
19	Coychurch Lower	Llangrallo Isaf	934 935
20	Cwm-du		————
21	Dulais Higher [Dylais H.]	Dulais Uchaf	841 904
22	Dulais Lower [Dylais L.]	Dulais Isaf	————
23	Dyffryn Clydach		————

No.	Parish name used	Correct Welsh form	Monument Nos.
24	Eglwys Brewys [Eglwysbrewis]		871
25	Eglwysilan		812
26	Ewenni [Ewenny]		924 955 975–981
27	Flemingston	Trefflemin	———
28	Gelli-gaer		804 805 842 843 881 892
29	Gileston	Silstwn	———
30	Glyncorrwg		808
31	Gowerton	Tre-gŵyr	———
32	Ilston	Llanilltud Gŵyr	———
33	Kenfig	Cynffig	971
34	Knelston	Llan-y-tair-mair	———
35	Laleston	Trelales	963 972
36	Lavernock	Larnog	———
37	Leckwith	Lecwydd	———
38	Lisvane	Llys-faen	———
39	Llanblethian	Llanfleiddan	———
40	Llancarfan		827 940
41	Llanddewi		———
42	Llandeilo Tal-y-bont		———
43	Llandŵ [Llandow]		———
44	Llandyfodwg		811
45	Llanedern [Llanedeyrn]		———
46	Llanfabon		———
47	Llan-fair		———
48	Llanfedw		———
49	Llanfythin	Llanfeuthin	———
50	Llan-gan		913 925 982
51	Llangeinwyr [Llangeinor]		809
52	Llangennith	Llangynydd	821 905
53	Llanguicke	Llan-giwg	986
54	Llangyfelach		823 882 883 931
55	Llangynwyd Higher	Llangynwyd Uchaf	———
56	Llangynwyd Lower	Llangynwyd Isaf	———
57	Llangynwyd Middle	Llangynwyd Ganol	988
58	Llanharan		———
59	Llanhari [Llanharry]		———
60	Llanilid		———
61	Llanilltern [Llanilterne]		850
62	Llanmadog [Llanmadoc]		844 865 866
63	Llanmaes	Llan-faes	———
64	Llanmihangel	Llanfihangel y Bont-faen	———
65	Llanrhidian Higher	Llanrhidian Uchaf	———
66	Llanrhidian Lower	Llanrhidian Isaf	951
67	Llansanwyr [Llansannor]		———
68	Llantrisant		888 992
69	Llantrithyd	Llantriddyd	———
70	Llantwit Fardre	Llanilltud Faerdref	———

No.	Parish name used	Correct Welsh form	Monument Nos.
71	Llantwit Major	Llanilltud Fawr	826 911 912 932 933 953 954 974
—	Llanvithyn (see Llanfythin)		
72	Llanwynno [Llanwonno]		863 889 890
73	Llyswyrny [Llysworney]		956
74	Loughor Borough	Casslwchwr	845
75	Marcroes [Marcross]		———
76	Mawr		801
77	Merthyr Mawr		807 824 847 917 918 927 928 952 964–970 987
78	Merthyr Tudful [Merthyr Tydfil]		862
79	Michaelston Higher	Llanfihangel-ynys-Afan	———
80	Michaelston-le-Pit	Llanfihangel-y-pwll	———
81	Monknash	Yr As Fawr	———
82	Nash	Yr As Fach	902
83	Neath	Castell-nedd	———
84	Neath Higher	Castell-nedd Uchaf	841
85	Neath Lower	Castell-nedd Isaf	———
86	Newcastle Higher	Castellnewydd Uchaf	922
87	Newton Nottage	Drenewydd yn Notais	———
88	Nicholaston	———	———
89	Oxwich	———	———
90	Oystermouth	Ystumllwynarth	1001
91	Penarth		828 938
92	Pen-coed		———
93	Pendeulwyn [Pendoylan]		———
94	Pen-llin [Penllyn]		———
95	Pen-maen		———
96	Pen-marc [Penmark]		———
97	Pennard		———
98	Penrice	Pen-rhys	———
99	Pen-tyrch		———
100	Peterston-super-Ely	Llanbedr-y-fro	———
101	Peterston-super-montem	Llanbedr-ar-fynydd	———
102	Pontypridd		812 891
103	Port Einon [Porteynon]		———
104	Porthkerry[1]	Porthceri	———
105	Port Talbot		825 846 848 849 868 870 884–887 901 906–910 914 919–921 929 961 973 991
106	Pyle	Y Pîl	971
107	Radur [Radyr]		———
108	Resolfen [Resolven]		———
109	Reynoldston	———	864
110	Rhigos	Rugos	802 803

[1] The unnumbered area on the back end-paper map between 96 and 3 is a detached portion of Porthkerry.

No.	Parish name used	Correct Welsh form	Monument Nos.
111	Rhondda		802 811
112	Rhosili [Rhossili]		———
113	Rhyd-y-gwern		———
114	Rhyndwyglydach [Rhyndwyclydach]		903
115	Rudry	Rhydri	———
116	St. Andrews Major	Saint Andras	———
117	St. Andrews Minor	———	———
118	St. Athan	Sain Tathan	———
119	St. Brides Major	Saint-y-brid	926 1002
120	St. Brides Minor	Llansanffraid-ar-Ogwr	———
121	St. Brides-super-Ely	Llansanffraid-ar-Elái	———
122	St. Donats	Sain Dunwyd	———
123	St. Fagans	Sain Ffagan	———
124	St. George	Sain Siorys	941
125	St. Hilary	Saint Hilari	———
126	St. Lythans	Llwyneliddon	———
127	St. Mary Hill	Eglwys Fair y Mynydd	———
128	St. Nicholas	Sain Nicolas	———
129	Sker	Y Sgêr	———
130	Stembridge	———	———
131	Sully	Sili	———
132	Swansea	Abertawe	———
133	Tongwynlais		———
134	Tonna		806 915
135	Tythegston Higher	Llandudwg Uchaf	———
136	Tythegston Lower	Llandudwg Isaf	916 962
137	Van	Y Fan	———
138	Welsh St. Donats	Llanddunwyd	———
139	Wenvoe	Gwenfô	———
140	Wick	Y Wig	———
141	Ynysawdre		———
142	Ynysymwn [Ynysymond]		———
143	Ystradowen		———
144	Land common to six parishes: Llanrhidian Higher & Lower, Nicholaston, Pen-maen, Penrice, Reynoldston		———

ABBREVIATED TITLES OF REFERENCES

Ann. Camb.	J. Williams 'ab Ithel' (ed.), *Annales Cambriae*, Rolls Series (London, 1860).
Arch. Camb.	*Archaeologia Cambrensis*. The Cambrian Archaeological Association.
Arch. in Wales	*Archaeology in Wales*. Council for British Archaeology, Group 2.
Arch. Journ.	*The Archaeological Journal*. The Royal Archaeological Institute.
Bartrum, *Tracts*	P. C. Bartrum, *Early Welsh Genealogical Tracts* (Cardiff, 1966).
B.B.C.S.	*Bulletin of the Board of Celtic Studies*. University of Wales.
B.M.	British Museum, London.
Brut (Peniarth)	T. Jones (ed.), *Brut y Tywysogyon*, Peniarth MS. 20 version (Cardiff, 1952). Board of Celtic Studies, History and Law Series, No. 11.
Camden, *Britannia*	W. Camden, *Britannia* ... (1 vol., ed. E. Gibson, London, 1695; 4 vols., ed. R. Gough, London, 1806).
Carlisle, *Top. Dict.*	N. Carlisle, *A Topographical Dictionary of Wales* (London, 1811).
Celt and Saxon	N. K. Chadwick (ed.), *Celt and Saxon: Studies in the Early British Border* (Cambridge, 1963).
C.I.I.C.	R. A. S. Macalister, *Corpus Inscriptionum Insularum Celticarum* (2 vols., Dublin, 1945).
Clark, *Cartae*	G. T. Clarke, *Cartae et alia munimenta quae ad dominium de Glamorgan pertinent* (6 vols., 2nd edn., Cardiff, 1910).
Collingwood, *Northumbrian Crosses*	W. G. Collingwood, *Northumbrian Crosses of the pre-Norman age* (London, 1921).
Davies, *W. Gower*	J. D. Davies, *The History of West Gower* (4 vols., Swansea, 1877, 1879, 1885, 1894).
E.C.M.S.	J. R. Allen, *The Early Christian Monuments of Scotland* (Edinburgh, 1903).
E.C.M.W.	V. E. Nash-Williams, *The Early Christian Monuments of Wales* (Cardiff, 1950).
Epis. Acts	J. Conway Davies (ed.), *Episcopal Acts and cognate documents relating to Welsh Dioceses, 1066–1272* (2 vols., Cardiff, 1948, 1953).
Henry, *Irish Art*	F. Henry, I: *Irish Art in the Early Christian Period (to 800 A.D.)* (London, 1965). III: *Irish Art in the Romanesque Period (1020–1170 A.D.*, London, 1970).
H.M.S.O.	Her Majesty's Stationery Office, London/Edinburgh.
Inv. Anglesey, Caerns., Herefs.	R.C.A.M. (Wales), *An Inventory of the Ancient Monuments in Anglesey* (1937); ... *Caernarvonshire* (3 vols., 1956, 1960, 1964); R.C.H.M. (England), *An Inventory of the Historical Monuments in Herefordshire* (3 vols., 1931, 1932, 1934). All H.M.S.O.

Jackson, *Lang. and Hist.*	K. Jackson, *Language and History in Early Britain* (Edinburgh, 1953).
Kermode, *Manx Crosses*	P. M. C. Kermode, *Manx Crosses* (London, 1907).
Lhuyd, *Parochialia*	E. Lhuyd, *Parochialia* (3 parts, *Arch. Camb.* supplements, 1909–11, ed. R. H. Morris).
Lib. Land.	J. G. Evans and J. Rhys (eds.), *Liber Landavensis. The text of the Book of Llan Dav* (Oxford, 1893).
Lloyd, *Hist. Wales*	J. E. Lloyd, *A History of Wales from the Earliest Times to the Edwardian Conquest* (2 vols., London, 1911).
Morgan, *E. Gower*	W. Ll. Morgan, *An Antiquarian Survey of East Gower* (London, 1899).
N.L.W.	National Library of Wales, Aberystwyth.
North Munster Studies	E. Rynne (ed.), *North Munster Studies* (Limerick, 1967).
O.D.	Ordnance Datum.
O.S.	Ordnance Survey.
P. and E. Wales	I. Ll. Foster and G. E. Daniel (eds.), *Prehistoric and Early Wales* (London, 1965).
Radford, *Ewenny*	C. A. R. Radford, *Ewenny Priory* (H.M.S.O. guide, 1952).
Radford, *Margam*	C. A. R. Radford, *Margam Stones Museum* (H.M.S.O. guide, 1949).
R.C.A.M.	The Royal Commission on Ancient and Historical Monuments in Wales.
R.C.H.M.	The Royal Commission on Ancient and Historical Monuments in England.
Roman Inscriptions	R. G. Collingwood and R. P. Wright, *The Roman Inscriptions of Britain: I, Inscriptions on Stone* (Oxford, 1965).
Stowe MSS.	In British Museum Library. Stowe MSS. 1023–4 date from about 1700.
Trans. Cymmr.	*Transactions of the Honourable Society of Cymmrodorion.*
Vitae Sanct.	A. W. Wade-Evans (ed.), *Vitae sanctorum Britanniae et genealogiae* (Cardiff, 1944). Board of Celtic Studies, History and Law Series, No. 9.
Westwood, *Lapid. Wall.*	J. O. Westwood, *Lapidarium Walliae: The Early Inscribed and Sculptured Stones of Wales* (Oxford, 1876–9).

PRESENTATION OF MATERIAL

General Arrangement. The entries in the Inventory are now arranged by types of structure, instead of by grouping together items of all periods which happen to lie within the boundaries of a given parish. The general discussion of each type of monument can therefore be accompanied by the complete set of relevant entries, and the material can be published in smaller sections which are individually less costly and easier to handle.

Volume I is concerned with those types of monument which seem generally to be earlier than the arrival of Norman influences. The remaining volumes will be as follows: II. Ecclesiastical Buildings; III. Castles and other defensive works; IV. Domestic Buildings (including those associated with farms); and V. Industrial and other late structures. Volume IV is likely to appear next, for the extremely rapid destruction of early houses has made it necessary to concentrate work on them. Detailed decisions as to possible arrangement and subdivision can only be decided after the material has been collected.

This first volume has been divided into three parts. *Part i* deals mainly with cairns and burial mounds, *Part ii* with hill-forts and with structures of Roman date, and *Part iii* with inscribed stones assigned to the Early Christian Period. The classification by types of structure corresponds fairly closely to a proper chronological sequence in terms of the classic Three-Age system, for which there is no satisfactory alternative, in the absence of precise dating.

Since the range of interest of the individual reader may lie within a single part of this Volume, the introductory material and indexes are repeated, modified in each part as necessary.

Monuments Included. Some structures cannot be classified satisfactorily by surface investigation, either because of their condition or because they present unusual features. The decision whether to include such marginal cases in the Inventory can only be based on a subjective judgement as to whether they are more likely than not to be genuine; any uncertainty is indicated in the descriptive entry, and rejected sites are listed at the ends of sections.

Form of Entries. These give a detailed description, illustrated where necessary. This is followed by the name of the parish; where the present civil parish differs from the original ecclesiastical parish both are named and indicated by (C) and (E) respectively. The last line gives the sheet number of the current 1/10,000 or 1/10,560 O.S. map; the National Grid reference, to eight figures, of the approximate centre of the monument or group; the date of survey, or of the most recent visit if no plan is given; and the sheet number of the obsolescent county series of 6″-to-one-mile O.S. maps. The note on condition given in former Inventories has been omitted; the information it conveyed is implicit in the entries themselves.

For the monuments described in this volume, the structural materials used were almost invariably obtained in the vicinity, and are only specified when this is known not to be the case.

Numbering of Entries. Entries are numbered consecutively throughout each volume, save that gaps have been left to allow for future discoveries. Within each section, the entries are normally arranged in order of 1/10,000 or 1/10,560 map sheets, that is by the N.W., N.E., S.W., and S.E. quarters of 10 km grid squares. Where this scheme would break up an assemblage of monuments (such as cairns) which seem to form a group, the separate items of the group are enumerated and described in succession after the first relevant entry; cross-references are given in the appropriate positions to any entries displaced by this arrangement.

A few structures found after the text had been completed have been recorded in their correct places with numbers such as 240a.

Names. Most early structures are anonymous, and are indicated on the map merely in descriptive terms. Where a traditional name is known, or a specific modern name is well established, this heads the entry. In other cases, the name of an adjacent farm, village, or natural feature is used for convenience of reference, even though its correct application may be to some other object; thus 'Fforest-newydd' heads an entry describing a small earthwork which lies some distance N.W. of the farm of that name. Unless there is a good reason for a change the names used by previous writers are retained.

Distribution Maps. The maps which accompany each section are intended primarily to show the distribution of the monuments. The background gives a generalised representation of the suitability of different areas for settlement, distinguishing by tints between the permeable and impermeable soils and by shading between the higher and lower ground. The most favourable territories, with permeable soils and at a low level, thus appear white, while the least favourable have the darkest colouring. The distributions of the different types of monument are shown by overprints.

Location of Monuments. The individual monuments shown on these maps are not numbered, since to do so would obscure the distribution pattern at the scale used (1/250,000, about ¼-inch to a mile. Even one inch to a mile is not a large enough scale to permit the exact location of small sites). The position of any particular monument, however, can be precisely fixed by its grid reference. Conversely, if the six-figure reference of a monument of a particular type is already known, it can be identified by use of the Index of Grid References (pp. 75–6); some structures will have escaped record, and information as to these would be appreciated (see p. x).

Parishes. The numbers of the monuments within each parish are given on pp. xvii–xxiv. Separate lists are given for Civil and Ecclesiastical parishes; the end-papers show maps of their boundaries. The Civil parishes are taken as in 1971. The boundaries of the Ecclesiastical parishes are those shown by the Tithe Award Surveys of *ca.* 1850; no attempt has been made to separate those which, like Kenfig and Pyle, are combined in a single survey.

Superimposed Structures of Different Periods. Occasionally structures of widely different date are superimposed. In such cases, the structure relevant to the present volume is described in detail, and a fairly full summary description is given of the other remains. Thus at Caerau, Ely (I ii 673) this volume contains a full account of the hill-fort, with a brief description of the medieval ringwork superimposed upon it; in Volume III the ringwork will be described in detail, with a note on the hill-fort.

Metric Measurements. In view of the forthcoming national adoption of the metric system, it has been used throughout; a conversion table to imperial units is given on pp. xxix–xxx. For the same reason, the system of scales used for the Caernarvonshire Inventory has been replaced by a sequence with the reduction factors 1:10,000, 5,000, 2,500, 1,000 and so on throughout the range required.

Most of the fieldwork had been completed before the Government's decision was made known, and as a result conversion has not always been possible without implying a degree of accuracy which would be unrealistic for the type of monument described; it is hoped that this will not prove misleading. Contours on plans have been left in feet, since in many cases to convert them satisfactorily would have required a fresh survey.

Authorship. The final form of the Inventory is the result of detailed discussion between the Commissioners and their staff; the Secretary acts as Editor. The authorship and compilation of the initial drafts are indicated at the end of the List of Staff (p. xvi).

CONVERSION TABLES

METRIC TO IMPERIAL

FOR fairly accurate conversion without reference to the tables, the following good approximate correspondences may be useful. More precise values are given in parenthesis.

    0·3 m   ⌒ 1 ft. (0·984 ft.)
    5 m   ⌒ 1 rod, pole, or perch of 16½ ft. (16·40 ft.)
    20 m   ⌒ 1 chain of 66 ft. (0·994 chain or 65·62 ft.)
    200 m   ⌒ 1 furlong (0·994 furlong)
    1 hectare ⌒ 2·5 acres (2·471 acres)

If the objective is merely to obtain a general mental impression of size, a metre may be looked upon as a long pace.

The linear tables are given to the nearest inch so that they can be used in combination if desired, but in applying them regard must be had to the degree of accuracy appropriate to the type of site; measurements of earthworks, for example, can seldom be determined more precisely than the nearest 0·3 m (1 ft.).

AREA—to the nearest 0·1 acre
Hectares by tenths

Ha	·0	·1	·2	·3	·4	·5	·6	·7	·8	·9
0	acres	0·2	0·5	0·7	1·0	1·2	1·5	1·7	2·0	2·2
1	2·5	2·7	3·0	3·2	3·5	3·7	4·0	4·2	4·4	4·7
2	4·9	5·2	5·4	5·7	5·9	6·2	6·4	6·7	6·9	7·2
3	7·4	7·7	7·9	8·2	8·4	8·6	8·9	9·1	9·4	9·6
4	9·9	10·1	10·4	10·6	10·9	11·1	11·4	11·6	11·9	12·1
5	12·4	12·6	12·8	13·1	13·3	13·6	13·8	14·1	14·3	14·6
6	14·8	15·1	15·3	15·6	15·8	16·1	16·3	16·6	16·8	17·1
7	17·3	17·5	17·8	18·0	18·3	18·5	18·8	19·0	19·3	19·5
8	19·8	20·0	20·3	20·5	20·8	21·0	21·3	21·5	21·7	22·0
9	22·2	22·5	22·7	23·0	23·2	23·5	23·7	24·0	24·2	24·5
10	24·7	25·0	25·2	25·5	25·7	25·9	26·2	26·4	26·7	26·9
11	27·2	27·4	27·7	27·9	28·2	28·4	28·7	28·9	29·2	29·4
12	29·7	29·9	30·1	30·4	30·6	30·9	31·1	31·4	31·6	31·9
13	32·1	32·4	32·6	32·9	33·1	33·4	33·6	33·9	34·1	34·3
14	34·6	34·8	35·1	35·3	35·6	35·8	36·1	36·3	36·6	36·8
15	37·1	37·3	37·6	37·8	38·1	38·3	38·5	38·8	39·0	39·3
16	39·5	39·8	40·0	40·3	40·5	40·8	41·0	41·3	41·5	41·8
17	42·0	42·3	42·5	42·7	43·0	43·2	43·5	43·7	44·0	44·2
18	44·5	44·7	45·0	45·2	45·5	45·7	46·0	46·2	46·5	46·7
19	47·0	47·2	47·4	47·7	47·9	48·2	48·4	48·7	48·9	49·2
20	49·4	49·7	49·9	50·2	50·4	50·7	50·9	51·2	51·4	51·6

LINEAR—to nearest inch

0–10·9 metres by decimetres

m	·0	·1	·2	·3	·4	·5	·6	·7	·8	·9
0	ft./ins.	0′4″	0′8″	1′0″	1′4″	1′8″	2′0″	2′4″	2′7″	2′11″
1	3′3″	3′7″	3′11″	4′3″	4′7″	4′11″	5′3″	5′7″	5′11″	6′3″
2	6′7″	6′11″	7′3″	7′7″	7′10″	8′2″	8′6″	8′10″	9′2″	9′6″
3	9′10″	10′2″	10′6″	10′10″	11′2″	11′6″	11′10″	12′2″	12′6″	12′10″
4	13′1″	13′5″	13′9″	14′1″	14′5″	14′9″	15′1″	15′5″	15′9″	16′1″
5	16′5″	16′9″	17′1″	17′5″	17′9″	18′1″	18′4″	18′8″	19′0″	19′4″
6	19′8″	20′0″	20′4″	20′8″	21′0″	21′4″	21′8″	22′0″	22′4″	22′8″
7	23′0″	23′4″	23′7″	23′11″	24′3″	24′7″	24′11″	25′3″	25′7″	25′11″
8	26′3″	26′7″	26′11″	27′3″	27′7″	27′11″	28′3″	28′7″	28′10″	29′2″
9	29′6″	29′10″	30′2″	30′6″	30′10″	31′2″	31′6″	31′10″	32′2″	32′6″
10	32′10″	33′2″	33′6″	33′10″	34′1″	34′5″	34′9″	35′1″	35′5″	35′9″

0–109 m by metres

m	0	1	2	3	4	5	6	7	8	9
0	ft./ins.	3′3″	6′7″	9′10″	13′1″	16′5″	19′8″	23′0″	26′3″	29′6″
10	32′10″	36′1″	39′4″	42′8″	45′11″	49′3″	52′6″	55′9″	59′1″	62′4″
20	65′7″	68′11″	72′2″	75′6″	78′4″	82′0″	85′4″	88′7″	91′10″	95′2″
30	98′5″	101′8″	105′0″	108′3″	111′7″	114′10″	118′1″	121′5″	124′8″	127′11″
40	131′3″	134′6″	137′10″	141′1″	144′4″	147′8″	150′11″	154′2″	157′6″	160′9″
50	164′1″	167′4″	170′7″	173′11″	177′2″	180′5″	183′9″	187′0″	190′3″	193′7″
60	196′10″	200′2″	203′5″	206′8″	210′0″	213′3″	216′6″	219′10″	223′1″	226′5″
70	229′8″	232′11″	236′3″	239′6″	242′9″	246′1″	249′4″	252′7″	255′11″	259′2″
80	262′6″	265′9″	269′0″	272′4″	275′7″	278′10″	282′2″	285′5″	288′9″	292′0″
90	295′3″	298′7″	301′10″	305′1″	308′5″	311′8″	315′0″	318′3″	321′6″	324′10″
100	328′1″	331′4″	334′8″	337′11″	341′2″	344′6″	347′9″	351′1″	354′4″	357′7″

0–1090 m by decametres

m	0	10	20	30	40	50	60	70	80	90
0	ft./ins.	32′10″	65′7″	98′5″	131′3″	164′1″	196′10″	229′8″	262′6″	295′3″
100	328′1″	360′11″	393′8″	426′6″	459′4″	492′2″	524′11″	557′9″	590′7″	623′4″
200	656′2″	689′0″	721′9″	754′7″	787′5″	820′3″	853′0″	885′10″	918′8″	951′5″
300	984′3″	1017′1″	1049′10″	1082′8″	1115′6″	1148′4″	1181′1″	1213′11″	1246′9″	1279′6″
400	1312′4″	1345′2″	1377′11″	1410′9″	1443′7″	1476′5″	1509′2″	1542′0″	1574′10″	1607′7″
500	1640′5″	1673′3″	1706′0″	1738′10″	1771′8″	1804′6″	1837′3″	1870′1″	1902′11″	1935′8″
600	1968′6″	2001′4″	2034′1″	2066′11″	2099′9″	2132′7″	2165′4″	2198′2″	2231′0″	2263′9″
700	2296′7″	2329′5″	2362′2″	2395′0″	2427′10″	2460′8″	2493′5″	2526′3″	2559′1″	2591′10″
800	2624′8″	2657′6″	2690′3″	2723′1″	2755′11″	2788′9″	2821′6″	2854′4″	2887′2″	2919′11″
900	2952′9″	2985′7″	3018′5″	3051′2″	3084′0″	3116′10″	3149′7″	3182′5″	3215′3″	3248′0″
1000	3280′10″	3313′8″	3346′6″	3379′3″	3412′1″	3444′11″	3477′8″	3510′6″	3543′4″	3576′1″

INVENTORY

PART III: THE EARLY CHRISTIAN PERIOD

INTRODUCTORY NOTE

THE transition from the Roman to the Early Christian period in Glamorgan is illustrated archaeologically by two contrasting sites—the villa at Llantwit Major (I ii 758) and the settlement 20 km to the east at Dinas Powys (p. 11).

The villa was a comfortable and civilised building, the centre of a prosperous farm, even though in its latest phases it may have been worked by servants and slaves on behalf of an absentee owner. So far as the available evidence goes, it reached the zenith of its prosperity in the middle of the 4th century, when the mosaic pavement was inserted. No later datable relics were found, but indications of declining standards suggest fairly long continuation of use, perhaps for half a century up to A.D. 400 or later. It stood on a site having no defensive advantages, and in its final form seems to have been unfortified.

The Dinas Powys settlement was also prosperous by the standards of its time, but in its earliest phase, assigned to the 5th century A.D., the only dwelling it contained seems to have been a timber hall 8 m wide and not more than 16 m long. Its position is naturally strong and it was further protected by rather slight artificial defences.

The circumstances of the decline and abandonment of the Llantwit Major villa are crucial for a knowledge of the transition period, but require further excavation to elucidate them. Storrie's recognition that most of the skeletons were massacre victims is likely to be correct, but at the time the building was apparently ruinous, though with walls still standing to some height. The formal, oriented burials did not take place until much later, when the whole site had been reduced almost to its present level. It is thus practically certain that these burials were not made by anyone occupying any part of the villa as now known. Similarly, the suggestion that the villa was the actual home of St. Illtud is not supported by any evidence; it would imply that occupation continued for several generations, leaving no trace. Nevertheless, most of the area of the villa and all its immediate environs are unexcavated, so the possibility remains that further discoveries may lead to revision of these conclusions.

There is no reason to doubt the validity of the historical tradition of the foundation, *ca.* A.D. 500, of the monastery of St. Illtud (Llanilltud Fawr, *anglice* Llantwit Major), not far from the Roman villa. Unfortunately, no structural trace of this important site has ever been recorded, but the existence of an important centre of early Christianity is confirmed by the distribution of inscribed stones. Similar evidence suggests another such centre at Margam, though the supporting traditions are lacking. These stones are the main relics of the period, and important collections of them, or of casts, are assembled at both these places, as well as at the National Museum of Wales.

I

Buildings which can be attributed to the Early Christian period are rare. The earliest is the post-built timber hall at Dinas Powys, perhaps never finished. Two later buildings at that site, still of the 7th century or earlier, can be inferred from the presence of gullies; their walls had been entirely removed, leaving no trace. Structures have also been discovered at Burry Holms (821, I ii 705), where the earliest visible remains are of the 12th century; but excavation showed that these corresponded to the last of a succession of buildings. The earliest, otherwise undated, consisted of a small wooden church, which stood in an oval enclosure bounded by a rough stone wall, resembling the 'cashels' of Ireland. Two similar enclosures (I ii 706, 707) exist near-by, but have not been excavated.

The slightness of these traces, which have been discovered only under conditions of highly skilled excavation, probably explains the apparent absence of buildings even at monasteries of major importance. There can be no doubt that the territory was fully utilised, at least by the time of the Norman invasions, and the dwellings of the native rulers must await discovery.

This period, also, sees in use the trackways which now follow the natural routes along the mountain ridges, and some may actually have been developed at this time. This is attested by inscribed stones beside them. Traffic along the ridges was also controlled by small cross-ridge dykes. Ruined chapels along these routes are structurally later, but may well occupy places already sacred in the Early Christian period.

These introductory notes have been concerned primarily with the slight and unimpressive evidence available on daily life in the Early Christian period. The numerous memorial stones and other religious monuments form a striking contrast; detailed consideration of them in the relevant section makes unnecessary any summary comment here.

COMMUNICATIONS

THE EARLY CHRISTIAN PERIOD

As in many other parts of Britain, some part of the earlier road system survived through the obscure transition to the Early Christian period. The present main east–west road through Glamorgan still follows, for much of its length, the line set out by Roman engineers; the obvious deviations caused by the collapse of bridges or the failure to repair sections which became founderous can never have been serious enough completely to interrupt its use. Though this served for through traffic, the villas and other settlements in the coastal region—the Vale of Glamorgan—must have been connected by a network of tracks now irrecoverably incorporated in the modern road system. The distribution of inscribed stones suggests that by the Early Christian period, although the direct engineered Roman road would still have been usable, its importance had been usurped by a track running nearer the coast through Llantwit Major and Merthyr Mawr. Such a track could well have developed earlier, to serve the villas near Llantwit Major and Barry, but its existence is purely inferential; no part of it can be demonstrated to exist today. For the Vale, then, although positive proof is clearly impossible, the distribution of Roman and later relics is in favour of the view that there was no drastic change in the pattern of the tracks and roads in use over the period of transition.

In the mountains, apart from the Roman roads from Neath and Cardiff to Brecon Gaer, and possibly Ffordd y Gyfraith (T7),[1] there is no positive evidence for any substantial use of the ridgeways during the Roman period; but from the 6th century onwards their importance seems to have been considerable, though still less than the routes through the Vale. Reasons for this change can only be conjectured.

While the general character of the road system at this time is thus fairly clear—one or more routes running east and west through the Vale, along the coastal strip, and towards Loughor, linked to the north by a number of mountain trackways—the details present some difficulty. The lowland trackways are lost in the network of modern metalled roads, while almost every mountain ridge is seamed with hollow trails which give an impression of great antiquity.

This impression, however, may well be illusory, for pack-horse traffic at any period produces much the same result, whether the goods carried are bronze axes or coal. For the Vale, some clue to the early roads is provided by the material collected and mapped by Professor William Rees,[2] but despite its great value this information cannot be taken as certainly valid for five centuries earlier.

It seems preferable, therefore, to accept only those roads for which there is positive evidence of use during the relevant period. This approach has the disadvantage that some genuinely ancient tracks will be rejected, but the alternative is liable to cover the map with a close mesh of lines, for many of which the arguments are wholly subjective; in particular, the system of ridgeways becomes identical with the geography of the mountain ridges.

Even the more critical approach retains seventeen separate stretches of track, corresponding to about twelve or thirteen routes across the mountains (map, Fig. 1), for which some evidence of use can be found during this period. They fall into two main groups. Those on the west (T1–3), seem to have led to the Llandovery district, while the remainder probably joined up with a route which left the line of Sarn Helen (T4) a little north of the county boundary to run roughly eastwards, finally curving north and separating into branches leading to Brecon and Bronllys. These routes outside Glamorgan are those indicated by Professor Rees's map. It seems likely that the general directions of traffic would have remained the same until the 14th century, even if the exact lines followed earlier may be open to doubt. Most of those in the easterly group (T5, T8–13, and probably T6 and 7) belong to the remarkable fan of tracks radiating from Mynydd Beili-glas, the point at which T5 descends the scarp of the mountains towards the county boundary. Until the '20s of this century, when the present motor road was built, this unmetalled hollow trail was the only direct exit from the Rhondda valley towards the north. Further east again, two tracks—called for convenience Heol Fawr and Heol Lâs (T15, 16)—are linked on Mynydd Eglwysilan and probably joined again at their northern ends, now lost in the mineral workings east of Merthyr Tudful.

The early names used to describe the roads are conveniently collected on Professor Rees's map. Almost all are purely descriptive, such as Cefn Ffordd (T5, T6, T13 and other minor tracks) on the ridges, or Portway, applied to parts of the Roman road and to a track from E. Aberthaw towards Wenvoe. The Cefn Gwyngul route (T13) is also termed Heol Adam, a name no longer applied to that track, but used on

---

[1] Numbers preceded by T refer to the list of ridgeways at the end of this chapter; others indicate monuments.
[2] W. Rees, *South Wales and the Border in the fourteenth century* (Ordnance Survey, 1933).

modern maps for part of the Roman road over Cefn Gelli-gaer (T16). The only specific name, Ffordd y Gyfraith ('Road of the Law', T7), has not been traced to its origin; it does not appear on Professor Rees's map.

The evidence for the date of use of the ridgeways takes two main forms. One is the presence of dykes built either to bar traffic or more probably to control it; one (812) shows what seems to be an original entrance-gap, and continued traffic along the tracks could have destroyed similar evidence elsewhere. These dykes are found on Tor Clawdd (801, T1); at Cefn Morfudd on the Cefn Mawr route (806, T5); near Ton Mawr (see p. 8b, T6); where the Mynydd Caerau route crosses Bwlch Garw (808, T8); after this track has joined that from Mynydd Llangeinwyr (T9), the latter is crossed by another dyke at Bwlch yr Afan (809); at Bwlch y Clwydd [sic] (811) at the north end of Mynydd William Meyrick (T12); all these routes except the first coalesce into the Cefn Mawr route (T5) a little west of where it penetrates Ffos Toncenglau (802) before descending the northern scarp. The Cefn Gwyngul track (T13) also joins these tracks east of Ffos Toncenglau, and is crossed by a dyke further to the east, Bedd Eiddil (810). The Heol Fawr route (T15) is barred on Mynydd Eglwysilan (812), south of its junction with Heol Lâs (T16); and the latter, on Cefn Gelli-gaer, where its course must lie on or near the Roman Road, is crossed by two dykes (805, 806).

The second piece of evidence is the presence of early inscribed stones on the ridges near the tracks. Among those already mentioned, stones are recorded near the tracks on Cefn Mawr (861, T5), Cefn Gwyngul (889 and 890, T13), Heol Fawr (891, T15), and the Roman section of Heol Lâs (842, 892, T16), as well as a stone now lost (p. 39a) which must have stood somewhere near the continuation of the Cefn Mawr track (T5) after its descent to the north of the mountains. Other trackways associated with stones but not barred by dykes are those on Mynydd Carnllechart (903, T2), Sarn Helen (841, 904, T4), Ffordd y Gyfraith (848, T7), Mynydd Merthyr (863, T14), and Cefn Brithdir (843, 881, T17); of these, that by Ffordd y Gyfraith lies only a little north of its junction with the Ton Mawr route, which is barred by a dyke.

Five of these stones were associated with churches or chapels: Llanwynno (889, 890); Eglwysilan (891); Capel Gwladys (892); and Capel Brithdir (843). This suggests that other ecclesiastical sites near the ridgeways may imply that the localities had early religious associations, though the present buildings are 12th-century or later. The tracks on Mynydd Merthyr (T14), Heol Fawr (T15) and Mynydd Llangeinwyr (T9) pass the remains of chapels at Cefn y Fan (Kyndynvaen or Capel Dynvaen on Professor Rees' map) and Forest, and the church at Llangeinwyr, respectively. The Mynydd Drumau—Cefn Gwryd route (T2) passes Llanguicke church, and branches of the Mynydd y Gaer track (T10) may have passed near the churches of Llandyfodwg and Peterston-super-montem. The evidence for the use of these two trackways in this period is in fact rather tenuous, but the former is one of the few where there is some evidence for use in the Bronze Age, while the latter seems a natural continuation of the route over Mynydd William Meyrick (T12).

The chapel of Llaneithrim is shown on Professor Rees's map as close beside the Mynydd Carnllechart track, but locally the position is said to be at SN 7008 0271, which is not so close to the line, though no more distant than Capel Gwladys from Heol Lâs.

South of the mountains, the continuous use (with minor deviations) of the Roman road from Cardiff to Neath is demonstrated by its survival. The probable monastic sites at Llandaf (829), and Margam (825) are related to it, as well as Ewenni (924) and the cluster of stones near Port Talbot (p. 21). The monasteries at Llancarfan (827), Llantwit Major (826) and Merthyr Mawr (824) imply an important track connecting these places. Its general direction is obvious enough, but its exact line is conjectural.

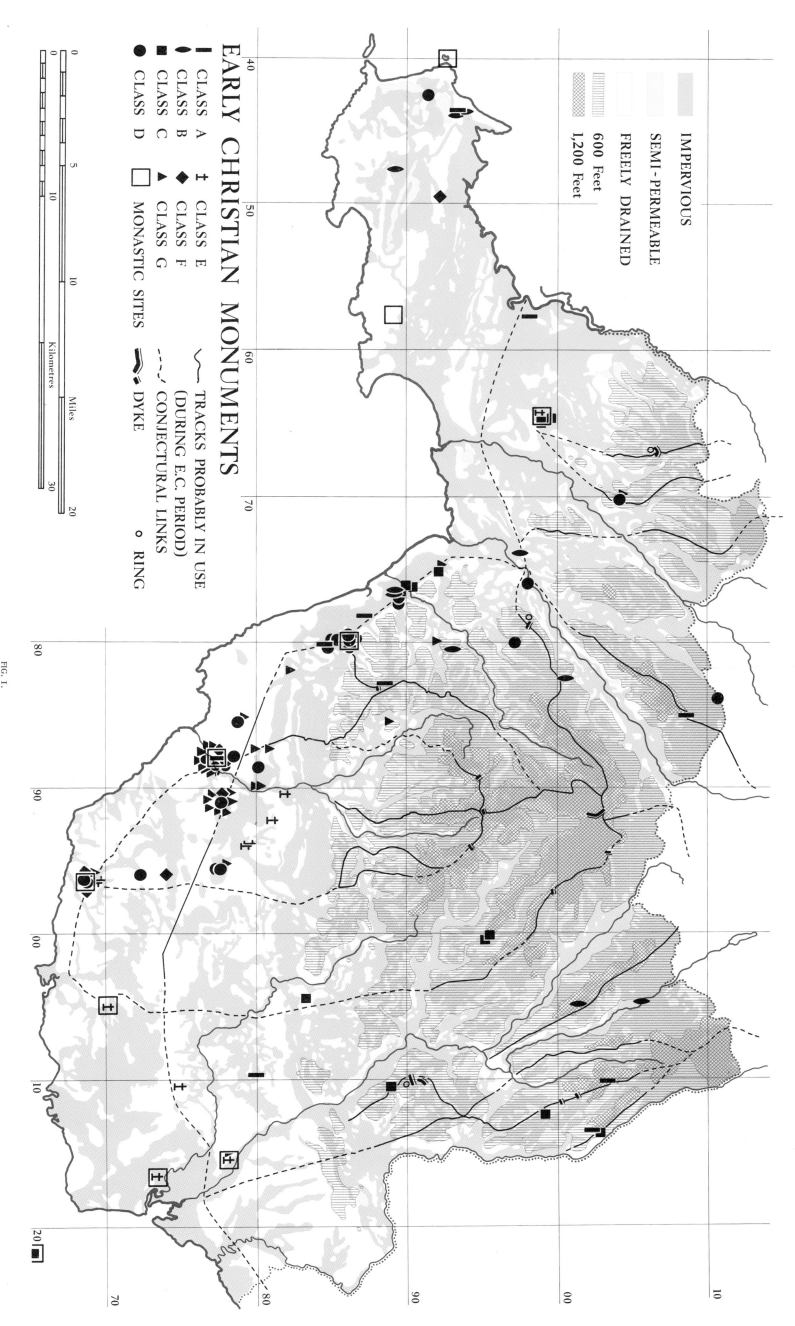

EARLY CHRISTIAN MONUMENTS

	CLASS A	⊢	CLASS E
	CLASS B	◆	CLASS F
	CLASS C	▲	CLASS G
●	CLASS D	☐	MONASTIC SITES

TRACKS PROBABLY IN USE
(DURING E.C. PERIOD)

CONJECTURAL LINKS

⌇ DYKE   ○ RING

IMPERVIOUS

SEMI-PERMEABLE

FREELY DRAINED

600 Feet

1,200 Feet

0   5   10   Miles   20
0   5   10   Kilometres   30

FIG. 1.
For explanation of soil mapping see 'The Physical Background' in Part i or Part ii of this Volume.

Ridgeways probably used during the Early Christian Period

No.	Name	Ends so far as known	
		South	North
T1	Tor Clawdd	ss 6650 9940	sn 6647 0986
T2	Mynydd Carnllechart	sn 6940 0243	sn 6896 0976
T3	(South section) Mynydd Drumau	ss 7228 9871	sn 7270 0153
T3	(North section) Cefn Gwryd	sn 7245 0565	sn 7363 1166
T4	Sarn Helen (Roman road)	sn 7931 0134	sn 8610 1075
T5	Cefn Mawr	ss 7807 9742	sn 9192 0470
T6	Ton Mawr (joins T7)	ss 8076 8623	ss 8302 8900
T7	Ffordd y Gyfraith	ss 8720 8030	ss 8600 9590
T8	Mynydd Caerau (joins T9)	ss 8812 9326	ss 9190 9487
T9	Mynydd Llangeinwyr (joins T5)	ss 9100 8500	sn 9056 0255
T10	Mynydd y Gaer (alternative to T11, probably continues as T12)	ss 9680 8540	ca. ss 9565 9255
T11	Cwmogwr Forest (alternative to T10, probably continues as T12)	ss 9680 8540	ca. ss 9615 9020
T12	Mynydd William Meyrick (joins T9)	ca. ss 9400 9442	ca. ss 9210 9512
T13	Cefn Gwyngul (joins T5)	st 0402 9170	ca. sn 9240 0317
T14	Mynydd Merthyr	st 0845 9550	sn 9982 0798
T15	Heol Fawr, Mynydd Eglwysilan	st 1280 8610	so 0740 0555
T16	Heol Lâs (and Heol Adam partly Roman) (meets T15 near 1250 9278)	st 1475 8788	so 0992 0525
T17	Cefn Brithdir	so 1462 0100	so 1110 0570
T18	Roman Road, Cardiff–Loughor		

DYKES

As noted above (p. 4), most of the ridges of the Glamorgan uplands are crossed by short lengths of rampart, apparently designed to control or prevent traffic along these natural routes. Many of these dykes were discovered, and their significance was first emphasised, by Sir Cyril and Lady Fox,[1] who argued from topographical and archaeological evidence that they were built in about the 8th or 9th centuries A.D., indicating the limits of mountain pasture controlled by the inhabitants of the adjacent lowland.

The evidence for date was at that time purely inferential. Recently, however, C. B. Crampton has demonstrated that four typical examples of the dykes were built after the growth of Ericaceae in the uplands had reached its maximum, which is consistent with the suggested dating.[2] One of the structures examined, however, (at Bwlch Garw, 808) seems to be appreciably earlier than the other three, though the nature of the evidence does not allow a precise estimate of the interval.

---

[1] Especially *B.B.C.S.*, VIII, iii (Nov. 1936), pp. 280–4; also VII, ii (May 1934), p. 221; iv (May 1935), pp. 418–19; IX, iv (May 1939), pp. 368–372; *A Hundred Years of Welsh Archaeology* (Cambrian Archaeol. Assoc., 1946), pp. 117–18.
[2] *B.B.C.S.*, XXI, iv (May 1966), pp. 376–90. The evidence for the plant succession is summarised in *B.B.C.S.*, XX, iv (May 1964), pp. 440–9.

All these dykes face towards traffic approaching from the north, and are sited to cross a narrow part of the ridge between natural obstacles. The positions chosen, however, seem to fall into two classes. In one, the rampart is placed so that it forms a line capable of defence; examples of this are Tor Clawdd (801), Ffos Toncenglau (802), probably Cefn Morfudd (806), Bwlch Garw (808) and Bwlch y Clwydd (811); Ffos Toncenglau and Bwlch y Clwydd incorporate dry stone walling or revetting. Those at Tyla-glas (804), Clawddtrawscae (805), Bwlch yr Afan (809), Bedd Eiddil (810), and Mynydd Eglwysilan (812) are not well situated for defence; neither is Bwlch y Lladron (803), but this may be no more than a parish boundary-mark. Most of these latter dykes are insignificant, and would require the addition of a hedge or palisade if they were to form any sort of obstacle to traffic.

At three of the sites, Tor Clawdd, Cefn Morfudd, and Mynydd Eglwysilan, a small, lightly embanked ringwork stands in a position behind the dyke suggesting that it served some function in relation to it; at Cefn Morfudd both the dyke and the ringwork are unfinished. The enclosing banks, however, are too slight to have provided any useful defence. Although these rings have been described in the entries relating to the adjacent dykes, the connection, though probable, is not established with certainty.

None of these cross-ridge dykes seems to be mentioned in any early document. The earthwork at Vervil (807), however, has been identified as a section of the boundary of Merthyr Mawr parish. It is clearly not of the same type as the others described here, but its purpose is obscure.

One other linear earthwork requires mention. This is the dyke which forms a large, roughly oblong enclosure around Senghennydd. Although there is no documentary record relating to it, it is almost certainly a medieval park pale.[3]

The dyke indicated on some maps from ss 9582 9362 to 9586 9373 (XXVII N.W.) is merely a short length of hollowed trackway.

---

[3] As suggested by Sir Cyril Fox, MS. notes at Ordnance Survey Office. It passes through ST 1020 9150, 1240 9125, 1373 8995, 1200 8805.

(801) DYKE WITH ADJACENT RINGWORK on Tor Clawdd (Fig. 2), an almost level plateau at about 300 m above O.D. On the N., the ground falls away steeply, and the top of the scarp has apparently been adapted to form a dyke. The remains have been very severely damaged by excavations for outcrop coal, and the existence of the dyke has been doubted, but is implied by the name. Its siting, also, is similar to that of other cross-ridge dykes.

The line has been traced[1] from the head of a steep-sided gulley (SN 6664 0625) just below the 275 m contour, through 6672 0627 and then in a gentler curve through 6680 0636 to 6705 0646, whence it runs almost straight to end at 6734 0631 by a patch of boggy ground in which a streamlet rises. The central part almost follows the 300 m contour, and there is a gap, apparently original, at 6694 0645.

The extensive disturbance obscures the form of a dyke, but towards its E. end it seems to have measured about 9 m overall; a section accidentally exposed in 1938 showed that the ditch was about 1·2 m deep from the present surface, with a flat bottom 0·9 m wide. Most of the scarp has been formed by cutting back the natural slope, but there is a slight bank now about 0·3 m high, along the top. Towards the W. end the remains are slighter.

On the plateau about 180 m S. of the dyke, almost central to the arc formed by its line, is a small *ringwork* (SN 6703 0630); it stands just W. of a straight artificial causeway leading to the gap in the dyke. The ring is 15·5 to 16·5 m in diameter within the enclosing bank, which is 2·1 to 3·3 m wide and 0·3 m high. There are traces of an external ditch 1·8 to 2·1 m wide on N.W. and S. On the S.E. is an entrance 2·1 m wide. Although the position relative to the dyke and causeway suggests that the structures may be associated, the ring resembles in some respects the large ring-cairns (such as Pebyll, I i 348) with which it has been included (I i 60). There are four small pits in the bank, one at the entrance, and two within the enclosure, which could be stone-holes.

The *causeway* is a flat-topped bank about 0·3 m high with a small ditch on each side. It measures about 9 m wide overall, and runs in a straight line N.W. for 460 m towards the gap in the dyke. Its object is clearly to carry a road across the shallow peat-bog S. of the dyke, but there is no evidence as to its age.

[1] Morgan, *E. Gower*, p. 36. B.B.C.S., IX, iv (May 1939), p. 371.

Llangyfelach (E), Mawr (C).

SN 60 N.E. (6664 0624–6734 0631)   10 x 62   VIII N.W.

TOR CLAWDD DYKE AND RING

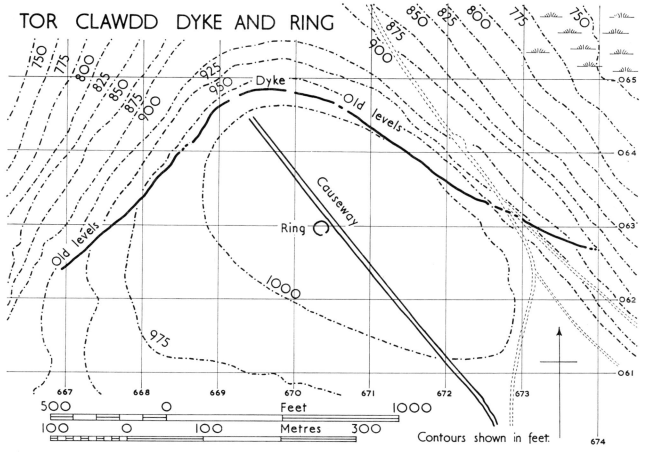

FIG. 2. No. 801.

(802) FFOS TONCENGLAU, a dyke barring passage from E. to W. along the ridge followed by the ancient trackway[1] known as Cefn Ffordd. Between the head of the Rhondda valley and the cliffs above Llyn Fawr the ridge narrows to about 1 km in width, and is traversed by a marshy saddle, with the ground on the W. rising in a steep scarp, in places precipitous, about 15 m high. The dyke follows this scarp, a little below its top, at levels ranging from about 490 m above O.D. at its S. end to 530 m at its N. It extends from SN 9188 0198 to SN 9172 0301, in two fairly direct but sinuous sections with a bend near the middle, at SN 9207 0255. There is a gap about 3 m wide at SN 9202 0238, where the natural scarp is lowest, and this seems to be original. It is now used by a forestry road, but in about 1935 there were indications of secondary narrowing. The Cefn Ffordd crosses the line of the dyke (here damaged) at the N. end, ascending the scarp by a terrace.

The dyke terminates on precipices. It seems originally to have been formed by a bank of earth, now about 4·3 m wide, revetted on the E. side with a fairly massive dry-stone wall, which where best preserved, near the gap, now stands about

1·2 m high. Near the ends, however, the stonework was either absent or more probably has slipped down the hillside, so that the structure appears as a grass-grown bank.

The dyke is not of great size, but is strongly placed, and could in fact have served as a military obstacle.

Investigation by C. B. Crampton has shown that the bank was built not long after the Ericaceae pollen had reached its maximum.[2]

[1] *B.B.C.S.*, VIII, iii (Nov. 1936), pp. 280–4.
[2] *Ibid.*, XXI, iv (May 1966), pp. 384–5.

Ystradyfodwg (E), Rhigos/Rhondda (C).
SN 90 S.W. (9188 0198–9172 0301)   6 x 60   X S.E.

(803) BANK, Bwlch y Lladron, at 500 m above O.D. The bank starts at the edge of a steep gully in the cliff at the N. and proceeds southwards along the boundary between Rhigos and Aberdâr parishes, with a gap 2·4 m wide for the cliff-top track to pass through. It is 2·1 m wide and 0·45 m high, of earth with stone facing. It fades out into marshy ground to the

S., from where the parish boundary coincides with Nant Rhydfelen. Although the situation, linking two natural obstacles, resembles early dykes in this area, the bank differs from these in having no ditch. It may have served merely to mark the boundary.

Aberdâr/Ystradyfodwg (E), Aberdâr/Rhigos (C).

SN 90 S.W. (9466 0335, N. end)   7 x 60   XI S.W.

(804) DYKE near Tyla-glas. A bank with a ditch on the N., about 5·5 m wide and 1 m high overall, crosses the ridge of Cefn Gelli-gaer about 275 m N. of its highest point, at the foot of a fairly steep descent at about 380 m above O.D. The W. end continues for about 15 m in a ploughed field and is then lost; the E. end terminates at the modern road, not on any natural obstacle.

B.B.C.S., VII, iv (May 1935), p. 419; VIII, iii (Nov. 1936), pp. 282–4.

Gelli-gaer.

SO 10 S.W. (1104 0124)   21 iv 64   XII S.E.

(805) DYKE E. of Clawddtrawscae, crossing the ridge of Cefn Gelli-gaer at ca. 370 m above O.D. It lies on open ground, and both ends stand clear of natural features. It is 90 m long N.E.–S.W., up to 0·9 m high, with a ditch at the N.W. side. The overall width is ca. 4·6 m. It is built of stones and earth in straight sections of length varying from 7 to 32 m; the S.W. half bends southwards slightly, but resumes the original line at the S.W. end. It is interrupted by a modern road and an earlier track.

B.B.C.S., VII, iv (May 1935), p. 418; VIII, iii (Nov. 1936), pp. 282–4.

Gelli-gaer.

SO 10 S.W. (1178 0027–1172 0021)   14 x 60   XIX N.E.

(806) DYKE WITH ADJACENT RING, Cefn Morfudd (Fig. 3). The N. end of this ridge is crossed by a dyke, apparently unfinished. Apart from a few recent gaps, it is well preserved. The E. end has been destroyed by an old mineral tramway, but must have been at about ss 7905 9803, at 260 m above O.D., at the head of a steep side valley of the Gwenffrwd. From here the line runs due W. for 247 m, to a gap, perhaps the site of an original opening (at 7869 9813), where a track crosses the dyke, at 270 m above O.D. This section has a profile consisting of a shallow ditch on the S., about 0·3 m deep, a bank about 1 m high, and a ditch about 0·6 m deep to the N.; their widths, respectively, are about 5·8, 5·8, and 4·3 m. After the gap, the dyke runs N.W. for a further 146 m, to 7869 9813. Over this stretch the bank and ditches are gradually reduced to a terrace with a steep N. scarp about 2·4 m high, and this is finally replaced by a slight bank about 1 m high which ends on the open summit of the ridge.

Fifty metres S.W. of the dyke near its unfinished end is an earthen ringwork (at ss 7682 9812) also apparently unfinished. It stands at 275 m above O.D. on a natural shelf at the edge of ground falling to the N.W. The enclosure is oval, 52 m from N.E. to S.W. by 40 m. Most of the N.W. side is invisible on the ground, though it can just be made out on aerial photographs. The defences elsewhere consist of a bank from 3·7 to 6·1 m wide, with an external ditch 3·7 to 5·5 m wide,

the overall height being about 1 m; the ditch fades out on the N.E. and S.W. as the crest of the natural slope is approached. On the N.E. is an entrance 4·9 m wide.

B.B.C.S., VIII, iii (Nov. 1936), pp. 281–4.

Llantwit-juxta-Neath (E), Tonna (C).

SS 78 N.E. (7905 9803–7869 9813)   30 iv 64   XVI S.W.

(807) VERVIL DYKE. The S.E. boundary of the ecclesiastical parish of Merthyr Mawr follows, for most of its length, the River Ogmore, but for about 365 m near the church it extends further to the S.E., to the Ewenni, forming an almost square salient. Along the E. side of this salient are the remains of a substantial bank and ditch, running almost straight for about 230 m between two rivers, from ss 8896 7733 to 8887 7753. The actual boundary follows the field-bank along the outer (W.) lip of the ditch, so that the structure lies within Coety ecclesiastical parish, and excludes the long tongue of land between the two rivers.

Two sections cut during 1937[1] showed that the overall width of the rampart was about 16 m, with a ditch originally 1·5 to 2·1 m deep. A berm 0·9 m wide separated it from the bank, which was much ploughed down but survived in one place to a height of 1·2 m. No revetment of timberwork was found. The excavators identify the remains with the 'cruc' (i.e. bank) mentioned in an early description of the boundaries of Merthyr Mawr,[2] implying a date sometime in the Dark Ages for its construction, but its purpose remains obscure.

[1] W. F. Grimes and H. J. Randall, Arch. Camb., XCVIII (1945), pp. 241–7. This is the earliest record of the structure.
[2] Lib. Land., p. 213.

Coety (E), Merthyr Mawr (C).

SS 87 N.W. (8896 7733–8887 7753)   27 vi 63   XL S.E.

A dyke, from ss 8337 8819 to 8312 8800, near the small fort Caer Blaen-y-cwm (I ii 657) is described in the entry relating to that monument.

(808) CLAWDD MAWR, Bwlch Garw.[1] The dyke runs almost straight for 192 m W.N.W. to E.S.E. at about 490 m above O.D. It is located roughly 15 m above the floor of a narrow saddle running E. from Mynydd Caerau, on a slope rising steeply westwards. The N. end lies at the head of a steep-sided natural gully, the S. on a steep slope. There is a gap where a track crosses, but this appears recent. The dyke has been formed by throwing earth downwards from a ditch on the upper side. Near the N. end, the bank and ditch measure about 7·5 m by about 1 m high overall, but the earthwork steadily decreases in size towards the S. end, where it is now merely a shelf about 1·5 m wide. There is no sign of stonework. The dyke was built just at the time when the Ericaceae pollen reached its maximum; it would seem, therefore, to have been appreciably earlier than the other three dykes studied by C. B. Crampton.[2]

[1] B.B.C.S., VII, ii (May 1934), p. 221; VIII, iii (Nov. 1936), pp. 282–4.
[2] Ibid., XXI, iv (May 1966), pp. 380–2.

Llangynwyd (E), Glyncorrwg (C).

SS 89 S.E. (8944 9486–8952 9470)   19 vi 62   XXVI N.E.

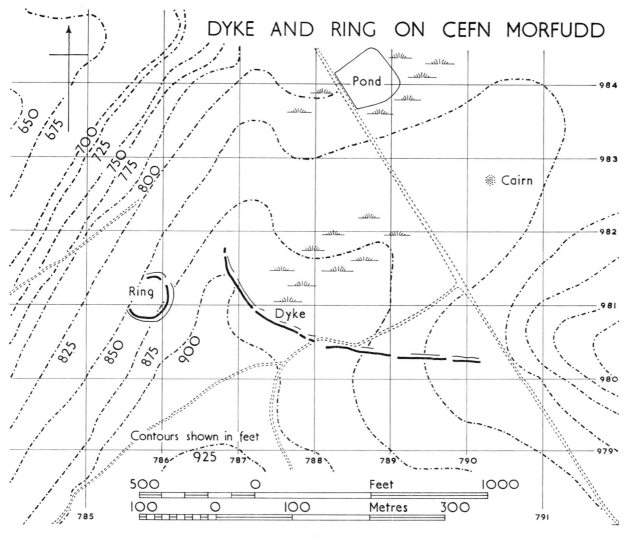

DYKE AND RING ON CEFN MORFUDD

Contours shown in feet

FIG. 3. No. 806.

(809) BWLCH YR AFAN,[1] crossing a saddle at about 520 m above O.D. The dyke runs almost straight for 192 m, W.S.W. to E.S.E. Its W. end coincides with the line of an old trackway, but does not reach any natural obstacle. Its E. end dies away in a patch of marsh. It is fairly uniform in character, composed of a ditch between two banks of equal size, 10·7 m wide by about 1 m high overall. An accidental disturbance showed that the S. bank (and thus probably the N. also) is of upcast from the ditch resting on about 75 mm of peat corresponding to the old surface. There is no stonework in the structure.

Examination by C. B. Crampton showed that the dyke was made not long after the Ericaceae pollen reached its maximum.[2]

[1] B.B.C.S., VII, ii (May 1934), p. 221; VIII, iii (Nov. 1936), pp. 282–4.
[2] Ibid., XXI, iv (May 1966), pp. 382–4.

Llangeinwyr.
SS 99 N.W. (9197 9510–9215 9515) 19 vi 62 XXVI N.E.

(810) DYKE, Bedd Eiddil,[1] in a saddle at about 390 m above O.D., the lowest crossing from Cwm Aman to Cwm Rhondda Fach. It is aligned E.–W. in such a way as to control the 'Cefn Ffordd' which runs from the N.W., along the N.E. side of Cwm Rhondda Fach, and continues along the ridge of Mynydd y Ffaldau towards Llanwynno. The dyke consists of a bank at the S. and ditch at the N., measuring 3·7 to 4·6 m wide overall and 0·6 to 0·9 m high overall where best preserved, near the crossing of the trackway. The W. end is obscured by the embankment of the modern road, but is just discernible emerging at the head of a watercourse below it.

DYKE AND RING ON MYNYDD EGLWYSILAN

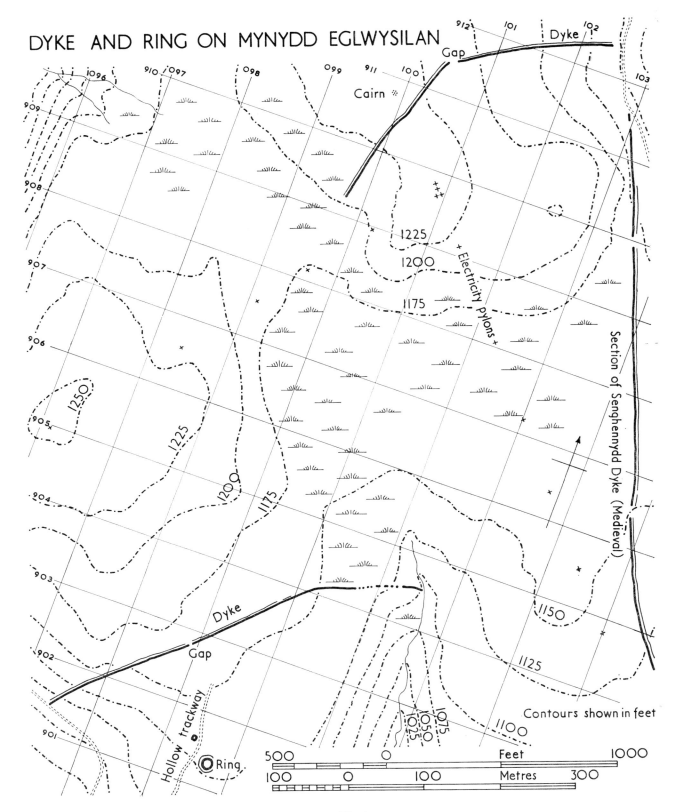

FIG. 4. No. 812.

The E. end fades as it passes into boggy ground. Examination by C. B. Crampton showed that the dyke had been constructed not long after the Ericaceae pollen had reached its maximum.[2]

[1] *B.B.C.S.*, VIII, iii (Nov. 1936), pp. 282–4.
[2] *Ibid.*, XXI, iv (May 1966), pp. 384–5.

Aberdâr.
SS 99 N.E. (9709 9968–9729 9968) 21 ii 62 XVIII N.W.

(811) BWLCH Y CLWYDD. The dyke runs roughly S.W. to N.E., almost straight, for 200 m across a narrow col, falling from 465 to 400 m above O.D. The position is naturally strong, the line chosen for the dyke being on a slope of about 1 in 3, overlooking the lowest part of the saddle from about 7·5 to 9·0 m above it. The main bank is 4·3 m wide and 1·5 m high, the lower (N.W.) face having been originally revetted, though now much robbed. There is no ditch, but along the N.E. half is a subsidiary bank 1·8 m wide and 0·6 m high, parallel to the main rampart and *ca.* 12·2 m from it to the N.W. This subsidiary bank may originally have extended further to the S., but is no longer visible. Two trackways penetrate the system, but it is not clear whether either gap is original.

B.B.C.S., VII, ii (May 1934), p. 221; VIII, iii (Nov. 1936), pp. 282–4. (The 'Lower Dyke'; the apparent 'Upper Dyke' seems to be the result of quarrying.)

Llandyfodwg/Ystradyfodwg(E), Llandyfodwg/Rhondda(C).
SS 99 S.W. (9399 9443–9406 9455) 10 x 60 XXVII N.W.

(812) DYKE WITH ADJACENT RINGWORK across the S. part of Mynydd Eglwysilan (Fig. 4). The dyke consists of a bank with ditch on the N.W.; it is in two sections connected by a stretch of marshy ground, and shows little sign of disturbance. The N. part, generally about 3·4 m across and 0·5 m high overall starts at 340 m above O.D. near the edge of the modern enclosures (ST 1024 9123), and climbs the ridge S.W. for about 210 m to a little over 370 m above O.D.; it then bends slightly S.S.W. for a similar distance, ending at about 360 m above O.D. in the small marshy valley of Pant Waungorrwg (ST 0997 9090). The marsh acts as its continuation for about 485 m to S.S.E., and the dyke reappears at about 340 m above O.D. close to the source of the stream Nant Corrwg (ST 1022 9047). This southern section is rather stronger, 5·2 m across by 0·8 m high overall. It runs S.S.W. for about 120 m and then bends to S.W. for a further 360 m, ending at about 335 m above O.D. near the modern enclosures (ST 0982 9016). There seem to be indications that the ground beyond each end of the dyke was originally marshy.

About 210 m from the S.W. end, near the highest point of the S. section (350 m above O.D.), there is a gap 1·8 m wide, probably original, where a track running from N. to S. crosses the line.

The *ringwork* (ST 1007 9014) lies near this track, about 165 m S. of the dyke. It is about 9 m in diameter, surrounded by a bank and external ditch measuring about 4·6 m by 1 m overall where best preserved; on the E., however, it is slighter, and the ditch is barely visible. There is no entrance.

A smaller *enclosure* stands 37·5 m to N.W. It is about 5 m square internally (axis 99°), surrounded by a slight ditch 0·6 m wide and 0·2 m deep with an external bank 1·5 m wide and 0·2 m high, with no entrance.

Eglwysilan (E), Eglwysilan/Pontypridd (C).
ST 09 S.E.–19 S.W.   13 x 60   XXVIII S.E.
(0982 9016–1024 9123)

DOMESTIC REMAINS

TRACES of secular domestic occupation are extremely rare in this period. A few caves were used, including Lesser Garth Cave (I i 19) and Minchin Hole (I i 12), where there was considerable evidence of use for the production of fine metal-work.

One important settlement of this period has been located by excavation at Dinas Powys,[1] where a 12th-century fortification incorporates and completely conceals an earlier defended site. During the 5th and 6th centuries A.D. an inland promontory with more or less precipitous sides was protected by a small rampart cut across the level southern approach. The bank consisted of a simple dump of clay and rubble without revetment, resting on the edge of a rock-cut ditch. The whole system was about 6 m wide and 2·7 m high overall. Access was by a steep, rocky path ascending the E. side of the promontory, overlooked from the recurved end of the rampart. The enclosed area was 0·1 ha.

[1] L. Alcock, *Dinas Powis* (Cardiff, 1963). The site is in Michaelston-le-Pit parish, ST 17 S.W. (1482 7225) XLVII N.W. See also I ii p. 17.

The structures were all of timber, and the sequence seems to have been as follows: the first building was a post-built hall with a hipped roof, 8 m wide, the length not determined; latter gullies indicate that this was succeeded by a rather irregular dwelling about 6 m by 12 m, with a smaller structure 5 m square adjacent. The latter were probably founded on sleeper-beams, so that the walls have left no traces.

The middens associated with these remains contained, among much kitchen refuse, imported Mediterranean and continental pottery, and the debris of metal-working.

Though this is the only domestic settlement as yet known in Glamorgan, it should be noted that its character was entirely unknown until its excavation, and that the original defences would have been superficially indistinguishable from a weak pre-Roman promontory fort. It therefore seems fully possible that other establishments of this kind remain unrecognised.

EARLY MONASTIC SITES

FROM the limited historical and archaeological evidence for the Christian Church in Glamorgan (as in Wales generally) before the Norman conquest, one of the few features of its organisation that can be deduced with some confidence is the existence of locally important centres which can be acceptably termed monasteries.[1] The probable locations of such ecclesiastical centres are indicated in this section. They are based on the few contemporary written works, the traditions embodied in the hagiological literature of the Conquest period, analogies from other Celtic areas, and on the few concentrations of inscribed and decorated stone monuments discussed in a later section of this Inventory. The sites concerned have no known structural remains earlier than the Norman period. In almost every instance the continuous use over the centuries of both a church and a churchyard precludes any expectation that such structural remains will be recovered. However, two island sites are included, on which limited excavations have provided evidence of occupation in this period, presumably as hermitages or retreats rather than as major ecclesiastical settlements.

Several of the early 'saints' of south-east Wales, whose *Lives* were compiled in the monastic milieu of the late 11th and 12th centuries, were reputed to have founded the monasteries that had survived until then under their patronage. Thus Illtud was regarded as the founder of Llanilltud Fawr (826, Llantwit Major), Cadog as that of Nantcarfan (827, Llancarfan), Cyngar was identified as the Docco who founded Llandough (828, either Llandough-by-Cowbridge or the more important establishment near Penarth) and Dyfrig (Dubricius) was made to have fostered an early Llandaf (829). Only in the case of Llanilltud Fawr is there more nearly contemporary evidence for such a personal link, uncontaminated by the pious imagination of the later hagiographers. The process of evangelisation in the area is unavoidably obscure, perhaps owing as much to the survival of the faith from the late Roman period as to missionary efforts from outside the area and derived ultimately from monasteries in Gaul. In either event, the local monastery seems to have been the base for such evangelisation, and it continued to function as the local centre of

[1] For recent summaries of the historical and archaeological evidence see *P. and E. Wales*, chap. 7 (L. Alcock) and chap. 8 (I. Ll. Foster); M. W. Barley and R. P. C. Hanson (eds.), *Christianity in Britain, 300–700* (Leicester, 1968), pp. 131–50 (W. H. Davies); E. G. Bowen, *Saints, Seaways and Settlements* (Cardiff, 1969).

pastoral ministry throughout the pre-Norman period. Linked to these major centres were a number of smaller dependent churches, as is implied by Gildas, but it is impossible to determine whether the distribution of dedications to early saints indicates early evangelisation by these saints or much later cults possibly influenced by monastic patronage.[2]

These monasteries differed in many important respects from continental monasticism based on the Rule of St. Benedict.[3] The community (the *clas*) was under an abbot (*abad*) who was normally a cleric, perhaps often a bishop, but the members (*claswyr*) were not necessarily all clerics or monks; they held property in common, but succession to office and property by hereditary right was recognised. Just how bishops were associated with such communities and whether there was any development towards diocesan organisation before the Norman Conquest remain unresolved problems of the early Welsh Church.[4] With the Norman reorganisation of the Church in Glamorgan, these establishments apart from Llandaf ceased to exist as such and continued only as parish churches dependent on other English or French Benedictine houses. Neither Llanilltud Fawr nor Llancarfan, the most important of them, survived even as a body of Augustinian Canons Regular as did similar Celtic monasteries in independent Wales, thus retaining something of their ancient identity.

If these early monastic settlements resembled those known in other Celtic areas,[5] they consisted of a number of small buildings grouped rather casually and enclosed by a bank or wall usually curvilinear in plan, possibly also by a wide shallow ditch. One or more of these buildings would have been a church, the principal one housing the shrine of the founder with the cemetery adjoining it. In addition to the small, separate huts for individual members of the community there would have been a guest-house, a scriptorium or library, a school and barns or other domestic buildings. At the more important settlements additional structures may have multiplied around the original monastic enclosure, or the larger enclosures may have been subdivided to separate the community from the laity attracted there, as with some surviving Irish examples, notably Clonard, Co. Meath.[6] The many 'canons' each endowed with a 'vill' mentioned in the late *Lives* of Cadog and Illtud may remotely echo such an enlarged settlement but more probably refer to dependent churches and lands.[7] One of the charters of Llancarfan appended to Lifris' *Life* of St. Cadog mentions a cross set up in a monastic enclosure,[8] and numerous crosses scattered within and around the enclosure are described in early Irish poetry and depicted on a crude plan of a monastery in the Book of Mulling.[9] Some of the surviving stone monuments would seem to confirm that this was a feature of monastic sites in Glamorgan (907, 931 and 938 below).

Most of the mainland sites under consideration are located in a sheltered valley near but not immediately on the sea coast (Fig. 1), and in each case there is a modest stream close to the spot. Early Celtic foundations in general apparently preferred low-lying ground or the lower valley slopes.[10] This coastal situation, while advantageous in an age of primarily sea-borne communications, made the monasteries vulnerable to Viking raiders, and the native annals record the despoiling in A.D. 988 of Llantwit Major and Llancarfan together with the major centres on the west coast.[11] It is also possible, but unprovable at present,

---

[2] E. G. Bowen, *op. cit.*, pp. 69–72, 81–111; O. Chadwick in N. K. Chadwick (ed.), *Studies in Early British History* (Cambridge, 1954), pp. 173–88.
[3] *Arch. Camb.*, CXI (1962), p. 6; *Epis. Acts*, II, pp. 463–77; *S. Wales & Mon. Record Soc.*, No. 2 (1950), pp. 130–9.
[4] *Epis. Acts*, II, pp. 480–7.
[5] *Arch. Camb.*, CXI (1962), pp. 1–24; Radford, *Margam*, pp. 14–15; Henry, *Irish Art*, I, pp. 76–91.
[6] E. R. Norman and J. K. S. St. Joseph, *The Early Development of Irish Society* (Cambridge, 1969), pp. 90–121.
[7] *Vitae Sanct.*, pp. 120, 210.
[8] *Ibid.*, p. 132.
[9] Henry, *Irish Art*, I, pp. 134–6.
[10] E. G. Bowen, *op. cit.*, pp. 107–10, 124–5.
[11] *Ann. Camb.*, s.a. 988; *Brut* (Peniarth), s.a. 987.

that these Glamorgan monasteries were deliberately set near centres of lay settlement, as with some Anglesey sites.[12]

Some other sites may be mentioned as probable ecclesiastical settlements though not known to be specifically monastic. At Ewenni (ss 912 778) where a priory was established in 1141 there is a concentration of early memorial stones, some of which are of earlier date, while the dedication of the church to St. Michael also suggests an 8th- or 9th-century foundation.[13] The three early monuments at Llanmadog (ss 438 934), together with its coastal situation and the survival of a handbell of Celtic type,[14] suggest that something more than merely a local church was established there. The *Life* of St. Cadog mentions 'Mammelliat' as the place where the religious of Llancarfan sought safety for the saint's relics in the early 11th century,[15] the word 'locus' by which it is described being unfortunately ambiguous as to whether a monastery was meant. But the identification of this place with Mamheilad near Pontypool, Monmouthshire (so 305 035)[16] seems unlikely if the invading force came from that easterly direction, as might be presumed. Another hitherto unidentified location in north or west Glamorgan should probably be sought. Llanfythin as a possible monastic site is discussed under Llancarfan (827).

---

[12] *Inv. Anglesey*, pp. xci–ii; E. G. Bowen, *op. cit.*, pp. 205–6.
[13] O. Chadwick, *op. cit.*, pp. 182–4.
[14] *Arch. Camb.* 1886, pp. 155–6; Davies, *W. Gower*, II, p. 66.
[15] *Vitae Sanct.*, p. 110.
[16] Lloyd, *Hist. Wales*, p. 351.

(821) BURRY HOLMS (Fig. 5). A group of four ruined buildings on the small tidal island of Burry Holms off the N.W. coast of Gower (see also I ii 612 above) had long been regarded as a possible monastic establishment of Celtic type, but only when excavations were undertaken in 1965–8[1] was the existence of a pre-Norman ecclesiastical settlement confirmed. The site lies on the flatter and sheltered E. part of the island nearest the mainland, at between 7 m and 15 m above O.D. The rectangular building in the shelter of the rising ground was shown to have been a 12th-century church consisting of a small nave (5·33 m by 3·42 m) and apsidal chancel (with radius of 1·35 m), the latter feature being subsequently replaced by a square-ended chancel. Partly covered by the footings of this building were four corner post-holes of an earlier wooden structure, 3·35 m by 3·05 m, aligned more N. of E. than the stone church. The filling of these holes showed that the posts had been removed in order to erect the later building, and one of them (at the S.E.) had been dug through an earlier disturbed burial.

Around the lower part of the site were remains of an enclosing wall or cashel built in at least two stages (I ii 705). The earlier wall, formed of an earthen bank revetted only by very small stones, was almost boat-shaped in plan except for a straight E. end wall aligned with the timber building and subsequently used as a foundation for the E. end of the square-ended chancel; the entry through the cashel lay on the S., facing the doorway of the stone church. In a later (12th-century) phase, the enclosure wall, consisting of a double line of grounders, was extended eastwards to complete a regular ovoid shape, and the entry was reduced in width with a thinner wall on its E. side.

Immediately S. of the cashel of the church site lay a complex of structures of several periods, but the 12th-century and earlier buildings which were traced on the W. part of this area had been extensively robbed. Below these features were the post-holes of two timber round huts, one adjacent to the cashel but at a higher level than the earliest form of this, the other and smaller one possibly of iron-age date.

The medieval and later structures to be described in a later volume include (S. of the church) a hall (10·2 m by 4·7 m) with rounded external corners, to which was added an annexe on the S. with a bench and stone-built table against its external S. gable end, suggesting a *scriptorium*. A small lime-kiln stood further to the S. Of the two rectangular buildings N. of the church, one (9·6 m by 3·8 m) was built into sloping ground with tiered stone seating in its W. half and a porch on the S., suggesting a school or assembly room; the other building at the N. end had been a two-storeyed structure of no great age, and a boundary wall linking this with the E. end of the church was also a recent feature.

The earliest documentary reference to the church here occurs in a confirmation charter (1195) of an early 12th-century grant of Llangennith to a French abbey,[2] and late medieval grants describe it as 'the hermitage of St. Kenydd-atte-Holme'.[3]

[1] By D. B. Hague on behalf of the Commission. *Arch. in Wales*, V (1965), No. 50; VI (1966), No. 49; VII (1967), No. 33; VIII (1968), No. 51. Final report forthcoming.
[2] *Epis. Acts*, I, D.25 (1095–1115).
[3] *Arch. Camb.*, 1893, p. 297.

Llangennith.

ss 49 s.w. (4009 9258)   1965–8   XXI s.w.

BURRY HOLMS

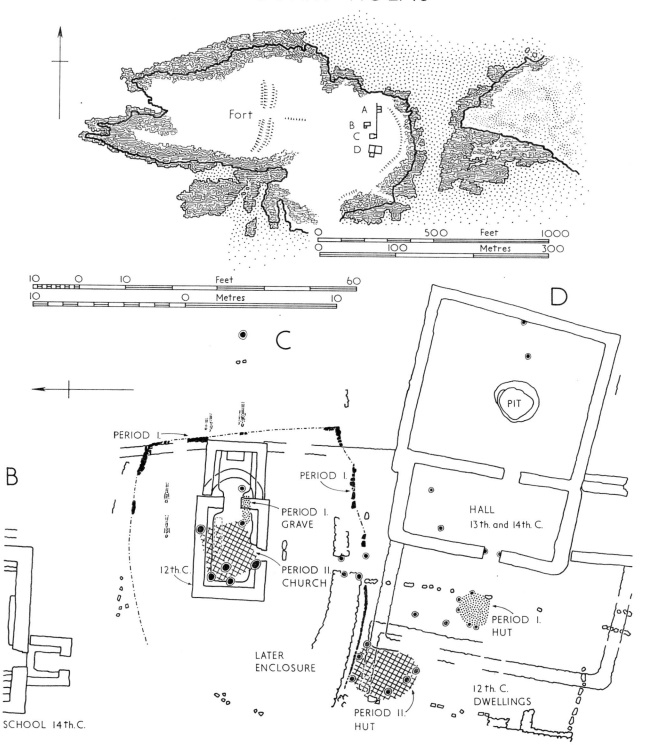

Fort

A
B
C
D

500 Feet 1000
100 Metres 300

10 0 10 Feet 60
10 0 Metres 10

C

D

PERIOD I.

PERIOD I.

PERIOD I.
GRAVE

PERIOD II.
CHURCH

12th.C.

B

PIT

HALL
13th. and 14th. C.

PERIOD I.
HUT

LATER
ENCLOSURE

12th. C.
DWELLINGS

PERIOD II.
HUT

SCHOOL 14th.C.

FIG. 5. No. 821.

16

(822) BISHOPSTON. The location of an early monastic settlement in this Gower village is based on certain phrases of the Book of Llandaf. The present form of the name, appearing in the early 13th century,[1] reflects the territorial rights of the bishops of Llandaf in this village, but the traditional Welsh name, Llandeilo Ferwallt,[2] occurs in presumed pre-12th-century entries in the Book of Llandaf variously in that form or as *Lan Mergualt* and *Llanferwalt*. In particular the title 'princeps' for the leading cleric there and the phrase 'in monasterio sancti cunuuri id est lann berugall'[3] point directly to the existence of a monastic community of the Celtic type.

It may be presumed that the site of this monastic settlement lay where the existing medieval church stands in a dell on the hillside of Bishopston Valley. There are no surviving features that might be associated with such a settlement.

[1] Clark, *Cartae*, II, p. 478; *Epis. Acts*, II, p. 705 (L. 340).
[2] Peniarth MS. 147 (an early list of parishes), in *Report on MSS. in the Welsh Language*, I, pt. ii (H.M.S.O., 1899), p. 919.
[3] *Lib. Land.*, pp. 145, 239; Lloyd, *Hist. Wales*, pp. 206, 269.

Bishopston.
SS 58 N.E. (5775 8936)   XXXII N.W.

(823) LLANGYFELACH. In the mid-12th-century Latin text of Rhigyfarch's *Life* of St. David the 'monasterium Langemelach' is reckoned as one of twelve monasteries founded by that saint, i.e. as one of the most ancient in Britain together with Glastonbury, Repton and Llantwit Major.[1] Another part of the text implies that this spot rather than the site of St. David's Cathedral was the saint's particular sanctuary where he received miraculous gifts from the patriarch of Jerusalem.[2]

The existence at the parish church of two 9th-century slabs (Nos. 882–3 below) and, more significantly, of the decorated base of a tall pillar-cross (No. 931) is corroborative evidence of an early ecclesiastical site of some importance. The part of the parish forming a manor belonging to the bishops of St. David's was still known as 'the clas' in the late 16th century, and a ruinous structure there was also called 'Y Llan'.[3] In addition, the churchyard is unusually large for what was until recently a sparsely populated rural parish, and its rounded outline may reflect that of an original monastic enclosure.

[1] J. W. James, *Rhigyfarch's Life of St. David* (Cardiff, 1967), p. 8 (in basic text); later additional text (as in *Vitae Sanct.*, p. 154) adds 'in regione Guhir'.
[2] J. W. James, *op. cit.*, p. 21; *Vitae Sanct.*, p. 164.
[3] Rice Merrick, Peniarth MS. 120, published in Lluyd, *Parochialia*, III, p. 146 (before recognition of true author).

Llangyfelach.
SS 69 N.W. (646 989)   XIV N.E.

(824) MERTHYR MAWR. Whether there was a monastic establishment at this site cannot be established satisfactorily,[1] and the present form of the place-name is not a reliable indication of its former importance.[2] But the number of pre-Norman monuments there, ranging from the late 5th century (No. 847) but chiefly belonging to the end of the period (Nos. 917–18, 952, 964–70, 987), probably indicates both its early origin and its relative standing at a later date. More particularly, the inscription on one of two slab-crosses from the vicinity (No. 928 together with No. 927) apparently recording a gift of property would be more likely to have been executed for a religious community than otherwise. The site has no topographical or structural features to strengthen this conjecture.

[1] A pre-Norman monastic site is indicated here on the O.S. *Map of Britain in the Dark Ages* (Ordnance Survey, 2nd edn. 1966).
[2] *Merthir Mimor, M. Myuor, Merthirmouoz* in the Book of Llandaf (*Lib. Land.*, pp. 31, 90, 212, 284), possibly indicating an original commemoration here of one *Myfor* or *Mofor* (cf. Llanofer, Monmouthshire), supplanted by the present dedication to St. Teilo (I. Williams, *Enwau Lleoedd* (Liverpool, 1945), p. 75; *Arch. Camb.*, LXXXIII (1928), p. 369); but for a contrary view that these forms represent *M. Mawr*, see *N.L.W. Journ.*, XI, No. 3 (1960), p. 199.

Merthyr Mawr.
SS 87 N.E. (8828 7753)   XL S.W.

(825) MARGAM. The great Cistercian abbey of Margam founded in 1147 preserved no record or tradition of an earlier monastery on the site,[1] but the existence of such a Celtic establishment may be inferred from the group of decorated and inscribed stones found in the immediate area of the Cistercian abbey.[2] These monuments belong to the later part of the period (late 9th–late 10th century), but the establishment may have begun much earlier. The large disc-headed slab-cross set in a socket-stone (the 'Conbelin' stone, 907) and first noted outside the churchyard would only be appropriate in the setting of a Celtic monastic enclosure, while the other pre-Norman stones were presumably associated with burials, one of them (910) found in the existing churchyard, S. of the church. This would suggest that the church of the Celtic monastery stood more or less on the site of the existing abbey church, but there are no topographical features that could indicate the extent of the monastic enclosure.

Radford, *Margam*, pp. 14–15.
[1] The name Margan (*sic*) pertains only to the district in the 12th century (Lloyd, *Hist. Wales*, p. 275 (n. 265)).
[2] Nos. 901, 907–10, forming part of the collection in Margam Stones Museum, three of them (901, 908–9) first recorded in the mid-19th century.

Margam (E), Port Talbot (C).
SS 88 N.E. (801 863)   XXXIII N.E.

(826) LLANTWIT MAJOR. The existence of an important monastery and school in the early 6th century under the direction of St. Illtud is attested in the early-7th-century *Life* of St. Samson,[1] and its location at this spot (Llanilltud Fawr) can hardly be resisted in the light of the place-name and evidence for a major monastery here in the 9th century and later. The 9th-century *Life* of St. Paul Aurelian speaks of the contemporary 'Iltuti monasterium';[2] and of the surviving monuments of that period at the site, one (No. 933) testifies that it was erected by an abbot Samson. The material in the Book of Llandaf, presumably originating in the period 9th–12th centuries, frequently refers to an 'abbas sancti Ilduti' or the 'abbas lannildut', while the less distorted evidence of the Llancarfan charters also gives 'Samson, abbas altaris sancti Eltuti'.[3] The *Life* of St. Illtud is a 12th-century work with little or no reliable information for the earlier history of the site, but

it describes the settlement established by the saint in the Hodnant valley ('pulcherrimus iste locorum') with its little dwelling, cemetery and oratory, to be followed by a church surrounded by a stone wall and a ditch.[4] The pre-Norman monuments from the churchyard (Nos. 911–12, 932–3, 953–4) show a relatively superior quality of carved decoration, and their inscriptions suggest the patronage of local rulers, at least to the extent of regarding the site as appropriate for the burial of such persons and therefore monastic.

An area of higher ground W. of the churchyard enclosed by a widely curving low bank and shallow ditch was formerly regarded as the site of a 'monastery'. Excavations of both the embankment and of structures within it in 1912–14[5] and 1937[6] established that the area had been occupied from the 12th century as a grange of Tewkesbury Abbey, to which the church of Llantwit Major and its possessions had been granted before 1135.[7] It was concluded that these excavations provided no evidence on 'the problem of the pre-Norman occupation of Llantwit Major'.[8] In the absence of such evidence, it may be assumed that the early monastery lay in the area of the existing churchyard and adjacent streets, but there are no topographical features which might reflect its boundary or plan.

[1] Lloyd, *Hist. Wales*, p. 144 (and refs. there cited); N. K. Chadwick, *Early Brittany* (Cardiff, 1969), pp. 250–5, 263–4; *Journ. Theol. Studies*, N.S. XVII, pt. 2 (1966), pp. 348, 378–9 (J. Morris).
[2] Lloyd, *Hist. Wales*, p. 144 (n. 100).
[3] *Vitae Sanct.*, p. 126.
[4] *Vitae Sanct.*, p. 202.
[5] By J. W Rodger, *Arch. Camb.*, 1915, pp. 141–56.
[6] By V. E. Nash-Williams, *B.B.C.S.*, XIV, iv (May 1952), pp. 313–333.
[7] *S. Wales & Mon. Rec. Soc.*, No. 2 (1950), pp. 140, 156–60.
[8] As n. 6.

Llantwit Major.
    SS 96 N.E. (966 687)   XLIX N.W.

(827) LLANCARFAN. A 'Lann Gharban' (= Gabran) is mentioned in the 9th- to 10th-century Irish *Lives* of St. Finnian,[1] implying a monastic site. Lifris' *Life* of St. Cadog and other writings which refer to an abbot of Nantcarfan are not earlier than the late 11th century, though the tradition they embody associating St. Cadog with S.E. Wales and this site in particular can be taken as valid.[2]

The unusually large churchyard, rounded in plan and set in the valley bottom beside a stream, may indicate the monastic enclosure. Preserved in the church is a fragment of a late-9th-century pillar-cross (940) which would have accorded with a monastery but could conceivably have come from some other place. It was held formerly that the monastery was located at Llanfythin, less than a mile to the N. of the church and the site of a grange of Margam Abbey.[3] A grant of land about 1190 to enlarge this grange refers to an 'old churchyard' there,[4] and the recent discovery at this spot of several burials of probable pre-Norman date has revived the suggestion.[5] That an ancient link existed between Llancarfan and Llanfythin is indicated by the claim in Cadog's *Life* that St. Meuthi (also known as Tatheus) was Cadog's teacher. It has also been claimed that the 'traditional' site lay a short distance S. of the churchyard where traces remain of footings of structures,[6] but

there is no specific reason or archaeological evidence for this identification.

In the material appended to Lifris' *Life* there is a detailed description of the monastery, supposedly in the time of Cadog,[7] but at best reflecting the monastery's possessions on the eve of the Norman Conquest. Several of the named prebends can be identified with hamlets in and adjacent to the parish,[8] but even so it is not possible to re-create a convincing picture of the Celtic monastery.

[1] C. Brooke in *Celt and Saxon*, p. 291 (n. 2).
[2] *Ibid.*, pp. 283–322; *Vitae Sanct.*, pp. 24–140; Lloyd, *Hist. Wales*, pp. 206, 276.
[3] At ST 0512 7125. *Arch. Camb.*, 1865, p. 345.
[4] Clark, *Cartae*, II, pp. 387–8; *Epis. Acts*, II, No. L.218.
[5] *Arch. in Wales*, IX (1969), No. 55.
[6] At 0515 7008. S. Baring-Gould and J. Fisher, *Lives of the British Saints* (London, 1907–13), II, p. 17; *Arch. Camb.*, LXXXVIII (1933), pp. 401–2.
[7] *Vitae Sanct.*, p. 120.
[8] W. J. Rees, *Lives of the Cambro-British Saints . . .* (Llandovery, 1853), pp. 379–80.

Llancarfan.
    ST 07 S.E. (051 702)   XLVI S.W.

(828) LLANDOUGH. The historical evidence for a monastic establishment here is all late. It consists of references to an abbot, first in Lifris' *Life* of St. Cadog, 'princeps altaris Docgwinni', 'prepositus altaris sancti Docgwini';[1] and in the material incorporated in the Book of Llandaf on 'abbas Docguinni' is frequently mentioned.[2] The archaeological evidence is specifically the one Early Christian monument on the site (938), an impressive and elaborate pillar-cross of the late 10th or early 11th century, which would be appropriate only to the enclosure of a major monastery, a status that is implied by the coupling of references to the abbot of Llandough in the Book of Llandaf with the abbots of Llantwit Major and Llancarfan.[3] The site has no topographical features to suggest the scale of the establishment, but its situation in a valley just out of sight of the coast is closely analogous to others such as Llantwit Major.

[1] *Vitae Sanct.*, pp. 134 and 132–3; *Celt and Saxon*, pp. 313–14 (C. Brooke).
[2] *Lib. Land.*, pp. 131, 140 and *passim*; *Trans. Cymmr.*, 1963, pt. 1, pp. 82–95. For the identity of Docus or Docguinnus see G. O. Pierce, *Place-names of Dinas Powys Hundred* (Cardiff, 1968), pp. 112–15; E. G. Bowen, *Saints, Seaways and Settlements* (Cardiff, 1969), p. 107; C. Brooke in *Celt and Saxon*, pp. 297–8.
[3] This status is also implied in Lifris' *Life* when Docguinnus is coupled with St. David and St. Teilo in receiving lands from St. Cadog, *Vitae Sanct.*, p. 72.

Llandough, Cogan, and Leckwith (E), Penarth (C).
    ST 17 S.E. (167 732)   XLVII N.W.

(829) LLANDAF. The question of the existence, much more the nature, of any pre-Norman establishment at Llandaf has been rendered problematical by virtue of the fact that almost all the relevant historical material was produced to further the interests of the Norman bishops of Llandaf, as to both the see itself and the extent of the newly-created diocese.[1] In the Book of Llandaf the predecessor of the cathedral is regularly

termed a 'monasterium' and even on occasion an 'arch-monastery'. But there are several pointers to the validity of the claim that there was such a monastery at this site, beginning with the fact that the cathedral was established where it is rather than in Cardiff, the *caput* of the Norman lordship. The site is topographically significant, being at the point where an early road, possibly the Roman road from Caerleon, crosses the River Taf.[2] The specific archaeological evidence is the surviving part of an elaborate pillar-cross (937) of the late 10th or early 11th century, such as might be associated with a monastic settlement, though not necessarily of equal status with Llantwit Major or Llancarfan.

[1] *Epis. Acts*, I, pp. 24, 33, 55–68, 119–33, 147–72, 181–6; II, pp. 480–2. C. Brooke in N. K. Chadwick (ed.), *Studies in the Early British Church* (Cambridge, 1958), pp. 204–42. C. Brooke in *Celt and Saxon*, pp. 315–322. *Morgannwg*, IV (1960), pp. 50–65.
[2] F. J. North, *The Stones of Llandaff Cathedral* (Cardiff, 1957), pp. 3–13.

Llandaf (E), Cardiff (C).
ST 17 N.E. (156 779)   XLIII S.W.

(830) FLATHOLM. The *Life* of St. Cadog refers to the island of 'Echni' or 'Eckni' as a place for Lenten retreat, together with 'Barren' which is taken to be Barry; and a further reference equates 'Eckni' with 'Holma'.[1] An account of a visit to the island in 1815 describes two graves with cross-decorated stones at head and foot, one of them an open slab-lined cist.[2] These stones, lying about 23 m E. of the farmhouse on the W. side of the island (at ST 2198 6498), within a walled enclosure of no great age, were again reported in 1890 and subsequently,[3] but did not include the slab recorded below as No. 893, and the surviving example is attributable to a post-Norman date. Recent excavations[4] in the area to the N.E. of the graves, noted as a monastic site on the 1921 edition of the O.S. map, found no traces of early medieval settlement, but evidence of occupation from the 12th century occurred near the farmhouse.

The tradition embodied in the *Life* of St. Cadog suggests that there was probably a hermitage here, but this provides no certain indication of how long-established this may have been.

[1] *Vitae Sanct.*, pp. 62, 92. These references are probably taken from the near-contemporary Latin *Lives* of St. Finnian like other material in this *Life* though not substantiated in the earlier Irish *Lives* (C. Brooke in *Celt and Saxon*, p. 292).
[2] *Memoire of Thomas Turner* by 'a relative' (London, 1875), p. 21.
[3] *Trans. Cardiff Nat. Soc.*, XXII (1890), pp. 105 *seq.*
[4] By H. B. A. Ratcliffe-Densham. *Ibid.*, LXXX (1948–50), pp. 19–23

Cardiff St. Mary (E), Cardiff (C).
ST 26 N.W. (219 649)   LI S.E.

INSCRIBED AND SCULPTURED STONES

EARLY CHRISTIAN MONUMENTS

IN their variety and range of types, the stone monuments of the Early Christian period in Glamorgan are more representative than those of any other county in Wales. It is thus possible to arrange them in groups that, broadly speaking, cover the whole range of Welsh monuments of this kind, according to the form of the monument and its decoration.

Class A	Inscribed stones of the early period	(Nos. 841 to 850)
B	Pillar-stones with incised cross	(Nos. 861 to 871)
C	Recumbent grave-slabs with incised cross	(Nos. 881 to 893)
D	Standing sculptured slabs, including sub-types	(Nos. 901 to 929)
E	Pillar-crosses, usually composite	(Nos. 931 to 941)
F	Other decorated stones	(Nos. 951 to 956)
G	Headstones and grave-slabs of the late period	(Nos. 961 to 988)

The first class corresponds to Group I of Nash-Williams' *The Early Christian Monuments of Wales* (*E.C.M.W.* in following references), and the monuments of his Group II belong to the second and third of these classes, the latter including some of his Group III, which is represented mainly by Classes D to F. Class G corresponds for the most part to his Group IV ('Transitional Romanesque Monuments') and includes a number of additions to the eighty-three entries for the county in *E.C.M.W.*[1] Within each class or sub-type, entries are given by their original location according to the sequence of quarter sheets of 10 km squares of O.S. 1:10,560 maps.

This arrangement by the type of monument is also to a limited extent a chronological sequence in that stones in Class A are not later than the early 7th century, those in Classes B and C fall between that date and the late 9th or early 10th century, those in Classes D and E extend from the 9th century to the 11th century (with some in Class F), and those in Classes F and G are mostly of the 11th and 12th centuries. In general these classes of monuments are broadly datable by comparative typology, but the particular considerations that apply are discussed below as well as in certain individual descriptions. Only two of them (Nos. 911 and 933) can be associated directly with historical evidence which in itself is not incontrovertible.

The monuments in Classes A, C and G were primarily tombstones or grave-markers, although only five of the first category feature the explicit phrase *hic iacit* ('here lies'). The setting up of crude pillar-stones may be derived from prehistoric practice as much as from Roman or continental memorials, and even at a somewhat later date it was not thought inappropriate to describe a group of standing stones at 'Cefn Celfi' near Pontardawe as the graves of three folk heroes, Cynon, Cynfael and Cynfeli.[2] In the 12th-century *Life* of St. Cadog the grave of the murdered Llywri is said to have been marked by an upright boulder.[3] Two at least of the shaped pillar-stones in Class B which have a single-name inscription (Nos. 862 and 867) may have marked graves, but use for other dedicatory functions or merely to serve as boundary marks is quite possible.[4] There is a similar diversity of function in the slabs of Class D. While the 'Samson' cross (No. 912) at Llantwit Major may have been erected to mark either the cist-burial found at its foot or the burial immediately beneath it,[5] the 'Conbelin' stone (No. 907) at Margam inscribed with similar phrases stood outside the churchyard, possibly serving as a boundary mark or, in view of the didactic element in its decoration, as a preaching point. Stone crosses with no clear memorial purpose such as those in Class E were a characteristic of major Celtic monasteries,[6] the best examples being the Llandough cross (No. 938) and the former cross at Llangyfelach evidenced by a base stone (No. 931). The inscription on the Ogmore stone (No. 926) apparently records a grant of land to a church (presumably the foundation at Merthyr Mawr) and also marks its boundary, as is probably true of some other stones (Nos. 919–20, 927–8); the stone recently found near Pen-y-fai (No. 922) was probably re-used in this way.[7] In two instances the stone may have been set up by a holy well (Nos. 923 from Cwm Gwenffrwd and 936 from near Bridgend), but the evidence for such an association is not conclusive.

These various functions of the monuments are not directly reflected in the various forms they take, which are to some extent limited by the nature of the available stone. In most instances this material is

---

[1] This Inventory describes 107 monuments including fragments, and others no longer surviving are noted in appendices to the appropriate classes. One stone is listed twice (Nos. 868 and 914) to represent two stages of use but is not duplicated in the above total. On the other hand, two entries describe monuments which, because they are broken, formed two separate entries respectively in *E.C.M.W.*; three reputed stones in the appendices also formed part of the total in *E.C.M.W.*

[2] *Proc. Brit. Acad.*, LIII (1967), p. 113; see also above, Vol. I, i, No. 542.

[3] *Vitae Sanct.*, pp. 66, 68.

[4] *Cf.* Henry, *Irish Art*, I, p. 54; see also above, Vol. I, i, p. 121.

[5] *Arch. Camb.*, 1903, pp. 56–64. A stone cross placed over the grave of St. Samson is mentioned in the 12-century *Life* of St. Illtud (*Vitae Sanct.*, p. 216).

[6] Henry, *Irish Art*, I, pp. 134–6.

[7] Boundary stones on monastic lands are mentioned in a later 12th-century grant to Margam (*Epis. Acts*, II, No. L.208).

coarse sandstone or schist from the immediate locality, and the Sutton stone used for some monuments of the 10th to 12th centuries occurs locally in the south and east of the county as well as at the known later quarries near Ogmore (at ss 864 754). Most of the stones in Class A are merely roughly squared pillar-stones, together with some re-used Roman material. Those in Classes B and C show more evidence of being dressed to a regular shape, notably the inscribed cylindrical column from Port Talbot (No. 867) and the stone from Carn Caca with expanded rounded head (No. 861); one pillar-stone at Llanmadog (No. 865) has a quasi-cruciform head, but is unlikely to be a prototype of the later pillar-crosses. These earlier monuments were inevitably crude like their counterparts in Ireland before the development of a native tradition of stone carving. Once the cross incised on the stone becomes its main feature it is possible to see a progressive development in both the form of the cross and the shaping of the stone itself. Not all stages from incised to fully sculptured forms are apparent in the surviving monuments of the county or even in those of Wales as a whole, but instances of decoration in low relief in imitation of incised forms can be noted on stones of Class C, in particular the fragment at Llanwynno (No. 889) and a weathered slab at Llangyfelach (No. 883). The more numerous standing slabs of Class D include two distinct types, those with a rounded head wider than the shaft below ('disc-headed' slabs, Nos. 903–13) and those in which the cross is formed of roughly equal segments of a rounded or rectangular panel ('panelled-cross' slabs, Nos. 914–25), the latter being a strictly local development. Their origin in the cross-decorated stones of Classes B and C seems clear, the Carn Caca stone (No. 861) in particular suggesting the tendency to make the cross-bearing rounded head distinct from the supporting shaft. The same tendency is apparent in some Irish slabs of pre-9th-century date,[8] though not developed there as in South Wales into the distinctive disc-headed form. The panelled-cross form more obviously derives from the common 'cross formy' of earlier memorials (e.g. No. 848, the 'Bodvoc' stone, and E.C.M.W. 17, 19–20, 280, 367), perhaps rendered in relief for the first time on No. 915 at Neath from which Nos. 916 and 921 follow directly, though others seem to derive from both this and No. 914, as is discussed further below. Such evidence as there is for pillar-crosses in their complete form points to Anglian rather than Irish influences, but the actual form of these can vary from a single squared pillar to a composite and elaborately moulded monument such as that at Llandough (No. 938). The head-stones of Class G are generally regularly shaped blocks with little carving in the round. It is characteristic of the monuments in Classes D to F that the later examples (i.e. late 10th- to 11th-century) are more elaborately decorated yet also more clumsily designed and executed than the earlier ones.

Though the main categories by form are readily distinguished, some monuments combine features of two or more types. Thus one slab with a cross-head at Merthyr Mawr (No. 928) has the bulbous angle-mouldings more characteristic of a group of pillar-crosses (Nos. 935–8), and another at Margam (the 'Grutne' stone, No. 910) combines the disc-head of one type of slab with the squared inscribed shaft of some pillar-crosses but tapered like slabs. With the 'Conbelin' stone (No. 907), a pedestal block that might be expected with a pillar-cross here supports a 'disc-headed' slab. The monuments of Classes C to G similarly share a common repertoire of decoration, iconography and inscriptional formulae. The chief characteristics of the formal decoration, consisting of plaitwork or fret-patterns,[9] are the avoidance of symmetry or repetition and, in terms of development, a progressive deterioration in execution until Romanesque patterns and forms prevail in place of native tradition. Hence, some monuments are listed

---

[8] E.g. the Killaghtee slab, Donegal (Henry, *Irish Art*, I, Pl. IV and p. 120); cross on Skellig Michael, Kerry (M. and L. de Paor, *Early Christian Ireland* (London, 3rd ed., 1961), Pl. 7); slab at Kirk Braddan, Isle of Man (*Proc. Soc. Ant. Scot.*, L (1916), pp. 52–3 and Fig. 5).

[9] For analysis of patterns according to Romilly Allen's classification, see *E.C.M.W.*, pp. 235–7. In descriptions of plaitwork, the number of cords is reckoned across the narrowest dimension even if this is a vertical dimension.

that may not strictly be 'pre-Norman' but, owing something to earlier trends, are included for the sake of consistency.

Several monuments of the earlier part of the period (Class A and some in Classes B and C) were apparently sited in close relation to Roman roads or ridgeway routes that may have been contemporary (see above, p. 4 and Fig. 1).[10] The stone from Clwydi Banwen (No. 841) stood close to the road connecting the Roman forts at Neath and Coelbren, while the one on Cefn Gelli-gaer (No. 842) stands near the road between Gelli-gaer and Penydarren forts. Two others formerly on the eastern outskirts of Port Talbot (Nos. 846, 849) were near the presumed line of the road towards the fort at Neath. At the same time it is worth remarking on the almost complete absence of any association of these monuments with known Roman sites, with the exception of the Roman altar re-used for a memorial (No. 845) at Loughor, in what was the most intensively Romanised area of Wales. Cefn y Brithdir is a ridge parallel to Cefn Gelli-gaer, and the stone inscribed 'Tegernacus' (No. 843) stood near a trackway along this ridge. The 'Bodvoc' stone (No. 848) stood beside a trackway along the plateau surface of Margam Mountain, and a lost stone (see Appendix to Class A) was presumably on an early route from the Neath Valley across Hirwaun Common towards Merthyr Tudful. If, as seems likely, these stones marked graves, they indicate the survival of an essentially pagan custom of wayside burial, to be supplanted gradually by churchyard burial. Only three stones of Class A seem to have been located originally at an ecclesiastical site (No. 844 at Llanmadog, No. 847 at Merthyr Mawr, and a stone formerly recorded at Llanrhidian), each within a mile of the coast and featuring other monuments of pre-Norman date. A coastal distribution characterises all but three of the stones in Class B, but those exceptions (Nos. 861–3) cannot be associated with established trackways. Several of them, such as Nos. 865–6 at Llanmadog and Nos. 867–8 at Port Talbot, seem to have been located at early ecclesiastical sites, and this is entirely so with the stones of Class C which may be compared with grave-slabs from similar sites in Ireland and the north of England.[11]

The later monuments are predominantly associated with ecclesiastical centres in the coastal lowland, particularly with the Celtic monastic foundations of Llantwit Major and Margam;[12] other such establishments at Llancarfan and Llandough are not so well reflected in their surviving monuments. Notable concentrations of pre-Norman stones occur at other ecclesiastical centres such as Ewenni, Llangyfelach and Merthyr Mawr for which there is little or no literary evidence of a specifically monastic establishment.[13] The area around Margam, including Port Talbot, has an unusually large number of monuments.[14] Six of these derive from sites on opposing banks of the River Afan (including one stone at the parish church but otherwise not located in origin) where the former line of the main road (and possibly also the Roman road) crossed the river. Both the west bank site ('The Croft', see No. 884) and the east bank site (two adjoining farms, Upper and Lower Court, now demolished) were also the location of a former medieval chapel;[15] but it is unlikely that either chapel was the 'capellam Sti Thomae . . . inter aquas de Avena et Neth' of a 12th-century charter,[16] and thus any connection with the earlier stone from Lower Court Farm inscribed TOME (No. 867) must remain quite uncertain.

---

[10] *Arch. Camb.*, XCIV (1939), pp. 30–41; *E.C.M.W.*, p. 4; E. G. Bowen, *The Settlements of the Celtic Saints in Wales* (Cardiff, 1954), pp. 24–5. But *cf.* L. Alcock in *P. and E. Wales*, p. 206.
[11] *Proc. Roy. Irish Acad.*, Vol. 61 (C, 1961), pp. 95–169; *Archaeologia*, LXXIV (1925), p. 258.
[12] At Llantwit Major, Nos. 911–12, 932–3, 953–4 and 974; at Margam (originally), Nos. 901, 907–10.
[13] At Ewenni, Nos. 924, 955, 975–81; at Llangyfelach, Nos. 882–3, 931; at Merthyr Mawr, Nos. 847, 917–18, 952, 964–70 and 987 (with Nos. 927–8 nearby).
[14] Nos. 846, 848–9, 867, 869–71, 884–7, 906, 919–21, 971 and 973.
[15] *Arch. Camb.*, LXXX (1925), p. 425; LXXXI (1926), pp. 193–7; *Trans. Port Talbot Hist. Soc.*, I, No. 1 (1963), p. 47.
[16] Clark, *Cartae*, I, p. 134. Three other chapels with the same dedication in the south of the county are specified in the same charter.

CLASS A: Inscribed Stones of the Early Period (Nos. 841–850) (Plates 1, 2)

Ten stones survive in the county with simple memorial inscriptions of the period 5th–7th centuries, and the inscriptions of two other stones now lost (see Appendix to Class A) should probably be added to their number. Though not as numerous as those in the south-western and north-western counties of Wales, they provide some evidence for the period succeeding the Roman occupation. Two of them are in fact Roman objects re-used to carry a memorial inscription, the Loughor altar (No. 845) and the Port Talbot milestone (No. 846). Two other stones in the Margam collection (Nos. 848–9) are neatly squared blocks that may represent Roman building material similarly re-used.

The inscriptions, surviving in varying degrees of completeness, are formed in Roman capitals and half-uncials, one (the 'Pumpeius' stone, No. 849) having a partially related inscription in ogam strokes which occur also on the re-used Roman altar (No. 845). In each case the inscription ranges along the length of the stone, to be read down the face of the upright pillar-stone or slab. The inscriptions show a development from those in which the letter-forms are entirely in fairly regular Roman capitals or cursive forms (Nos. 844, 847, and probably 841), through those with a few half-uncials (Nos. 846, 848–9), to two with a high proportion of half-uncials (Nos. 843 and 850). This development considered in relation to the whole *corpus* of Welsh inscriptions provides the basis for approximate dating within the period 5th–7th century.[17] Divergences from standard forms of letters are not peculiar to the inscriptions under review: the horizontal final I in Nos. 841, 848, 850 (and possibly 844) occurs widely over the whole period; the S-shaped G in Nos. 843 and 848 derives from the usual cursive form seen in No. 844; the A with indented cross-bar in Nos. 848 and 850 is common, though the inverted form in No. 848 is unique; the tilted A-s in No. 843, seemingly a compromise with the half-uncial letter, occur on the stone at Llansadyrnin, Carmarthenshire (*E.C.M.W.* 166); the M with closed loop in No. 850 also has parallels as indicated below; ligatured letters occurring on more than half these inscriptions are quite usual.

The two ogam-inscribed stones with their inscriptions of specifically Celtic type (i.e. the name alone and in the genitive case, or name with affiliation) point to a slight extension into south-east Wales of the Irish element so prevalent in south-west Wales; this is echoed in one inscription (No. 842 on Cefn Gelligaer) which apparently consisted only of the name in the genitive. In all the others, excepting the Latin inscription on the 'Pumpeius' stone (No. 849) which is uncertainly related to its ogam inscription, these Celtic features are combined with the classically derived *hic iacit* (Nos. 841, 847 and Appendix (i) being possible but uncertain instances). The unusual formula used on the Port Talbot milestone (No. 846) may be taken as an alternative rendering of the normal indication of affiliation. The vertical alignment of all the surviving inscriptions is indicative of how widely diffused in time and distribution such basically non-Roman influences could become. Similarly, the purely Roman names occurring on Nos. 843, 846–9 are in three instances (Nos. 843, 848–9) associated with Celtic names, of which another example is seen in isolation on No. 850.

In three instances an 'enclosure' is (or was) associated with a stone, but of these the one that surrounds the site of the 'Bodvoc' stone (No. 848) is a bronze-age ring-cairn (Ii 271). The 'two small circular entrenchments like cock-pits' that were described thus at the site of the Clwydi Banwen stone (No. 841) in 1695[18] were more plausibly recognised as ruined barrows in 1853 before their destruction.[19] There remains one

---

[17] *Inv. Anglesey*, p. xciv and Appendix V; *E.C.M.W.*, pp. 10–13 and Appendix I; Jackson, *Lang. and Hist.*, pp. 158–64; *cf. P. and E. Wales*, pp. 200–202.

[18] Camden, *Britannia* (ed. Gibson), p. 620.

[19] *Arch. Camb.*, 1865,, p. 59.

FIG. 6.

Forms of crosses on stones of Class B (except *m*). Scale $\frac{1}{10}$: (*a*) Neath (869), S. face; (*b*) ibid., N. face; (*c*) Pontrhydyfen (870); (*d*) Port Talbot (868); (*e*) Mynydd Merthyr (863); (*f*) Carn Caca (861); (*g*) Llanmadog (865); (*h*) Port Talbot (867), cross *a*; (*i*) ibid., cross *b*; (*j*) ibid., cross *c*; (*k*) Reynoldston (864), S. E. face; (*l*) ibid., N. W. face; (*m*) Mynydd Margam (848), Class A; (*n*) Merthyr Tudful (862); (*o*) Llanmadog (866).

instance where the bank survives with an inscribed stone, the monument on Cefn Gelli-gaer (No. 842). If, as suggested by Lhuyd's description in 1693, there was a burial cist at the centre of the enclosure, this may be another instance of a bronze-age site re-used or 'sanctified' by an Early Christian memorial, though the form of the bank does not accord so well with typical ring-cairns. On the other hand, there remains the possibility that the whole structure, inscribed stone, bank and possible cist, is of the Early Christian period.

CLASS B: *Pillar-stones with Incised Cross (Nos. 861–871) (Plates 3, 4)*

All eleven stones in this group were shaped to stand upright, their most prominent feature being a cross incised at the head. The various forms of the cross are depicted in Fig. 6. The plain linear Latin cross occurs on four stones, in one case twice (No. 869), and appears beside two plain outline crosses on the Port Talbot column (No. 867). The elaborated forms are usually based on an equal-armed cross, in one instance framed in a ring, while the ring-cross itself occurs only twice, with extended stem (Nos. 862 and 868).

These particular stones also provide the few indications of approximate date for this type of monument. Three stones (from Merthyr Tudful, Port Talbot and Neath, Nos. 862, 867, 871) carry a single-name inscription in developed half-uncials, suggesting an 8th- to 9th-century date. The stone from Port Talbot originally decorated with an incised ring-cross (No. 868) may be attributed to about the 7th or 8th century because this is a primitive form of cross, and because it was re-shaped in the late 9th or early 10th century. The plain linear crosses on the stone from near Neath (No. 869) closely resemble that on a similar Irish pillar-stone which has an inscription dating it to *ca.* 700, while the decorated block at Llanmadog (No. 866) also has Irish parallels thought to be of 9th-century date. With the Reynoldston pillar-stone (No. 864), the shallow decorative plaitwork indicates a later stage of development in which decoration begins to extend from the cross over the general surface of the stone.

CLASS C: *Recumbent Grave-slabs with Incised Cross (Nos. 881–893) (Plates 4, 5)*

Distinguishable from the pillar-stones of Class B are a number of cross-decorated slabs which it may be presumed were intended to lie recumbent over graves. In most cases, the cross extends the full length of the slab where complete, either incised or in low relief. One slab at Port Talbot decorated on both faces (No. 887) may have been re-used as an upright head-stone (set in a socket-stone such as those listed as Nos. 986–8 below), but could also have been re-used as a recumbent slab like the Bargoed slab (No. 881) which almost certainly was so re-used. Also included in this group is a small slab with an incised figure from a probable grave at Eglwysilan (No. 891).

On seven slabs the form of the cross is basically linear (Fig. 7), ranging from the simplest Latin cross of the Flatholm slab (No. 893) to elaborated ringed forms like Nos. 888 (with subordinate crosses), 892 and 881 with ring-and-dot devices in a rectangular frame. The design of one Llanwynno fragment (No. 889) is virtually the same device as the latter but rendered in false relief, the incised ring-and-dot becoming a carved ring-and-hollow, and the double-incised frame becoming a groove. It is possible to see in this the first development from incised decoration towards carving in relief and ultimately to sculptured ornament.[20] The much-weathered slab at Llangyfelach (No. 883) also has traces of raised ring-and-hollow devices; its ring-cross with outline stem below foreshadows the developed ring-cross with carved interlace seen in Nos. 882, 885–6. The ring-cross is one of the commonest forms on Irish recumbent slabs but usually has

---

[20] *Cf.* Henry, *Irish Art*, I, pp. 123, 130.

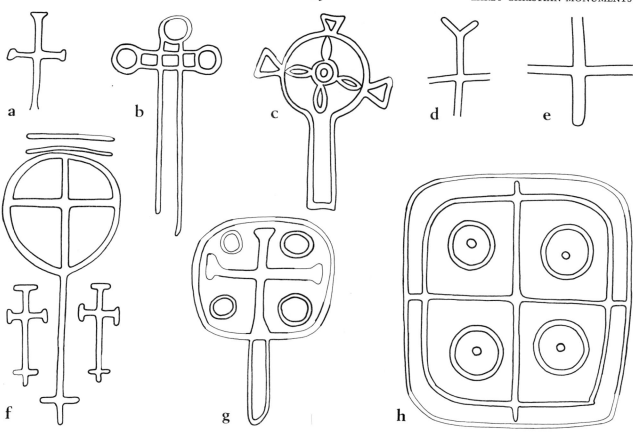

FIG. 7.

Forms of crosses on stones of Class C. Scale approx. $\frac{1}{10}$: (*a*) Port Talbot (884); (*b*) Port Talbot (887); (*c*) Gelli-gaer (892); (*d*) Llanwynno (890); (*e*) Flatholm (893); (*f*) Llantrisant (888); (*g*) Llangyfelach (883); (*h*) Brithdir (881).

less decoration than these three slabs.[21] Though Irish slabs and ornamental manuscripts provide many parallels for these 'expansional crosses', it does not follow that they derive directly from Irish work, and an independent but similar development from Merovingian prototypes is quite possible. It must also remain debatable whether the 'Celtic cross' form seen in these three slabs is to be derived from the incised ring-cross (as is suggested by the Llangyfelach slab) or from wooden free-standing crosses with arm-supporting struts becoming the segments of a wide ring.

Four of the slabs are inscribed, but of these only one inscription (No. 882) is complete, reading CRUX $\overline{\text{XPI}}$ (*The Cross of Christ*), a formula probably derived from Irish slabs[22] occurring again on No. 884 with an incomplete personal name and also on two standing slabs (Nos. 908, 910 below). Another at Baglan (No. 886) with the personal name BRANCU was probably completed by *fecit*, a formula indicated on No. 885 with other letters. No historical information can be gleaned from these inscriptions, but they strengthen the association with other types of slabs local to ecclesiastical centres on the Glamorgan coast.

---

[21] *Proc. Roy. Irish Acad.*, Vol. 61 (C, 1961), pp. 124–5.
[22] W. F. Wakeman, *A Survey of the Antiquarian Remains on the Island of Inismurray* (London, 1893), pp. 81, 83–4.

The lettering on these inscriptions is entirely in half-uncials, indicating broadly the period from the 7th to the 10th centuries, and it is unlikely that any of these slabs is earlier;[23] slabs later than the upper dating limit are treated in Class G below. Closer dating within that range is sometimes possible on the basis of stylistic comparisons with other monuments. The cross on both the Port Talbot fragment (No. 884) and a slab at Llanwynno (No. 890) resembles that on the pillar-stone near Neath (No. 869) attributed by analogy with an Irish stone to *ca.* 700, and the inscriptional formula on the first of these is on Irish slabs limited to the 8th century.[24] The ringed cross with external triangular terminals on a slab at Gelli-gaer (No. 892) is found on some Irish grave-slabs, and also on the Moylough belt-reliquary attributed to the early 8th century.[25] The elaborated expansional cross seen on the better-preserved slab at Llangyfelach (No. 882) and on a Port Talbot fragment (No. 885) and the Baglan slab (No. 886) shows a development which on Irish slabs is datable to the late 9th and 10th centuries, though combining this with a ringed form of cross which is mainly characteristic of the 9th century in Ireland. On this Llangyfelach slab (No. 882) are double-beaded plaits closely paralleled by the Gwnnws stone, Cardiganshire (*E.C.M.W.* 125), which has an inscription indicating an early 9th-century date.

CLASS D: Standing Sculptured Slabs (Nos. 901–929) (Plates 5–20)

Erect slabs with carved decoration in low relief form the most numerous single type of Early Christian monument in the county, with twenty-nine surviving examples. Apart from the two distinctive sub-types already referred to above ('disc-headed' and 'panelled-cross' types), there are two slabs displaying a ringed cross on a surface otherwise plain, from Margam (No. 901) and Nash (No. 902), and three other slabs with some features in common, from Ogmore (No. 926) and near Merthyr Mawr (Nos. 927–8).

Traces of inscriptions in varying degrees of completeness occur on twelve stones of this group, all with the exception of the Margam 'Conbelin' stone (No. 907) placed in horizontal lines below the cross-head of the slab. Inscriptions on disc-headed slabs (Plate 12) are set in small panels subordinate to the decorative scheme, except for the 'Grutne' stone at Margam (No. 910) in which, as with the panelled-cross slabs, the inscription fills the main face of the shaft. The incised lettering is in the rounded half-uncials of contemporary manuscripts, embracing variant forms of E, M and S (Nos. 910–12, 920, 926) and such other manuscript features as abbreviated words (*pro*, Nos. 907–8; *dei, deo*, Nos. 910, 920, 926; *Christi*, No. 908; and *et*, Nos. 908, 911, 926–8), with marks of abbreviation (No. 908), and word-separation by dots (Nos. 908, 910, 920, 926). On some apparently uninscribed slabs an inscription may have been painted rather than incised, e.g. Nos. 916, 922, and there is some indication that on the 'Samson' cross at Llantwit Major (No. 912) the incised letters were coloured for emphasis.[26] On the other hand the stone from Eglwys Nynnid (No. 921) suggests an attempt was made to remove the incised letters, possibly for secondary use of the stone, and this may have obtained in the case of some apparently uninscribed stones. Some blunders in the cutting of inscriptions may be ascribed to illiterate copying of written patterns, e.g. NNI in No. 908, the omitted N and I of No. 910, the intrusive I of No. 911, the corrected minims of IM in No. 912, and Q for G in No. 919 (where *petri* may be a blunder for *petra*).

The phraseology of these inscriptions extends beyond mere commemoration or dedication (as on the 'Samson' cross, No. 912, W. face). One phrase especially characteristic of the area (but not exclusively so) records the making of the cross by *X pro anima Y* (Nos. 907–8, 910–11, 920–3) and in two other cases by

[23] *Proc. Roy. Irish Acad.*, Vol. 61 (C, 1961), p. 156.
[24] *Ibid.*, pp. 151–2.
[25] *Ibid.*, Fig. 13 (8) and Pl. XXX (1); Henry, *Irish Art*, I, p. 116 and Pl. 35.
[26] *Arch. Camb.*, 1893, p. 327; *cf. Archaeologia*, LXXXIX (1943), p. 40.

X pro anima eius (Nos. 912, 927; *cf.* also No. 933). Other formal phrases, essentially deriving from an ecclesiastical context with documentary forms providing prototypes are *in nomine D(e)i Summi* (Nos. 910–911, 920, 926, 928; *cf.* also No. 933) and *in grefium* (for *graphium*) *in proprium usque in diem iudici(i)* (No. 928). These phrases with their free syntax and such variations as *proparabit, properabit, propararet* and *preparauit* (all for *preparavit*; *cf.* No. 933) indicate how far removed from strictly classical forms the contemporary use of Latin had become. Some of the personal names have similar or related forms in manuscripts derived ultimately from the pre-conquest period,[27] but there can be no certainty in identifying names that correspond. The 'king' named Samson on No. 912 at Llantwit Major is not known in any of the king-lists or genealogies relating to the area, but the Houelt (*Hywel*), son of Res (*Rhys*), on No. 911 may be accepted as the king of Glywysing who is attested in the late 9th century independently of the genealogies. Of the four names on the W. face of the 'Samson' stone (No. 912), the first, *Iltuti*, may be taken as a dedication of the slab to St. Illtud as founder or patron of the monastic establishment at Llantwit Major, the others also being regarded as possible early patrons similarly commemorated. Two local figures (? rulers) seem to be coupled together in the dedications on the Ogmore and Merthyr Mawr stones (Nos. 926–7): Glywys (as *Gliguis* and *Gliussi*) is stated in the *Life* of St. Cadog to have been that saint's grandfather from whom the kingdom of Glywysing was named,[28] and a 'Merthir Gliuis' appears as a place-name in the Book of Llandaf;[29] of *Nertat* or *Nerttan*, the other name linked with his, nothing further is known. The *Arthmail* on the Ogmore stone (No. 926), a late form of the name occurring on No. 933 at Llantwit Major as *Artmali*, cannot in this instance be identified with the king (or kings) named Arthfael in the genealogies.

With the greater number of examples in this class, some typological sequences might be sought, in which elements of both form and decoration have to be considered together. It would seem a natural development for the simple cross-decorated grave-slabs of Class C to have been set upright in the course of the 8th and 9th centuries, and then become progressively elaborated. But this cannot be demonstrated by examples, for the Margam plain slab (No. 901) which most nearly seems to belong to such a transitional stage (and was certainly an erect not a recumbent slab) has the pierced hollows of some Manx slabs attributable to the 10th century, and thus belongs to a later stage. The other comparable rectangular slab with a similar ringed cross of plaitwork from Nash Manor (No. 902) derives its flat relief and iconography from combined Manx and Irish influences, and is thus likely to be of similar date; the small rectangular panels especially (with the figures of SS. Paul and Anthony and also possibly David the harpist) recall the sculptural panels of Irish high crosses. This, the tallest of the monolithic slabs, may be purposely symbolical in its proportions, the height being six times the width as with the human frame.[30] The early prototypes of disc-headed slabs (Plates 5–13) were suggested above, but there must be an unrepresented interim stage between these and such slabs as the 'Enniaun' stone at Margam (No. 908) and the 'Houelt' stone at Llantwit Major (911), for which their inscriptions and style of decoration, owing something to Irish work, indicate a mid-9th-century date. The others of this type, apart from that at Llangennith (No. 905) which is probably also 9th-century, show a progressive deterioration in style and form, the coarser plaitwork in the two composite slabs at Margam and Llantwit Major (Nos. 907 and 912) of the 10th century, debased key-patterns (on the Coelbren stone No. 904) and plaitwork (on two stones at Margam, Nos. 906, 909) by the following century. The form of the cross in each case filling the disc-head is predominantly the ringed cross potent which of itself varies only slightly. The plain incised outline form with central square on the

---

[27] See references cited with Nos. 907–8, 912.
[28] *Vitae Sanct.*, pp. 24, 118 (*Vita B. Cadoci*, Prefatio and ch. 45); Bartrum, *Tracts*, p. 24.
[29] *Lib. Land.*, p. 225.
[30] *Cf.* Henry, *Irish Art*, II, p. 142, citing St. Augustine.

Llanguicke fragment (No. 903) is enclosed in an incised circular frame,[31] but normally the cross is in low relief with its arm-ends linked by panelled arcs of a ring. The late, 'hybrid' nature of the 'Conbelin' stone at Margam (No. 907) is reflected in its central ringed boss and stem carried down the shaft on one face. On the 'Enniaun' stone (No. 908) the cross is expansional rather than potent, with squared arm-ends and hollowed angles, but it derives from the same (probably Irish) stylistic source. With two other Margam stones (Nos. 909–10) the cross forms are characteristically Northumbrian and North British, the latter showing in its square proportions and inscribed panelled shaft a rather hybrid character.

The 'panelled-cross' slabs (Plates 14–18) in contrast show little decoration beyond the cross itself. With the notable exception of the re-shaped pillar-stone from Port Talbot (No. 914), their patterns all derive from the cross formy in two acceptable sequences. The simplest and thus presumably earliest form is on the Neath stone (No. 915), with sunken wedge-shaped panels or 'arms'. As repeated on the Eglwys Nynnid stone (No. 921), Tythegston slab (No. 916) and the Merthyr Mawr fragment (No. 918, back), the 'arms' become separated from the hub which also develops from a sunken roundel to a raised ringed boss; the inter-arm decoration of incised crosses is replaced on the Eglwys Nynnid stone by incised rings which become ringed pellets on the Tythegston slab. A separate but parallel sequence can be seen on five other stones in which the cross formy is outlined by raised ribs. Its simplest form is the Pen-y-fai stone (No. 922), with an incised ring at the hub and ringed pellets in the lower spandrels; then the hub becomes a ringed raised boss (Nos. 917–20), still with spandrel pellets, but the surrounding frame becomes more dominant as on the 'Ilci' stone at Margam (No. 920) and there is plait-work of a debased kind. With this group should be linked the round-headed slab from Cwm Gwenffrwd (No. 923), although the form of its cross is less obviously 'spoked'. In both strands of development the lower part of the slab (or 'shaft') becomes increasingly important, usually featuring an incised inscription. The embryonic 'arms' of a free-standing cross seen on the 'Ilquici' stone at Margam (No. 919)[32] are even more pronounced on the broken slab at Merthyr Mawr (No. 918), and this motif has clearly affected the design of the smaller slab at Tythegston (No. 916).

The remaining six slabs (Nos. 924–9) show looser design and more extensive but debased ornament characteristic of a later stage of development, i.e. into the 11th century. On the two broken slabs at Ewenni and Llan-gan (Nos. 924–5) the cross formy is in relief but is still framed; on the large inscribed slab-cross at Merthyr Mawr (No. 928) this has become freed from the two-dimensional frame and quite distinct from the rest of the slab. The row of vertical frets seen on the Llan-gan slab and the knotwork of the arms also appear on this Merthyr Mawr cross. The plaitwork of the other broken slab at Merthyr Mawr (No. 927), though elaborate and filling each of three faces, is somewhat disorganised, and the key-patterns filling one face of its companion stone (No. 928) are poorly made in comparison with those on the earlier 'Houelt' stone at Llantwit Major (No. 911). The enlarged angle-mouldings of the Merthyr Mawr cross-slab, as also to a lesser extent those on the 'Ilquici' stone (No. 919), reflect the influence of some late pillar-crosses in producing hybrid forms, aesthetically inept.

Some late slabs were provided with a pedestal, as is evidenced by the base tenon occurring on the 'Grutne' stone at Margam (No. 910) and the Ogmore Castle stone (No. 926). The massive disc-head of the 'Conbelin' stone at Margam (No. 907) clearly requires the large, squared base that supports the slab, and the Llan-gan slab (No. 913) was probably supported in this way originally. With the 'Samson' slab at Llantwit Major (No. 912) on the other hand, the slab was tall enough (3·1 m) to be set upright without a pedestal,

---

[31] A type that is frequent at Clonmacnois but not elsewhere in Ireland (*Proc. Roy. Irish Acad.*, Vol. 61 (C, 1961), p. 112), possibly derived originally from Byzantium (*ibid.*, p. 115).

[32] *Cf.* the Netherton Cross, Hamilton, Lanarkshire (*E.C.M.S.*, 411 and *Proc. Soc. Ant. Scot.*, XCII (1958–9), pp. 49–50), which also features arms of a cross formy, spirals and concentric rings.

but the disc-head was formed of a separate stone with a tenon resting in the mortised top of the slab. Such variations are to be explained by the nature of the available stone rather than any specific aesthetic concepts, but as with the 'Conbelin' stone (No. 907) the opportunity was taken to extend the decorative repertoire.

This repertoire consists largely of plaitwork with derived knotwork, of key or fret patterns, and of crude human or animal figures in low relief. Both plaitwork and knotwork can occur as single, double or, on the 'Enniaun' stone at Margam (No. 908), triple strands, the later examples tending to be less tightly set than in the earlier. It appears at its most complex yet effective on the Llangennith slab (No. 905) in symmetrical knotwork derived from twenty-two-cord plait. As well as the Stafford-knot, the triquetra (possibly symbolising The Trinity) and figure-of-eight knot, there occurs also a knot of two intertwined oval loops (e.g. Nos. 907–8, 912) which seems to have a symbolic significance. Animal-head terminals to knotwork occur once only, on the 'Conbelin' stone (No. 907). Pellets are to be found both in plaitwork (No. 927 at Merthyr Mawr) and in key-patterns (Nos. 911–12 at Llantwit Major), but the ringed pellet found chiefly on 'panelled-cross' slabs would seem to have a particular though unknown significance; it is probably a developed form of the incised ring-and-dot device occurring on Nos. 902, 906, 913 and 921.[33]

Three slabs bear a Crucifixion scene, but on only one of them at Llan-gan (No. 913) is the figure of Christ portrayed, accompanied in this instance by the figures of the sponge-bearer and the lance-bearer as was usual in rendering this scene on the contemporary Irish crosses or slabs.[34] In the two other instances, the Nash slab (No. 902) and the 'Conbelin' stone (No. 907), the cross is formalised but has the figure of St. Mary the Virgin and St. John at the foot; as rendered on the great Margam cross (No. 907), the iconography may be Anglo-Saxon but it is akin stylistically to Irish manuscript decoration. An additional figure on the Llan-gan slab below that of Christ is not so readily identifiable: it may be, as on the Gosforth cross, St. Mary Magdalen holding a phial of ointment,[35] or that of Adam (for mankind) redeemed by Christ's blood;[36] a similar figure, holding alternatively a bow or a horn, is associated with David on Manx and Irish crosses.[37] Two small-scale and weathered scenes also on the Nash slab can only tentatively be identified as representing David the Harpist and the Meeting of St. Anthony and St. Paul, both themes commonly occurring in Early Christian art, especially on Irish high-crosses. The figures in the 'orans' posture on the Pontardawe and Coelbren slabs (Nos. 903–4) may be taken as representing respectively a cleric and a lay-man, without closer identification than their garments.[38] There remains the panel on one side of the base of the great Margam cross with the allegorical scene of a hunt: two mounted figures, each 'sanctified' by a triquetra knot, pursue a stag with hounds, a scene perhaps representing SS. Peter and Paul, 'those two most fiery steeds of the Spirit of God'.[39]

CLASS E: Pillar-crosses (Nos. 931–941) (Plates 20–25)

Eleven monuments are represented by the stones in this group, but only the Coychurch and Llandough crosses (Nos. 934 and 938) are complete enough to be regarded as fully representative. As might be expected, such large-scale monuments are primarily associated with the important ecclesiastical settlements on the

---

[33] On this device, see *Ogam*, XIII (1961), p. 290.

[34] Henry, *Irish Art*, I, p. 148; *ibid.*, II, pp. 159–62.

[35] Collingwood, *Northumbrian Crosses*, p. 104 and Fig. 184.

[36] O. M. Dalton, *Early Christian Art* (Oxford, 1925); *cf.* also the figure of St. Peter at the foot of the cross in metalwork (Henry, *L'Art Irlandais* III, p. 194).

[37] Kermode, *Manx Crosses*, No. 104, Pl. LIV; *Journ. Roy. Soc. Ant. Ireland*, LXXIX (1949), pp. 40 f.

[38] For a recent discussion of 'orantes' figures on Irish stones, see *Journ. Roy. Soc. Ant. Ireland*, C, pt. 2 (1970), pp. 212–21.

[39] A phrase of St. Columbanus quoted in Henry, *Irish Art*, II, p. 151.

coastal plain (p. 13 above), the only exceptions being two fragmentary cross-heads (Nos. 939, 941) and also 'Carreg Fedyddiol' (No. 936) from the Ogmore Valley near Bridgend.

The pillar-crosses have been particularly vulnerable to loss and damage because they were probably in each case composite structures. The basic form is a square shaft surmounted by a separate equal-armed cross-head. In at least two instances, at Llangyfelach (No. 931) and Llandough (No. 938), the shaft rests on a pedestal base, but in four others (Nos. 932–3, 935–6) it was set in the ground without a pedestal. On the Coychurch cross (No. 934) the neck below the cross-head becomes an extension of the shaft (which is probably the form of cross-head originally on Nos. 935–6), and with the crosses at Llandaf and Llandough (Nos. 937–8) it has become an upper shaft equal in height to the main shaft. A development of this kind would be more plausible for these monuments than an imitation of wooden processional crosses, for the grossly enlarged collar on the Llandough cross is required primarily for structural stability rather than serving as a misunderstood copy of this feature on Anglo-Saxon crosses.[40] Two of the four cross-heads that survive are of Anglian type with splayed arms, No. 934 at Coychurch and 939 from Coety, only the former having had a ring linking the arms. One fragment of a cross-head from St. George (No. 941) is of Celtic type with squared arms linked by a ring and with hollowed angles. The Llandaf cross-head (No. 937) is a compromise between these two types and has a rudimentary ring.[41] A characteristic of four crosses (Nos. 935–8) is the exaggerated emphasis given to the angle-mouldings, a feature otherwise found only on the hybrid slab at Merthyr Mawr (No. 928 above) and on two Breconshire stones (E.C.M.W. 47, 65), of which the latter from Llanynys may be the stylistic progenitor. Three other shafts at Llantwit Major (Nos. 932–3) and Llancarfan (No. 940) have plain squared angles and are probably earlier in date. The chamfered angles of the Coychurch cross (No. 934) are almost certainly due to re-shaping of the shaft in the later medieval period, and its original form remains somewhat uncertain.

Four of these stones carry inscriptions, but on the Llancarfan stone (No. 940) the letters are secondary and give no complete word. The single word IRBICI on the Llandough cross (No. 938) is presumably the name of the person commemorated by the cross or responsible for its erection; as *Erbic*, this name occurs several times in The Book of Llandaf (associated with St. Teilo as well as with later bishops and rulers) but in no context suitable for identification or dating.[42] The much-eroded inscription on the second Coychurch shaft (No. 935) gives EBISSA(R?), a probable personal name which may be compared with EBISAR on the 'Samson' cross (No. 912) at Llantwit Major. Its last line can be read QUE[SCIT] and it is thus almost certainly associated with an interment; the only other occurrence of this word on Welsh pre-Norman inscriptions is on the Bishop Abraham stone at St. David's datable to the late 11th century (E.C.M.W. 382), and though it was used on Gaulish memorials from a much earlier date these two instances in Wales point to renewed Continental influences at this period. In contrast, the inscribed shaft at Llantwit Major (No. 933) provides the longest and most complete inscription in the county. Its lettering, in half-uncials as are the others mentioned above, is less careful than comparable inscriptions such as the 'Enniaun' stone at Margam (No. 908) or the 'Houelt' stone at Llantwit Major (No. 911) but it shows similar manuscript characteristics, phraseology and irregular Latin as those discussed in Class D above. The letter forms are especially close to those on the Caldy Island slab (E.C.M.W. 301), dated to the early 9th century. The particular form of plaitwork in its one decorative panel is not necessarily later than the 9th century (as

---

[40] Cf. *Arch. Journ.*, CXVII (1960), pp. 71–8; *Arch. Camb.*, LXXXVIII (1933), p. 393.

[41] The sketch of the Llandough cross (No. 938) in Stowe MS. 1024, fo. 19, shows the upper shaft surmounted by a shaped stone that is better interpreted as the lower limb of an Anglian cross-head than as the capping found on some Irish crosses, e.g. Ahenny, Durrow or the Cross of Muiredach at Monasterboice.

[42] But cf. *Arch. Camb.*, LXXXVIII (1933), pp. 393–5 (R. A. S. Macalister).

is argued in *E.C.M.W.*), so that the identification of IUTHAHELO REX with Ithel ab Athrwys, king of Gwent (d. 848), can hardly be resisted.[43] The rulers of Gwent and Glywysing were of the same stock and may have regarded Llanilltud Fawr (Llantwit Major) with particular patronal interest. It is less certain whether the ARTMALI of the inscription (*cf.* the later form of the name ARTHMAIL on No. 926) should be identified with the recorded ruler Artmail, father of Meurig who died in 849, and apparently a cousin to Athrwys.[44] The abbot Samson named here (with APATI for *abbati*) must be distinguished from two persons so named on a later slab at the same place (No. 912 above). The remaining name, TECAN, occurs in the Llandaf documents as *Teican* but is not that of a local ruler.

As with the stones of the preceding group, the decoration consists of plaitwork, knotwork, or key and fret patterns; only on the Llandough cross (No. 938) are there animal and human figures. Though particular patterns may recur, e.g. S-shaped knotwork on the Llandaf cross (No. 937, S. side) and on the Llandough cross (N. side), or figure-of-eight knots on the latter (W. side) and on the Llancarfan stone (No. 940), yet on any one monument there is an obvious desire for variety and the avoidance of complete symmetry. The best examples of decoration are on the earlier stones (Nos. 931–3, 940), which are also characterised by simplicity of form, notably 932 (Llantwit Major) in which one panel of plaitwork incorporates four cruciform breaks. In the later pillar-crosses the ornament is less restrained in extent but more clumsy and degenerate in execution (e.g. Nos. 935–7). On the Bridgend and Llandough crosses (Nos. 936 and 938) even the enlarged angle-mouldings are covered with plaitwork, framed at top and base by moulded bands. Though much of the decoration on the shaft of the Coychurch cross (No. 934) has been obliterated, the row of bold pellets on the collar is an unusual feature, recurring only on the cross at Nunnykirk, Northumbria.[45] The key-patterns of the base at Llangyfelach (No. 931) and plaitwork of the fragmentary cross-head from St. George (No. 941) so closely follow similar decoration on the 'Houelt' stone and 'Enniaun' stone (Nos. 911 and 908) respectively that direct imitation is a possibility. A very different form of decoration seems to have been provided for on the otherwise unornamented face of the Coety cross-head (No. 939), probably consisting of inset enamels or jewels. The pyramidal base of the Llandough cross (No. 938) has four figured panels, two of them showing a man's head and shoulders, possibly an early attempt at portraiture rather than being simply symbolical; another panel with a man on horseback recalls the 'hunting scene' of the great Margam cross (No. 907), as well as including the knot of two intertwined loops on that stone and others in Class D. The remaining panel with five diminutive figures in a row is reminiscent of the scripture panels of Irish high-crosses, but here also the iconography cannot be interpreted.

CLASS F: Other Decorated Stones (Nos. 951–956) (Plates 26, 27)

A few stones attributable to the pre-Norman period are not appropriate to any of the categories considered above, and are brought together in this class. All of them have carved decoration in low relief, but in each case the original form and function of the monument is obscure. The long boulder at Llanrhidian (No. 951) may have been part of a lintel, for only one face is decorated and it has tenon-like ends; it is too irregular in shape to have formed part of a sarcophagus. The cylindrical pillar at Llantwit Major (No. 953) was almost certainly one of at least a pair of similar stones, and is corroborated by another fragment there (No. 954), possibly supporting an inscribed upright slab. But if regarded as an enlarged version of the angle

---

[43] Harleian MS. 3859 (28) in Bartrum, *Tracts*, p. 12; *Brut* (Peniarth) and *Ann. Camb. s.a.*; his great-grandfather was named Iudhail, but an early 8th-century date for this stone would be unacceptable. The Ithel ab Idwallawn of Peniarth MSS. 131 and 178 (Bartrum, *Tracts*, pp. 105 and 122) was not certainly a ruler and an 11th-century date would be very late, but these pedigrees are in any case late and less trustworthy.

[44] The association with a king Ithel makes possible an identification with Arthfael, son of Hywel ap Rhys and father of the Cadell whose death is recorded in 942.

[45] Collingwood, *Northumbrian Crosses*, p. 106.

mouldings of the Llandough cross (No. 938) it is not impossible that there were originally four such columns clasping the shaft of a very large pillar-cross.

The extremely stylised decoration on the Llanrhidian boulder has no close parallel on Welsh monuments other than the pillar at Llanbadarn Fawr, Cardiganshire (*E.C.M.W.* 111), and its inspiration is clearly Irish in the rendering both of the garments of the human figures and of the accompanying animal figures. The scene is not readily identifiable, but is more likely to represent the Meeting of St. Paul and St. Anthony in the desert (*cf.* the Nash slab, No. 902) than Adam and Eve in the Garden of Eden. Parallels for its various stylistic features cited below suggest it is of 9th- or 10th-century date. On the Llantwit Major column (No. 953) the double-beaded plaitwork is typically varied in each panel but is slightly debased; the form and decoration, with an unusual chevron pattern, suggest a 10th- or 11th-century date. The remaining three fragments show a combination of native Celtic and Romanesque styles: Nos. 952 and 955 at Merthyr Mawr and Ewenni (one almost an exact copy of the other) have double-beaded plaitwork incorporating a square with looped angles that occurs on the Newcastle (Bridgend) slab (No. 984) and other memorials of the 12th century; on the Llyswyrny fragment (No. 956), the Romanesque pattern of diaper squares borders a pattern of debased spirals. One feature of the latter stone, a serpent-like creature of wavy lines, curiously echoes the surface rendering of one of the animals on the Llanrhidian stone.

CLASS G: Headstones and Grave-slabs of the Late Period (Nos. 961–988) (Plates 28, 29)

In form and decoration, the stones in this category show the replacement of native tradition by styles derived from the Continent. Though hastened by political events at the end of the 11th century, this process was not determined by the establishment of Norman rule in ecclesiastical and secular affairs, and the period of transition extends over both the 11th and 12th centuries. The characteristic headstone introduced is a thick, square-headed block such as that at Baglan (No. 961; see also Nos. 965–6, 972 and 977). Some smaller slabs that may have been recumbent are round-headed, e.g. No. 967 at Merthyr Mawr and No. 980 at Ewenni, the former probably re-shaped in secondary use. The round-headed stone at Pyle (No. 971) may have served as a boundary stone rather than as a gravestone. Two recumbent slabs at Newcastle (Bridgend, Nos. 983–4) are also massive, one modelled on a tomb-chest. Included in this category are three plain socket-stones (Nos. 986–8) into which, presumably, thin cross-incised slabs were set upright;[46] one stone at Merthyr Mawr (No. 969) may have been set up thus, but is more likely to have been recumbent.

The form of cross on these stones (Fig. 8) is predominantly either a cross potent or a ringed cross of arcs (often a cross formy with rounded arm-ends); outline crosses (Latin and Greek types) also occur. While some are merely incised (e.g. Nos. 961, 965 or 972), others are quite deeply set in false relief, e.g. Nos. 967, 977 or 981. Amongst these, No. 977 at Ewenni is a cross-potent with a spike at the foot, probably reflecting the form of wooden prototypes, a feature of some pre-Norman slabs in Anglesey and Ireland.[47] The six-leaf marigold on one stone at Merthyr Mawr (No. 967) is a comparatively rare instance. Two unusual forms of cross are the four incised rings on the back of a stone from Laleston (No. 972), and the two ringed crosses on the slab at Newcastle (Bridgend) (No. 983), probably with two smaller crosses in a group representing The Crucifixion. The closest approach to carving in relief is a rounded block from Laleston (No. 963) that may be part of a headstone of Saxon type without the slight projections (or 'ears') for the arm-ends.[48]

---

[46] *Proc. Roy. Irish Acad.*, Vol. 61 (C, 1961), p. 100.
[47] *Inv. Anglesey*, p. c; *Proc. Roy. Irish Acad.*, Vol. 61 (C, 1961), p. 139 Figs. 6, 16.
[48] *Cf. Arch Camb.*, 1891, p. 114.

FIG. 8.

Forms of crosses on stones of Class G. Scale $\frac{1}{10}$: (*a*) Merthyr Mawr (969); (*b*) Ewenni (980); (*c*) Llantwit Major (974); (*d–e*) Merthyr Mawr (967); (*f*) Ewenni (981); (*g*) Merthyr Mawr (966); (*h*) Llan-gan (982); (*i–j*) Laleston (972); (*k*) Pyle (971); (*l*) Merthyr Mawr (964); (*m*) Ewenni (977); (*n*) Ewenni (975); (*o*) Ewenni (976); (*p*) Merthyr Mawr (965); (*q*) Ewenni (978); (*r*) Baglan (961).

Carved decoration apart from the cross itself occurs only on the coped slab at Newcastle (Bridgend) (No. 984) which is also inscribed. This has a processional cross carved in low relief with surrounding panels of plain plaitwork merely incised and squares with looped angles (*cf.* Nos. 952 and 955); one vertical side of this originally prostrate slab has a pattern of arcading, suggesting that it rested in a recess probably inside the church. The lettering of its inscription reflects the mingling of styles in its decoration; one of the names, GVLGVEN, may be a later form of GELUGUI(N) on a Port Talbot stone (No. 884).

CHIEF COLLECTIONS OF MONUMENTS

(a) *National Museum of Wales, Cardiff.*
   Nos. 843, 861, 863, 870, 892, 902, 922–3, 926, 941, 963.
(b) *Margam Stones Museum* (in the custody of the Department of the Environment, formerly the Ministry of Public Building and Works, in the Old School House on the N. side of the churchyard).
   Nos. 846, 848–9, 867–8 (also 914), 885, 901, 906–10, 919–21, 936, 972.
(c) *Merthyr Mawr Parish Church* (under temporary shelter on the N. side of the churchyard).
   Nos. 847, 917–18, 952, 964–70, 987.
(d) *Ewenni Priory Church* (in the custody of the Department of the Environment, in the South Transept of the church).
   Nos. 924, 955, 975–81.
(e) *Llantwit Major Parish Church* (at the W. end of the Western Nave).
   Nos. 911–12, 932–3, 953–4, 974.
(f) *Museum of the Royal Institution of South Wales, Swansea.*
   Nos. 841, 845, 903 (part), 904.

Concordance Table with *E.C.M.W.*

E.C.M.W.	*Inventory*	*E.C.M.W.*	*Inventory*	*E.C.M.W.*	*Inventory*
191	886	218	951	245/6	965
192	939	219	888	247	966
193	935	220	911	248	862
194	934	221	932	249	863
195	891	222	912	250	902
196	924	223	933	251	869
197	842	224	953	251a	915
198	849	225	p. 64a	252	936
199	971	226	954	253	984
200	921	227	889	254	983
201	p. 64a	228	845	255	926
202	963	229	848	256	903
203	972	230	973	257	870
204	940	231	908	258	846
205	937	232	901	259	867
206	938	233	910	260	884
207	913	234	907	261	885
208	925	235	909	262	868/914
209	905	236	919	263	906
210	903	237	920	263a	887
211	882	238	847	264	p. 64a
212	931	239	927	265	923
213	883	240	928	266	864
214	850	241	917	267	941
215	844	242	918	268	841
216	865	243	952	269	904
217	866	244	955	270	843
				270a	916

841–850. CLASS A: INSCRIBED STONES OF THE EARLY PERIOD

(841) CLWYDI BANWEN, Cefn Hirfynydd. The surviving fragment of a pillar-stone (Plate 1), 1·1 m long, 20 cm wide and 24 cm thick, represents about half the original length and width, formed of a hard laminated sandstone. The complete inscription was in two lines (at least) read down the length of the face, of which the first line remains incomplete, with traces of the second line. The fracture of the stone antedates its first recorded notice by Lhuyd about 1693,[1] and flaking of the face has made the reading of some letters uncertain.

The first word has been read as M̂ACARITIN—with ligatured MA, but the A-s have no cross-bar, and the M is partly formed by surface-flaking (though read as such in 1693). It is possible to read the initial letter as an inverted V followed by I, while the C is followed by another inverted V with open angle.[2] The second word is clearly F̂ILI in two ligatures. As given by Lhuyd the line ends with BERICC—, but the edge of the fracture occurring at the fifth letter makes the latter part unconfirmable. This fifth letter is A (with cross-bar) rather than a very angular C. The whole line would thus read VICVRITIN— FILI BERIA[C—('Of Vicuritinus, the son of Beria(cus)'). The lettering, in crude Roman capitals, shows a reversed N, the R-s with an open loop, a tall B with separated loops, the ligatures mentioned and horizontal terminal I in the first and last words. The traces of the second line do not confirm the normal *hic iacit* ('here lies'), but six letters are indicated. The inscription is of early 6th-century date.

Its original location at Clwydi Banwen by Lhuyd is confirmed by Strange,[3] but before 1800 the stone was removed to The Gnoll, Neath, and subsequently damaged.[4] Since 1920 it has been in the Museum of the Royal Institution, Swansea, though mounted in an inverted position.

E.C.M.W. 268; *C.I.I.C.* 403; *Arch. Camb.*, LXXXV (1930), p. 124; *ibid.*, XCIV (1939), p. 32.
[1] Camden, *Britannia* (ed. Gibson), p. 620; Stowe MS. 1024, fo. 8; Lhuyd, *Parochialia*, III, pp. 69–70.
[2] For an inverted V, see *E.C.M.W.* 297, 132 and *C.I.I.C.* 461.
[3] *Archaeologia*, I (1769), p. 323 with wrong illustration; *ibid.*, IV, p. 7.
[4] *Arch. Camb.*, 1865, pp. 59–62; 1920, p. 370.

Cadoxton-juxta-Neath (E),
Neath Higher/Dulais Higher (C).

SN 80 N.E. (8519 0855)   4 vi 64   IV S.W.

(842) CEFN GELLI-GAER. A roughly squared pillar-stone (Plate 2) set in a small enclosure stands about 425 m above O.D. on this ridge close to the Roman road from Gelli-gaer to Penydarren. The stone, of the local Pennant series and possibly reduced in length, is 2·4 m long, 25 cm wide on the inscribed face and 40 cm thick at the base, leaning to the N. at about 45° from vertical.

When first noted in 1693 by Lhuyd[1] the inscription near the base of the N. face consisted of seven letters down the face but was severely mutilated before 1862.[2] Only the final three letters survive undamaged, reading IHI with half-uncial H. The complete word (presumably a personal name) as sketched by Lhuyd would seem to have been REFSOIHI, with half-uncial R and S; the lower curve of the O survives, possibly to be read as D. Alternative readings have been TEF(? or S) ROIHI (*E.C.M.W.* 'based on a rubbing made in 1898') and NEFROIHI (*C.I.I.C.*). The mixed character of the letters suggests a late 6th- or early 7th-century date.

The enclosure formed by a low bank 2·0 m wide and 0·3 m high is horseshoe-shaped, roughly 8·0 m by 9·0 m and open on the S.E. side where the stone is situated. Lhuyd described a square 'bed', presumably a cist, inside the enclosure and thought it had been for a burial, but all that remains is a depression apparently caused by digging. The whole structure may thus represent the remains of a bronze-age burial (the cist and mound) in which the stone either was set originally and was later inscribed or was entirely a later feature, but in its disturbed condition there can be no certainty as to its age.

E.C.M.W. 197; *C.I.I.C.* 1006; *Arch. Camb.*, XCIV (1939), p. 34.
[1] Camden, *Britannia* (ed. Gibson), p. 616; Stowe MS. 1023, fo. 164; *Arch. Camb.*, 1848, pp. 309–10 (letter of Lhuyd).
[2] *Arch. Camb.*, 1862, p. 134; *cf. ibid.*, 1875, p. 370.

Gelli-gaer.

SO 10 S.W. (1034 0340)   9 xii 64   XII S.E.

(843) CAPEL BRITHDIR, Bargoed. Stone (Plate 2) from near the site of Capel Brithdir at *ca.* 390 m above O.D. The massive irregular upright slab of the local carboniferous measures is 2·25 m (+ *ca.* 15 cm) high, 1·0 m at its widest, and 17 cm to 22 cm thick. The rough surface bears a Latin inscription vertically down the face in four lines: TEGERNA/CUS FILI/US MARTI / HIC IACIT ('Tegernacus, son of Marti(us), lies here'). Although the E-s conform to Roman capitals, other letters approximate more to half-uncials, especially the R-s, N, S-s, M and U-s (the flattened U of *Filius* beginning the third line is just traceable). The S-shaped G also occurs locally on No. 848; the A-s are turned sideways to resemble the half-uncial form. These characteristics point to an early 7th-century date for the inscription.[1] Modern initials have been scratched above and below the original. The stone was placed in the National Museum of Wales in 1923.

E.C.M.W. 270; *C.I.I.C.* 404; *Arch. Camb.*, 1862, p. 130.
[1] The suggestion (*C.I.I.C.* 404) that there are traces of Ogam cannot be maintained; a 7th-century date for Ogams would also be most unusual.

Gelli-gaer.

SO 10 S.W. (1375 0262)   8 xii 64   XIII S.W.

(844) LLANMADOG, Gower. The stone (Plate 1) discovered in 1861 built into the former rectory, subsequently fractured and re-set in the internal sill of the S.E. window of the nave of St. Madog's Church.[1] The surviving portion of the pillar-stone, lacking part of the head and the lower part, is 66 cm long and 15 cm wide, of local Old Red Sandstone. The inscription is in two lines to read downwards (when the stone was originally upright):]VECTI F̂ILÎVS /]GV̂ANI HIC IACIT ('Of . . . vectus, son of . . . guanus; he lies here'). The letters are all Roman capitals, with enlarged A-s; the ligatured FI and LI of *Filius* is a usual feature (*cf.* No. 848), and

there is one other ligature (VA). The lower curve of a letter preceding the first letter of line 1 has been variously read as D, G or P but is indeterminable. It is possible that line 2 is complete as it stands.[2] The inscription can be dated as late 5th- to early 6th-century.

E.C.M.W. 215; *C.I.I.C.* 406; Jackson, *Lang. and Hist.*, p. 385 (n. 4).
[1] Davies, *W. Gower*, II, p. 76.
[2] *Arch. Camb.*, 1895, pp. 180–1.

Llanmadog.
　SS 49 S.W. (4388 9343)　　5 vi 64　　　　XXI N.E.

(845) LOUGHOR. A Roman altar (Plate 2), found at Loughor[1] (see above, I ii 733) has a damaged inscription in Ogams on one angle below the capital. The stone itself, 1·1 m tall and 53 cm square but tapering slightly below the moulded edges of the capital, is of local sandstone, much weathered. The surviving Ogams were first noted in 1857[2] and may be read upwards as]L[ ]V (or L) ICA. A single vowel notch remains immediately before the strokes for V (or L) but does not necessarily represent A; the final vowel notch is on the chamfered under-edge of the capital. The inscription, presumably giving a personal name,[3] indicates a re-using of the stone as a memorial in the 5th or early 6th century. The stone is preserved in the Museum of the Royal Institution, Swansea.

E.C.M.W. 228; *C.I.I.C.* 405; *Arch. Camb.*, 1873, pp. 198, 286.
[1] Carlisle, *Top. Dict.*, s.v. Lloughor.
[2] *Arch. Camb.*, 1869, p. 261 (with Plate).
[3] Rhys, reading '. . L . . LICA' (*Arch. Camb.*, 1895, pp. 182–3), refers to the Goidelic *lica* ('stone'), but there is no common formula with that word which occurs only once in Irish Ogam inscriptions (*C.I.I.C.* 10). Cf. R. A. S. Macalister's reading GRAVICA (*C.I.I.C.* 405).

Loughor.
　SS 59 N.E. (5753 9816)　　21 vi 62　　　XIV S.W.

(846) PORT TALBOT. The squared sandstone pillar (Plate 1) originally serving as a Roman milestone and found in 1839 on the outskirts of Port Talbot (No. 755 (iii)) was re-used inverted for a Latin memorial inscription on the opposite face. This inscription, in one line down the face originally, reads HIC IACIT CANTVSVS PATER PAVLINVS ('Here lies Cantusus—his father was Paulinus'). The letters are picked out in Roman capitals with no separation of words; the H is the single half-uncial letter, some of the A-s and T-s are enlarged, the C-s have expanded terminals and the R a short tail; there is one ligature (AV). If *pater* is to be equated with the second name rather than the first, in contrast to the usual formula with *filius*, this rendering is unique. The Paulinus named here is unlikely to have been a historically known person such as St. Illtud's pupil. The inscription is of the 6th century.

The stone, formerly in Margam Abbey Church, is in Margam Stones Museum, set up as for a milestone.

E.C.M.W. 258; *Roman Inscriptions*, 2254; *C.I.I.C.* 407; Radford, *Margam*, No. 1.

Margam (E), Port Talbot (C).
　SS 78 N.E. (7834 8733)　　12 xi 64　　　XXXIII N.W.

(847) MERTHYR MAWR. A fragment of a pillar-stone with rounded head (Plate 1) of local Pennant sandstone, found on the site of St. Teilo's Church, Merthyr Mawr, just before 1856.[1] The surviving portion, representing rather less than half the presumed original full length, is 73 cm long, 45 cm wide (51 cm at maximum width), and varies in thickness from 7 cm to 17 cm. Of the Latin inscription in two lines read down the face there survives: PAVLI[/ FILI M[('Of Paulus (or Paulinus), son of M . . .'). The letters are well-formed Roman capitals, fairly deep-cut; the enlarged A is a common characteristic, the F less so. There is a strong presumption that the first name would in its complete form be PAVLINI (for Paulinus), of fairly common occurrence; but the letter following M (indicated only by part of the stem forming the edge of the fracture) might equally have been A or E. The inscription most probably dates from the later 5th century.

The face opposite to the inscription bears an incised emblem which is probably a later (? 9th-century) addition. This emblem (Plate 1) can be regarded as the Greek *omega* letter, but may alternatively represent part of an incompleted cross with splayed arms springing from a central ring-boss, just perceptible (as on Nos. 918, 922).

The stone has been set under a temporary shelter on the N. side of the churchyard.

E.C.M.W. 238; *C.I.I.C.* 410; Jackson, *Lang. and Hist.*, p. 323.
[1] *Arch. Camb.*, 1856, pp. 251, 319.

Merthyr Mawr.
　SS 87 N.E. (8828 7753)　　9 ix 64　　　XL S.W.

(848) MYNYDD MARGAM. A well-squared pillar-stone (Plate 1) formerly standing on a low mound (I i 271) on Mynydd Margam at 340 m above O.D. when it was known as 'Carreg Kythyrogg'.[1] It is of local material, 1·01 m (plus *ca.* 15 cm) long, 33 cm wide narrowing to 28 cm and 22 cm thick. The inscription is in four lines read down the face: BODVOC— HIC IACIT / FILIVS CATOTIGIRNI / PRONEPVS ETERNALI / VEDOMAV— ('Of Bodvocus—he lies here, the son of Catotigirnus and great-grandson of Eternalis Vedomavus'). The lettering is almost entirely in Roman capitals with a single half-uncial H; the A-s, with angular cross-bar, are inverted, and the R-s in the third line have a horizontal tail. For the 'S' form of G, compare No. 843. There are three ligatures, FI and LI (twice), and the horizontal terminal I occurs twice, in the first and last words. The inscription dates from the 6th century.

On the upper surface of the stone is an incised cross formy (Fig. 6, m) which is not necessarily later than the inscription.[2] The stone had been mutilated by modern *graffiti* and an O.S. bench mark before being moved to Margam Museum, its present location. It has been replaced by a modern replica.

E.C.M.W. 229; *C.I.I.C.* 408; Radford, *Margam*, No. 3; *Arch. Camb.*, 1859, pp. 287–92; XCIV (1939), p. 36.
[1] Stowe MS. 1024, fos. 10 and 16.
[2] Two slabs with small additional crosses similarly placed on the upper edge are recorded at Kilberrihert, Co. Tipperary (P. Ó. hEailidhe, 'The Crosses and Slabs at St. Berrihert's Kyle' in *North Munster Studies*).

Margam (E), Port Talbot (C).
　SS 88 N.W. (8306 8878)　　12 xi 64　　　XXXIII N.E.

(849) EGLWYS NYNNID, near Margam (Plate 2). A roughly squared pillar-stone of Rhaetic sandstone with Ogam and Latin inscriptions. It is 1·35 m above ground at its highest edge, 35 cm wide on the inscribed face, and 52 cm tapering to 45 cm in thickness. Its original location near Eglwys Nynnid was attested in 1578,[1] but it would seem to have been set up (or re-set) beside the road known as Water Street in the mid-18th century.[2] It is now in Margam Museum.

The Ogam characters on the upper left angle of the face read upwards, those on the right edge downwards; much of the inscription is made uncertain by subsequent damage to the angles. The left-hand angle gives: P [O or A] P followed by an uncertain number of vowel notches, probably representing POPIAS, a personal name.[3] The right-hand angle may be read: R(O)L[. . .]N[. . .]M[. . .]Q[ ]LLUNA, presumably part of a name. The gaps from fractures are each large enough to have carried more than one letter and not necessarily vowel notches only; the gap between M and Q is far more than would be filled solely with A to make the common MAQI. The U is indicated by the unusual 'forfid' form of a loop rather than notches (cf. C.I.I.C. 240).

The Latin inscription set in two lines down the length of the face reads PVMPEIVS / CARANTORIVS, formed of fairly regular but debased Roman capitals with a single ligature; the E is half-uncial, the S-s elongated, and both R-s have an open loop with short tail. These features indicate a mid-6th-century date.

While the Roman name Pumpeius (for Pompeius) is probably rendered in the Ogams by an early Irish equivalent such as Popias, there seems to be no correlation in the remainder of the two inscriptions. The name Carantorius may well be an artificial Latinisation of Carantori.[4] It is unlikely that Ogam characters formerly existed along the upper edge of the face but the two angles nonetheless form a single inscription. A bench-mark has been cut on the adjacent right-hand face.

E.C.M.W. 198; C.I.I.C. 409; Radford, Margam, No. 2.
[1] Merrick, Morg. Arch., p. 5; cf. Lhuyd, Parochialia, III, p. 125. For the place-name, see Arch. Camb., CXVIII (1969), pp. 144–5. No. 921 is also from this spot.
[2] Camden, Britannia (ed. Gough), II, p. 495.
[3] Arch. Camb., 1899, pp. 132–5 (Rhys).
[4] Jackson, Lang. and Hist., pp. 624–7.

Margam (E), Port Talbot (C).
   SS 88 S.W. (8033 8446)   12 xi 64   XXXIII S.E.

(850) CAPEL LLANILLTERN. The stone (Plate 1) was formerly built into the external face of the E. wall of the church[1] but subsequently was re-set horizontally in the internal face of the N. wall of the nave. It is a probably naturally squared pillar-stone of local rough schist, 1·22 m long and 27 cm wide on the inscribed face (which is all that is visible). When in its original vertical position the stone had the Latin inscription at its upper end, read vertically downwards in two lines: VENDVMAGL—/ HIC IACIT ('Of Vendumaglus; he lies here'). The letters combine Roman capitals with half-uncials (the latter being E, D, M, G, L, H, T), and also a horizontal terminal I at the end of the first line. The A-s both have an angular cross-bar as in No. 848, and the abnormal form of M can be paralleled (probably but not decisively) on two other inscriptions of roughly the same period, viz. E.C.M.W. 124, 287 (cf. also No. 984). Almost all the letters have expanded terminals. The mixed character of the lettering points to a late 6th-century or early 7th-century date.

E.C.M.W. 214; C.I.I.C. 1028; Jackson, Lang. and Hist., p. 386.
[1] Arch. Camb., 1871, p. 260; 1901, p. 64. In view of Lhuyd's record in Stowe MS. 1023, fo. 86, the suggestion in Arch. Camb., LXXIX (1924), p. 219, that it was brought from a reputed monastic site can be dismissed.

St. Fagans with Llanilterne (E), Llanilltern (C).
   ST 07 N.E. (0951 7996)   11 ix 64   XLII N.E.

FIG. 9.
Hirwaun, inscription of lost stone (i), recorded in 1827.

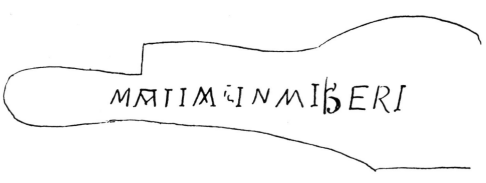

Near the Milldam at Lhan Rhidian Westward

MΛΤΙΜᏀΙΝΜΙᏰERI

FIG. 10.

Llanrhidian, drawing by Lhuyd of lost stone (ii).

Lost Stones

(i) HIRWAUN. An inscribed stone was reported in 1827[1] to be on 'ros Hirwaun Wrgan' or Hirwaun Common, W. of Aberdâr.[2] The inscription illustrated in the original publication (reproduced here as Fig. 9 with tones reversed) is in four (horizontal?) lines, apparently reading ERECOR / MAGLORI / CVNIIAC / FICIT. The letters are all Roman capitals except for cursive forms of G and L, a feature which together with the proper name elements establishes a strong case for accepting it as an authentic Early Christian inscription of the late 5th century.

ERECOR as a non-Roman personal name seems incomplete, for a final I would be expected; it is also possible that an initial letter is missing. Such a name may be cognate with Irish ERACOBI and ERAQETAI on *C.I.I.C.* 84. The second line makes an acceptable personal name with its first element one that is common in names of the period (*v.* No. 850).[3]

The third and fourth lines require some elucidation. CVN (or CVNI) is again a common element of personal names,[4] CVNIIAC[I] or CVNIIAC[VS] being acceptable forms. FICIT for *fecit* is possible though not paralleled, but it is also possible that the form of the stone (which cannot be known) would enable FIC to be read either as HIC or as ligatured FILI, with IAC / IT added at the ends of these two lines. In such a reconstruction the inscription would read ERECOR[I] / MAGLORI / CVNI / HIC IAC / IT or . . . CVNI / FILI / IAC / CIT.

[1] *Lleuad yr Oes: neu Amgeueddfa* (sic) *Fisol o Wybodaeth mewn Crefydd*, Mawrth, 1827, p. 160 (Abertawe). Acknowledgement must be made to Mr. R. J. Thomas, editor of *Geiriadur Prifysgol Cymru*, for drawing attention to this entry.

[2] 'Hirwaun Wrgan' was the name applied to the area on the MS. Ordnance Survey Map of 1812. Search of the area and local enquiry have not hitherto yielded any result, and extensive open-cast mining reduces the possibility of re-discovering the stone.

[3] It was in fact anticipated by Jackson, *Lang. and Hist.*, p. 625, with *Maglorix, from which are derived *Maglorius* (a Breton saint) and the modern Welsh *Meilyr*.

[4] *Cf.* CVNACI and CVNALIPI, *Inv. Caerns.*, II, No. 1015 and *E.C.M.W.* 105 (also *E.C.M.W.* 9, 70, 142, 172, 384 and 402). Despite MAGLOCVNI on a stone at Nevern, Pembs. (*E.C.M.W.* 353) it does not seem possible to treat MAGLORICVNI as one name, although this would resolve some of the difficulty of rendering.

Ystradyfodwg/Aberdâr (E), Rhigos/Aberdâr (C).
    (SN 95 05 approximately)   X N.E., S.E., XI N.W., S.W.

(ii) LLANRHIDIAN. An inscribed pillar-stone was sketched by Lhuyd 'near the milldam at Lhan Rhidian Westward',[1] a site that is still visible W. of the parish church. The inscription as recorded (Fig. 10), apparently in one line down the face, is difficult to interpret even though most of the letters are Roman capitals. The letters after an initial M may represent an unbarred A with half-uncial G, suggesting a *Magli–* form of name, but such a reading is quite uncertain. There is also a B with separated loops as occurs on the Clwydi Banwen stone (No. 841), dated to the early 6th century.

[1] Stowe MS. 1024, fo. 9. Another inscribed stone recorded as at the same site (fo. 61) would seem to have been a medieval grave-slab reading 'Maledictus sit qui . . .', but is not identifiable with one discovered there in 1885 and stated to be in Norman-French (*Arch. Camb.*, 1886, p. 335).

Llanrhidian (E), Ll. Lower (C).
    SS 49 S.E. (496 922)   XXII S.W.

861–870. CLASS B: PILLAR-STONES WITH INCISED CROSS

(861) CARN CACA. A pillar-stone (Plate 3) of local sandstone, found (not *in situ*) in 1953 on this ridge E. of Melincourt in the Vale of Neath. It is roughly squared, 28 cm wide at the shaft with slightly expanded rounded head 40 cm wide; its overall length of 1·01 m includes the spreading undressed base, the thickness varying from 17 cm to 7 cm. At the head within an irregular incised ring is an equal-armed cross with short bar-terminals (Fig. 6, f); in each of the inter-arm spaces a dot is picked out (*cf.* No. 870, and *E.C.M.W.* 131, 173, 178, 361). Its date would fall in the range 7th to 9th century. It is now in the National Museum of Wales.

Arch. Camb., CXII (1963), pp. 185–7.

Llantwit-juxta-Neath (E), Clyne (C).

    SN 80 S.W. (826 006)   8 xii 64   XVI N.E.

(862) MERTHYR TUDFUL. A pillar-stone (Plate 3) with ring-cross and inscription, formerly built into the E. gable wall of St. Tudful's Church. The stone, of Old Red Sandstone (which occurs a few miles to the N.), has been reduced in length and width, surviving 1·0 m long, 13 cm wide and 12 cm thick. At the head, the simply incised ringed cross has expanded terminals of trifid form at the sides and on the stem, but is incomplete (Fig. 6, n); there seems not to have been an expanded terminal at the head of the ring. The inscription in regular half-uncials read down the length of the face consists of the one word ARTBEU, the name of the person commemorated. The stone, whose earliest recorded location was in the fabric of the church before the rebuilding, is placed against the internal N. wall of the N. Aisle. 8th- or 9th-century.

E.C.M.W. 248; *C.I.I.C.* 1025; *Arch. Camb.*, 1858, p. 163; 1901 p. 61; Jackson, *Lang. and Hist.*, p. 373.

Merthyr Tudful.

    SO 00 N.W. (0496 0582)   30 x 65   XII N.W.

(863) MYNYDD MERTHYR. A pillar-stone (Plate 3), found in 1925 at Panwaen Pwll-gwellt, just W. of the parish boundary. Of local Pennant sandstone and lacking part of the head, it is 1·35 m long by 25 cm and 13 cm thick. The upper part of the face, slightly bevelled and smoothed, has a roughly incised linear Latin cross with elongated plain stem (Fig. 6, e). The upper terminals are crossletted with roughly semicircular frames. Its date is 7th- to 9th-century. The stone is in the National Museum of Wales.

E.C.M.W. 249; *Arch. Camb.*, LXXXV (1930), p. 396.

Llanwynno.

    SO 00 S.E. (0503 0157)   8 xii 64   XII S.W.

(864) REYNOLDSTON. A sandstone pillar with incised crosses and decoration (Plate 3) noted near Reynoldston, Gower, before 1877 and re-set as a modern memorial.[1] It is 1·65 m high above the modern socket, 33 cm wide tapering to 25 cm and 20 cm thick. Part of the head has fractured off, together with some flaking of the faces. On the N.W. face is a double cross

(Fig. 6, l), 38 cm by 28 cm, formed of an outline equal-armed cross enclosing a linear cross with outline cross-arms and two lozenge-shaped hollows at the intersections. The S.E. face has at the head an incised equal-armed cross (Fig. 6, k) 25 cm square, with triangular expanded terminals (part fractured away) and smaller linear crosses in the inter-arm spaces; there is also some suggestion of an incised ring connecting the terminals. Immediately under this is an incised pattern of double-beaded plaitwork with two Stafford knots at the top, covering most of the face. Below the panel is a bifurcated inturned terminal, part of an incised device (mostly flaked away) which could have been either a double-scroll figure (as *E.C.M.W.* 31, or a linear cross with similar terminals (as e.g. *Proc. Roy. Irish Acad.*, 61 (C, 1961), Fig. 8 (Nos. 7–11)). The features that are common to this and the inscribed stone at Llanddeti (*E.C.M.W.* 46) suggest a 9th-century date.

E.C.M.W. 266.
[1] Davies, *W. Gower*, I, p. 3.

Reynoldston.

    SS 48 N.E. (4788 8929)   2 vi 64   XXXI N.W.

(865) LLANMADOG. Pillar-stone (Plate 3) found in Llanmadog churchyard in 1864[1] and more recently re-set upright inside the church in a recess at the W. end of the nave. The undressed stone with expanded head is 1·55 m high, 45 cm wide at the head, with shaft 35 cm wide increasing to 50 cm at the base, and 7 cm thick. The incised linear cross on the widest part of the face (Fig. 6, g) has superficial traces of terminal bars on the cross-arms only, returned in opposite directions. It is probably of 7th- to 9th-century date.

E.C.M.W. 216.
[1] Davies, *W. Gower*, II, p. 73.

Llanmadog.

    SS 49 S.W. (4388 9343)   5 vi 64   XXI N.E.

(866) LLANMADOG. Broken pillar-stone with two incised crosses (Plate 4), found at Llanmadog 'in the wall of the churchyard in 1864',[1] and recently re-set inside the church in a recess at the W. end of the nave. The surviving fragment measures 53–61 cm by 53 cm by 44 cm. The upper edge as now re-set bears a Latin cross with wedge-shaped crosslets on the cross-arms, 29 cm by 23 cm. The adjacent face has a larger equal-armed cross with crosslets terminating each member, the base one elongated, and the intersection ringed unsymmetrically (Fig. 6, o). The larger cross can probably be dated to the 9th century by analogy with Irish examples,[2] suggesting that the smaller cross is rather earlier in date.

E.C.M.W. 217.
[1] Davies, *W. Gower*, II, p. 73.
[2] *Proc. Roy. Irish Acad.*, Vol. 61 (C, 1961), p. 126.

Llanmadog.

    SS 49 S.W. (4388 9343)   5 vi 64   XXI N.E.

(867) PORT TALBOT. Cylindrical pillar-stone (Plate 3) with three incised crosses (Fig. 6, h i j) and an inscription noted

before 1847 at Lower Court (Cwrt Isaf), a farmhouse formerly near Port Talbot; it was subsequently moved to Margam and is now in Margam Stones Museum. When discovered, the upper part had been fractured off and its length was recorded as about 1·5 m, of which 1·14 m is now exposed; the diameter is 38 cm. Cross (a) on the S. side as now set is a linear Latin cross 38 cm tall and cut as a broad groove with slightly splayed arms (the upper arm lost by fracture). The two other crosses, (b) to W. and (c) to N., are larger and in outline form with regularly splayed arms; they are virtually identical but the upper limb of (c) is lost by fracture. Below the cross-arm of (c) an inscription in half-uncials set horizontally and divided centrally by the lower limb of the cross reads TOME, for *Thomae* ('Of Thomas'). The name either refers to the person commemorated or, less probably, indicates a dedication (of the site) to St. Thomas the Apostle (see p. 21). The inscription and larger crosses suggest an 8th- or 9th-century date, but this may have been a re-using of the stone with an earlier linear cross.

E.C.M.W. 259; *C.I.I.C.* 1017; *Arch. Camb.*, 1857, pp. 55, 57; Radford, *Margam*, No. 4.

Margam (E), Port Talbot (C).
SS 78 N.E. (7651 8958)　12 xi 64　　　XXV S.W.

(868) PORT TALBOT. A slab-like stone first used for an incised cross, subsequently re-dressed as panelled-cross slab (and described more fully under No. 914). At the head of one face (the back as re-set upright) is a deeply incised linear ring-cross (Fig. 6, d) with prolonged stem, 48 cm in length. The stem is cut by an upturned semicircle, possibly a conventional symbol for a boat[1]. The cross is of 7th- or 8th-century date.

E.C.M.W. 262; *Arch. Camb.*, 1857, pp. 55, 59; XCIV (1939), pp. 17–18; Radford, *Margam*, No. 15.

[1] A common device, with examples in Ireland at Inismurray (W. F. Wakeman, *A Survey of the Antiquarian Remains on the Island of Inismurray* (London, 1893), p. 135 and Fig. 68; *Proc. Roy. Irish Acad.*, Vol. 61 (C, 1961), p. 139 and Fig. 8), and Killadeas (*ibid.*, Fig. 9); and in Scotland at Drumore, Wigtownshire (*Proc. Soc. Ant. Scot.*, LXXIV (1939–40), p. 72 and Fig. 4) and Kirkmadrine, Galloway (three).

Margam (E), Port Talbot (C).
SS 78 N.E. (7670 8941)　12 xi 64　　　XXV S.W.

(869) NEATH. Pillar-stone with two incised crosses (Plate 3), standing N. of the main road westwards from Neath near the site of Court Herbert. It is naturally shaped with squared but irregular sides and three-sided canted head, 2·13 m high, 48 cm wide and 15 cm thick. On the N. face is a rough Latin cross (Fig. 6, b) with narrow grooves, 50 cm by 22 cm, with bifurcated upper terminals and plain but abraded foot. The slightly larger and more refined cross on the opposite face (Fig. 6, a) has expanded, almost wedge-shaped, upper terminals with plain foot, and is cut as a wider groove. The stone and its original (N.) cross is of 7th- to 8th-century date,[1] while the cross on the S. face is likely to be later (probably 9th-century) than the other.

E.C.M.W. 251; *Arch. Camb.*, 1876, p. 35.
[1] Cf. *E.C.M.W.* 301; Henry, *Irish Art*, I, p. 119 and Pl. 49.

Cadoxton-juxta-Neath (E), Blaenhonddan (C).
SS 79 N.W. (7409 9763)　9 x 64　　　XV S.E.

(870) PONT-RHYD-Y-FEN. Pillar-stone (Plate 3) found in 1929 in a wall of the farm-yard at Penhydd-fawr.[1] It is a local sandstone, reduced in width and possibly in length, now 1·01 m long, 37 cm wide tapering to 17 cm at the base, and 10 cm thick at the head increasing to 20 cm at the base. The face, worn down by probable use as a threshold (with holes for door-posts and a bolt) and by flaking, has traces of a linear cross of unusual form at the head. The equal-armed cross (Fig. 6, c) has crosslets with wedge-shaped terminals and with a dot in each inter-arm space of all four crosslets. The side-arm crosslets are contained each within a semicircle with diagonal rays towards the centre; the bifid terminals of these rays almost make a circle around the intersection of the main cross. The stone, in the National Museum of Wales, is probably of the 9th or 10th century.

E.C.M.W. 257; *Arch. Camb.*, LXXXV (1930), pp. 394–5.
[1] Ex. inf. Professor W. F. Grimes.

Margam (E), Port Talbot (C).
SS 89 s.w. (8063 9312 approx.)　8 xii 64　　　XXV N.E.

(871) NEATH. Pillar-stone, with inscription and incised crosses, built horizontally into the base of a buttress on the E. side of the easternmost range of conventual buildings at the Cistercian abbey of Neath. One face and the head of the shaped rectangular stone of Pennant sandstone are exposed. The flattened head, 33 cms wide and 18 cms thick but tapering, is decorated with two incised plain Latin crosses, aligned within a subrectangular incised frame.[1] The face, apparently 120 cms long, has at the top (when upright) an incised plain Latin cross, 12 cms tall; below it the inscription along the length of the face consists of one word in half-uncials, reading (unusually) upwards towards the head, B (E) L G I C U, presumably a proper name.[2] In its present state, the reading must be a tentative one. The form of the monument, analogous to the Merthyr Tudful stone (No. 862), and its lettering indicate a 7th-8th-century date.

[1] Cf. *E.C.M.W.* 48, 331.
[2] Perhaps cognate with 'Beili'; cf. 'Belyau filia Brachan' in the genealogies, Bartrum, *Tracts*, p. 16 ('De Situ Brecheniauc' 12 (19)).

Cadoxton-juxta-Neath (E), Dyffryn Clydach (C).
SS 79 N.W. (7383 9735)　20 ix 73　　　XV S.E.

881–893. CLASS C: RECUMBENT GRAVE-SLABS WITH INCISED CROSS

(881) BRITHDIR, Bargoed. A slab with incised crosses (Plate 4) was found in 1960 during demolition of Capel Brithdir, a modern chapel on an older site near Bargoed. It is roughly square, 65 cm by 61 cm and 10 cm thick, of Pennant sandstone, probably approximating to its original size. On

one face is a simple linear cross with double stem. The whole of the other face is filled by a linear equal-armed cross combined with a roughly rectangular frame (Fig. 7, h), the cross-arms formed by single incised lines, the frame by a double line. In each of the inter-arm spaces is a centrally placed ring with a central dot, to be distinguished from the commoner ring-and-hollow (Nos. 916, 919–21), for which the nearest parallel is provided by No. 887. The slab, probably recumbent and re-used for the second cross device, may be dated as 7th- to 9th-century. It is at present at the National Museum of Wales.

Arch. Camb., CXII (1963), pp. 184–5.

Gelli-gaer.
    SO 10 S.W. (1375 0262) 8 xii 64   XIII S.W.

(882) LLANGYFELACH. A damaged slab with carved cross and inscription (Plate 5) found in 1913 in the floor of the parish church[1] and re-set on the internal face of the N. wall of the nave there. The rectangular gritstone slab, 110 cm by 57 cm, has been trimmed down from its original dimensions and one upper angle has fractured off; its thickness cannot be ascertained. A ringed Latin cross in false relief, formed of paired cords interlaced at the centre, extends to each edge, the expanded arm-ends forming triquetra knots. Each arc of the ring set within the arm-ends consists of a double-beaded single twist, squared at the ends. A similar form of cross occurs on Irish recumbent slabs[2] but is not usually combined with a ring as in this case. Parallel to the stem of the cross an incised Latin inscription reads (downwards) CRUX · $\overline{\text{XPI}}$ ('The cross of Christ'), in rounded half-uncials with single punctuation dot and mark of abbreviation (for *Christi*). The slab is of the 9th century.

E.C.M.W. 211; *C.I.I.C.* 1010.
[1] *Arch. Camb.*, 1920, p. 361.
[2] *Proc. Roy. Irish Acad.*, Vol. 61 (C, 1961), p. 124 and Fig. 26.

Llangyfelach.
    SS 69 N.W. (6461 9897) 9 x 64   XIV N.E.

(883) LLANGYFELACH. A slab with incised framed ring-cross (Fig. 11), forming the lintel of a doorway on the N. side of the detached tower in the churchyard. The rectangular sandstone slab, set on edge and lacking part of the foot, is 1·32 m long, 56 cm wide and 13 cm thick; the face is largely flaked away. At the head, an equal-armed cross (Fig. 7, g) with slightly enlarged terminals is set in an incised ring, joined at the foot. In each of the inter-arm spaces is a ring-and-hollow (*cf.* No. 889 and *E.C.M.W.* 52, 125, 344), one entirely flaked off. Below the ring-cross is a stem in outline with rounded foot; markings beneath this suggest a more elaborate terminal but are too faint for certainty. The whole cross is contained within an incised, rectangular (?) frame close to the edges of the slab. It probably dates from the 9th century.

E.C.M.W. 213; *C.I.I.C.* under 1010.

Llangyfelach.
    SS 69 N.W. (6464 9894) 9 x 64   XIV N.E.

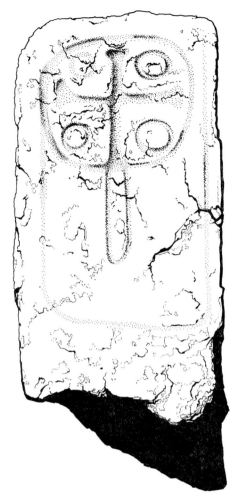

FIG. 11.
Llangyfelach, cross-decorated slab (883). Scale $\frac{1}{10}$.

(884) PORT TALBOT. Part of squared slab (Plate 5), with incised cross and inscription, probably originally recumbent. It was discovered in 1869 in the demolition of The Croft, a farmstead formerly near Aberafan (now Port Talbot), possibly the site of a medieval chapel,[1] and was deposited ultimately in the National Museum of Wales. The fragment, 28 cm by 25 cm in width and 10 cm thick, is of Pennant sandstone, but is split in two pieces. The face bears an incised Latin cross (Fig. 7, a) 25 cm by 14 cm, with slightly enlarged terminals (almost wedge-shaped). Inscribed to the left of it in horizontal lines is CRU / X / XPI, and to the right inscribed vertically GELUGUI[/ N, in rounded half-uncials. The latter, probably incomplete, word presumably names the person commemorated as on comparable Irish slabs (but *cf.* No. 886). It is probably of 8th- or 9th-century date.

E.C.M.W. 260; *C.I.I.C.* 1004.
[1] *Arch. Camb.*, LXXX (1925), p. 424; (see also p. 21).

Aberavon (E), Port Talbot (C).
SS 78 N.E. (7633 8998 approx.)   8 xii 64   XXV S.W.

(885) PORT TALBOT. A broken slab with carved cross and partial inscription (Plate 5), found in 1900 during the demolition of a building 'known as Hen Gapel which stood on Upper Court Farm',[1] and more recently deposited at Margam Stones Museum. The surviving part of the sandstone slab, 33 cm wide and 47 cm in maximum length and 8 cm thick (split from a greater original thickness), has a ringed cross carved in false relief within a circular frame. The equal-armed cross is formed by double-beaded but weathered cords set diagonally round a sunken centre and twisted to form expanded squared arm-ends of which the three upper ones are filled with double-beaded loops. The arcs of the ring, coincident with the arm-ends within the circular surround, are each formed of a double-beaded twist in two lobes, the inter-arm spaces being deeply sunken. The cords of the lowest arm-end merge into three-cord double-beaded plaitwork carried down in a vertical panel to form the shaft of the cross.

Part of a Latin inscription on both sides of the shaft reads down the face FEC[on the right and C[/ UT[on the left, cut in rounded half-uncials. The slab is of the late 9th or early 10th century.

E.C.M.W. 261; *C.I.I.C.* 1003.
[1] *Arch. Camb.*, LXXXI (1926), pp. 193–7.

Margam (E), Port Talbot (C).
SS 78 N.E. (7670 8955)   12 xi 64   XXV S.W.

(886) BAGLAN. An incomplete slab with carved cross and part inscription (Plate 5) found about 1850 in the churchyard of the old church at Baglan[1] and more recently re-set in the internal vestry wall of St. Catherine's Church, Baglan.[2] On the surviving part of the rectangular sandstone slab, 70 cm by 43 cm, is a ringed cross in false relief formed by double-beaded cords outlining a Greek cross with rounded angles and making squared Stafford-knots in the lower arm-ends. At the upper arm-end the cords instead of interlacing merge into a squared panel of narrow double-beaded knotwork, while at the foot the smaller knot rests on a stem in the form of a square panel of eight-cord knotwork incorporating a central cruciform break. The double-beaded arcs of the ring joining the arm-ends make circular inter-arm spaces. To the right of the stem an incomplete Latin inscription is incised down the face in rounded half-uncials, reading +BRANCU · F[ ]; the complete inscription presumably included the word *fecit*. By Irish parallels[3] the slab should belong to the late 9th or early 10th century.

E.C.M.W. 191; *C.I.I.C.* 1005.
[1] *Arch. Camb.*, 1851, p. 145 (J. O. Westwood).
[2] At SS 7527 9223 (XXV S.W.).
[3] *Proc. Roy. Irish Acad.*, Vol. 61 (C, 1961), pp. 129–31, 142.

Baglan (E), Port Talbot (C).
SS 79 S.E. (7535 9228)   7 x 64   XXV N.W.

(887) PORT TALBOT. (Plate 4), first noted in the churchyard of St. Mary's Church, Port Talbot. The roughly shaped and weathered slab, 65 cm long and 30 cm wide, has a slightly rounded head and is 7·5 cm thick. On each face is an incised outline Latin cross of intersecting arms with open-ended foot (Fig. 7, b). The expansional arm-ends are formed by an incised ring, those on the less weathered face incorporating a central dot. Crosses of similar design occur on Irish slabs datable to the 9th to 11th centuries,[1] and on a slab at Bryngwyn, Radnorshire (*E.C.M.W.* 405), with a rounded head suggestive of a late date, as here. The slab stands loose in the porch of St. Mary's Church.

Although slabs with two cross-decorated faces are known at some Irish sites,[2] serving as headstones, it is possible that this slab was originally recumbent and was re-used with a second cross imitating the original; the less weathered cross is cut across a flaked surface, but the upper arm-end of the other and possibly earlier cross is partly weathered away.

E.C.M.W. 263a.
[1] *Proc. Roy. Irish Acad.*, Vol. 61 (C, 1961), p. 131 and Fig. 21.
[2] P. Ó. hEailidhe, 'The Crosses and Slabs at St. Berrihert's Kyle', in *North Munster Studies*, p. 123.

Aberavon (E), Port Talbot (C).
SS 79 S.E. (7629 9011)   7 x 64   XXV S.W.

(888) LLANTRISANT. (Plate 4), formerly built into the external N. face of Llantrisant parish church and recently placed inside the church (loose at E. end of S. Aisle). The rectangular slab, 1·0 m long, 33 cm wide and 10 cm thick, is of local shaly material, somewhat flaked, and was probably originally recumbent. The central ring-cross filling the width of the slab has a linear Latin cross, its stem extending below with cross-letted terminal (Fig. 7, f). On each side of the stem is a smaller linear Latin cross with bifid upper terminals and trifid stem. Two parallel lines at the head of the slab may represent the titular inscription of a Crucifixion (as suggested in *E.C.M.W.*; *cf.* also *E.C.M.W.* 328). Similar grouping of three (or usually five) crosses occurs on Irish slabs and continental monuments, all belonging to a date in the range 7th–9th century.

E.C.M.W. 219; *Arch. Camb.*, 1893, p. 348.

Llantrisant.
ST 08 S.W. (0464 8342)   11 ix 64   XXXVI S.W.

(889) LLANWYNNO. Fragment of slab (Plate 4) of sandstone, found in 1893 in repairs to the fabric of the parish church. The fragment, 33 cm by 20 cm and 6 cm thick, has an equal-armed cross in a sub-rectangular ring formed by broad shallow grooves, with part of a stem below the ring. Each of the inter-spaces left in relief has a hollow, and two smaller hollows or dots occur beside the stem. Similar designs on pillar-stones date to the period 7th–9th century (*E.C.M.W.* 52, 133), but the same pattern of 'discs' in relief with internal hollows occurs on No. 913 of somewhat later date. The stone is set on a corbel on the internal S. wall of the nave of the church.

E.C.M.W. 227; *Arch. Camb.*, 1902, p. 308.

Llanwynno.
ST 09 N.W. (0300 9561)   10 xii 64   XVIII S.E.

(890) LLANWYNNO. Slab with incised Latin cross, built into the internal S. wall of the nave of St. Gwynno's Church, forming one vertical side of a recess.[1] The rectangular slab of Pennant sandstone, reduced for re-use, is 37 cm by 19 cm and about 5 cm thick. The cross (Fig. 7, d) of which one bifurcated terminal remains, probably resembled originally that on the pillar-stone near Neath (No. 869), suggesting a 7th- or 8th-century date.

[1] Thanks are due to Mr. J. K. Knight of the Department of the Environment for drawing attention to this stone.

Llanwynno.
ST 09 N.W. (0300 9561) 23 vii 71   XVIII S.E.

(891) EGLWYSILAN. Figured slab (Plate 5) found in 1904 in the churchyard of St. Ilan's Church, and preserved inside the church (mounted on the N. wall). The slab of Pennant sandstone is roughly rectangular but weathered, its dimensions 68 cm by 40 cm and 16 cm thick apart from a rough ridge at the upper edge of the face. Centrally in the upper half of the face an outline human figure is incised, 30 cm tall standing facing front; the facial features are crudely rendered on a rounded head with long neck, the arms being extended and the legs slightly bent at the knees. The left hand holds a buckler, and slung at the waist is a long sword with pommel and quillons, falling behind the figure who seems to be wearing a short tunic.

Although the figure recalls certain representations of a Celtic warrior god,[1] and probably derives from pagan Celtic tradition, the iconography could belong to an Early Christian context[2] and the figure may represent David the warrior king or simply the person interred. The girt sword (as against the spear held by pagan Celtic figures) suggests the slab belongs to the period 8th–10th centuries A.D.

E.C.M.W. 195.
[1] In particular an incised slab from Maryport, Cumberland (A. Ross, *Pagan Celtic Britain* (London, 1967), Fig. 128 and Pl. 63c).
[2] Cf. incised profile of David the Warrior on a stone at Carndonagh (Henry, *Irish Art*, I, pp. 129–30 and Pl. 59).

Eglwysilan (E), Pontypridd (C).
ST 18 N.W. (1064 8903) 9 xii 64   XXVIII S.E.

(892) GELLI-GAER. Slab with incised ring-cross (Plate 4), found about 1906 at the site of Capel Gwladys, Gelli-gaer, and preserved at the parish church (set inside the S. porch). The slab of Pennant sandstone, 1·2 m long and 13 cm thick, is now wedge-shaped, tapering from 71 cm at the head to 27 cm, most of the left-hand edge having fractured off; part of the surface is defaced by flaking, and the lower part is worn smooth by probable use as a step. The cross in the upper half (Fig. 7, c) is formed of a four-leaf marigold springing from a central ring-and-dot, all enclosed within a ring which is prolonged below as an outline stem with closed foot. The arm-ends outside the ring are outline triangles.[1] In each of the angles at the head of the slab is an incised ring (cf. No. 919). The slab is probably datable to the 8th or 9th century.

B.B.C.S., VIII, ii (May 1936), p. 162; *Trans. Cardiff Nat. Soc.*, XLIV (1911), p. 31.

[1] Cf. No. 862 and *Proc. Roy. Irish Acad.*, Vol. 61 (C, 1961), Fig. 13(8) and Pl. XXX (1).

Gelli-gaer.
ST 19 N.W. (1249 9928) 9 xii 64   XIX N.E.

(893) FLATHOLM (Plate 4). Found in 1942 'built into the base of the extreme south end of the wall which forms the west boundary of the garden',[1] and now in the National Museum of Wales. The rectangular stone, possibly cut down from a larger recumbent slab, is 42 cm by 26 cm and 11 cm thick. On one face is a Latin equal-armed cross (Fig. 7, e), formed by broad and deeply pecked grooves, with a central dot. Like similar crosses on pillar-stones (E.C.M.W. 356, 407), it is of the period 7th to 9th centuries.

[1] *Trans. Cardiff Nat. Soc.*, LXXX (1948–50), p. 22.

Cardiff St. Mary (E), Cardiff (C).
ST 26 N.W. (2190 6492) 8 xii 64   LI S.E.

901–928. CLASS D: STANDING SCULPTURED SLABS

(a) Plain Slabs (901–902)

(901) MARGAM. Incomplete slab with carved cross (Plate 6), added to the lapidary collection at Margam Abbey about 1855[1] and presumably discovered in the locality; it remains in Margam Stones Museum. The roughly trimmed rectangular slab of local Pennant sandstone, 48 cm wide and 13 cm thick, is less than its original length and is also set upright with buried base, the visible height being 1·07 m. A ringed cross carved in false relief with pierced inter-arm spaces[2] fills the width of the face but lacks the upper arm and upper arcs of the ring; the surviving arms have been re-set after fracturing off. The slightly expanded arms are formed of four-cord double-beaded plaitwork linked around the hub which is a sunk panel filled by a plain twist of two lobes. On the lowest arm, three-cord plaitwork is expanded to fill the long vertical panel of the shaft and as four-cord plaits it terminates in a double Stafford-knot. The surviving arcs of the ring, coincident with the arm-ends, consist of double-beaded knotwork based on pairs of interlaced loops, including a 'free-ring'.

The slab probably dates from the 10th century.

E.C.M.W. 232; Radford, *Margam*, No. 11.
[1] Westwood, *Lapid. Wal.*, p. 30 and Pl. XIX (1).
[2] Pierced hollows occur on two Manx slabs of comparable date (Kermode, *Manx Crosses*, Nos. 89 (Pl. XL) and 97 (Pl. XLVII)).

Margam (E), Port Talbot (C).
SS 88 N.W. (8017 8633) 12 xi 64   XXXIII N.E.

(902) NASH. Slab with carved cross (Plate 20), noted shortly before 1899 at Nash Manor[1] and more recently placed in the National Museum of Wales. The exceptionally tall sandstone slab, 2·65 m high,[2] is dressed to a uniform rectangular form 44 cm wide and 15 cm thick (partly affected by weathering), with a slight set-back at the top edge that may have secured a capping stone, and with slightly projecting base butts on the narrow faces. One face is decorated with carving in low relief,

forming three panels separated by plain areas, all much weathered and marked by striations.

At the head a ringed cross with hollow angles and squared expanded arm-ends fills the width of the face, showing vestiges of plaitwork; the hub is marked by a sunken roundel with a slight boss and central dot. The ring, of less width than the arms, is nicked at each exterior junction with the arm-ends. The lowest arm develops into a slightly splayed shaft, on each side of which is a standing figure in profile, facing the cross with one arm extended; they probably represent the Blessed Virgin Mary and St. John.[3] Below the shaft is an incised ring-and-dot, and below that again near each edge of the face is a sunken roundel, possibly part of a design that has been lost by weathering of the face.[4]

The slightly sunken central panel that extends across the width of the face contains a weathered carving in low relief but not readily identifiable. Its semi-upright posture makes it unlikely to be an animal (though there is a suggestion of a horned head), and as the legs appear to be crossed the sitting figure may represent David holding a harp.[5]

The lowest panel, similarly sunken but shorter, contains two weathered figures in profile seated face to face, each holding a staff. They probably represent St. Anthony and St. Paul in the desert; very faint traces remain of both the round loaf set between them and the bird that brought it.[6]

The slab has no close analogy amongst other slabs in Wales, and its apparently shallow and restrained decoration (even allowing for the effect of considerable weathering) may relate it to certain slabs in northern Britain. It is probably of 10th-century date.

E.C.M.W. 250.
[1] *Arch. Camb.*, 1899, p. 80.
[2] On the possible symbolism of these proportions see p. 27.
[3] The apparent representation of long plaited hair (as on No. 907) is an accident of surface flaking.
[4] Cf. *Ogam*, XIII (1961), p. 290.
[5] For representations of David the Musician on Irish crosses, *v.* Henry, *Irish Art*, I, p. 130; II, pp. 107, 173, and Pl. 91; on a Scottish slab, *E.C.M.S.*, Fig. 275a (Monifieth); and on a Manx slab, Kermode, *Manx Crosses*, No. 104, Pl. LIV (Kirk Michael).
[6] For this scene on Irish crosses, *v.* Henry, *Irish Art*, I, p. 149 and Pl. 70; II, pp. 147–8, 151, and H. M. Roe, *The High Crosses of Kells* (Meath Arch. and Hist. Soc., 1959), p. 43; on a Scottish slab, *E.C.M.S.*, Fig. 305B (Dunfallandy); on a Manx slab, Kermode, *Manx Crosses*, No. 67, Pl. XXVI (Maughold parish). The latter is not necessarily pre-Scandinavian; *v.* B. R. S. and E. M. Megaw, 'The Norse Heritage of the Isle of Man' in C. Fox and B. Dickins (eds.), *The Early Cultures of North-west Europe* (Cambridge, 1950).

Llanblethian (E), Nash (C).
SS 97 S.E. (9623 7294)   8 xii 64   XLV N.W.

(b) 'Disc-headed' Slabs (903–913)

(903) PONTARDAWE. Two incomplete portions of a slab-cross (Plate 6), part of the disc-head remaining at St. Ciwg's Church, Llanguicke,[1] part of the shaft now at the Museum of the Royal Institution, Swansea.[2] A description and sketch of the monument, broken but apparently *in situ*, about 1693 by Lhuyd[3] establishes its form and the correlation of the surviving fragments; that account also suggests its original location was in the damaged cist of a ruined cairn on Mynydd Gellionnen

(I i 85), E. of the Unitarian Chapel.[4] The stone is described by Lhuyd as 'about a yard and a half high', i.e. about 1·4 m, and his sketch shows the shaft as splayed (*cf.* Nos. 908, 911). Both the head and the shaft are decorated with ornament incised and carved in low relief.

The disc-head, of Pennant sandstone 7·5 cm thick and 79 cm in diameter, lacks the lowest third by fracture and the edge is also damaged. One face is filled with an incised ringed cross potent with large central square but is otherwise undecorated. The edge and other face are plain.

The shaft, of similar local stone, survives as a fractured slab 1·16 m tall, with splayed sides 48 cm in width at the base. Its maximum thickness at the base is 24 cm, tapering to 11·5 cm at the top. Part of the top and right-hand edge (from the front) are lost by fracture. A rough shoulder on the same side, below which level the main face is plain, shows that the lowest third of the stone was buried. The rest of the main face is occupied by the representation in low relief of a full-length figure facing front with uplifted bent arms (one only surviving) and vested in a squared garment that fills the width of the slab. Facial features, hair and the opened hand (mostly weathered) are rendered naturistically but crudely, with two out-turned shod feet depicted below the garment. On the edges of this garment (probably a chasuble with orphreys) is a continuous band of plain four-cord plaitwork, merging on the left-hand side into rigid plaits, apparently double-beaded. The posture (conventionally one of prayer) and the rendering of the 'vestment' have much in common with similar representations in Irish metalwork and illumination of the pre-Norman period.[5] The stone is probably of 9th-century date.

E.C.M.W. 210 (disc-head) and 256 (shaft); *Arch. Camb.*, 1917, p. 425; 1920, p. 373.
[1] Recorded at Llanguicke in 1869 but provenance not then known (*Arch. Camb.*, 1869, p. 188); transferred to the church *ca.* 1890 (Morgan, E. Gower, p. 55), i.e. at SN 7237 0558.
[2] Formerly, from 1801 to 1965, the shaft was built into the external N.E. end of the Unitarian Chapel on Mynydd Gellionnen (SN 7008 0415). Before the rebuilding of the chapel it had been in use as a gate-post or as a mounting block (Morgan, as n. 1 and information from Chapel records).
[3] B.M. Stowe MS. 1023, fo. 27, quoted in part of Morgan, E. Gower, pp. 48–9, and in part in *Trans. Cymmr.*, 1965, pt. i, p. 78, f.n. 41 (F. V. Emery).
[4] At SN 7029 0428. In Stowe MS. 1023 it 'stood upright in a Small Carn' which is drawn as a rectangle with chamfered corners, suggesting the cist referred to.
[5] Henry, *Irish Art*, I, Pl. 46 (the Athlone plaque) and Pl. 57 (the St. Matthew figure in the Book of Durrow), both attributed to the late 7th century.

Llangyfelach (E), Rhyndwyglydach (C).
SN 70 S.W. (7029 0428)   9 ix 64   VIII S.E.

(904) COELBREN, Cefn Hirfynydd. Fragment of shaft (Plate 6) of probable disc-headed slab-cross, found on Cefn Hirfynydd[1] and after standing in the grounds of The Gnoll, Neath, is now preserved at the Museum of the Royal Institution, Swansea. The stone, a coarse sandstone slab fractured and incomplete on all edges, is 76 cm tall and 25 cm thick. The main face, 45 cm wide at most (the width increasing to 56 cm at the back), has carved decoration in low relief. At the top this

forms the lowest sector of a ringed cross potent of which the squared arm-end and part of an arm survive, outlined by plain beading and filled with a disjointed pattern of frets. One arc of the ring remains (with traces of another) as a panel flush with the arm-end, similarly outlined and filled with straight frets.

In the space below, a full-length figure stands facing front with raised arms bent in the conventional posture of prayer; the head, rounded and hairless, and facial features are crudely rendered. The figure is clothed in a belted kilt with flared pleating that apparently does not cover the knees.[2] Descending from each elbow is a narrow band of diagonal frets, possibly representing plaitwork (cf. No. 903 above). The degenerate decoration of the cross-head suggests a 10th-century date.

E.C.M.W. 269; Arch. Camb., 1865, pp. 63–4 (Westwood).
[1] 'Not far from Capel Coelbren' (Arch. Camb., 1886, p. 339), i.e. in area SN 84 10.
[2] Kilted figures occur on Scottish slabs at Balblair and Golspie, Proc. Soc. Ant. Scot., LXXIV (1939–40), Pls. XVII and XXVIII; in Merovingian work, see Le Blant, Nouveau Recueil des Inscriptions Chrétiennes de la Gaule (Paris, 1892), p. 62.

Cadoxton-juxta-Neath (E), Dulais Higher (C).
    SN 81 S.W. (84 10 approx.)   4 vi 64   IV S.W.

(905) LLANGENNITH. Fragment of shaft (Plate 7) of probable disc-headed slab-cross found in the parish church[1] where it is set inverted on the internal W. wall. The sandstone slab, 1·4 m tall and 7·5 cm thick (probably half the original thickness), is splayed from its original top width of 50 cm towards the base. The whole face between plain rounded angle-mouldings is filled with continuous knotwork carved in low relief, consisting of twelve horizontal rows each of five knots, with some irregularities and incorporating one central cruciform break. The knots derive from plain loose twenty-two-cord plaitwork, of which the completion is traceable at the base; the pattern would have merged into the design on the cross-head, presumably of disc type. The stone is probably of 9th-century date.

E.C.M.W. 209; Arch. Camb., 1899, pp. 5, 13, 37, 56–7.
[1] Davies, W. Gower, III, p. 84.

Llangennith.
    SS 49 S.W. (4287 9141)   5 vi 64   XXI S.E.

(906) PORT TALBOT. (Plate 5). From the site of a medieval chapel at Upper Court Farm formerly near Port Talbot,[1] added to the lapidary collection at Margam about 1921 where it remains.[2] The slab of local Pennant sandstone, 10 cm thick, is much weathered and two-thirds of the head together with one edge of the splayed shaft have been lost by fracture; the surviving visible height is 68 cm. It is decorated with lightly carved ornament on both main faces and on the surviving narrow side.

The disc-head, originally 56 cm in diameter, has on both faces a ringed cross potent extending to the edge-moulding. On the wide face (as it survives, the N. face as now set), the arms and squared arm-ends are outlined by a continuous plain beading. The panels thus formed are filled with crudely

rendered plaitwork linked round the hub, which is marked by an incised ring with a central hole. The arcs of the ring, symmetrical with the disc-head, are indicated only by incised lines. On these arcs and on the inter-arm spaces are traces of a decorative pattern of sunk 'dots' and incised rings with a 'dot'. The surviving angle-moulding of the shaft below this is returned to meet the lowest arm-end, while the shaft itself forms one panel filled with varied patterns of frets imitating plaitwork.

On the opposite (or S.) face the arms of the cross and the arcs of the ring are formed in separate panels outlined by plain beading. These panels and the squared hub are filled with indeterminate patterns in low relief, that in the one complete arm-end tending towards debased scrolls or spirals (cf. No. 956), that in the arc of the ring probably a two-cord twist. The surviving angle-moulding of the shaft forms a cable-twist. In the middle of the shaft a vertical panel is filled with diagonal frets in imitation of a diagonal key-pattern, the spaces on each side being filled with indeterminate patterns of frets.

The surviving narrow side of the disc-head (on the E.) shows a series of small square panels each containing five sunk 'dots' grouped as four around one (cf. the same device on No. 914). The panelled side of the shaft below is filled with a plain two-cord twist, mostly eroded. The other narrow side of the shaft has indeterminate traces of decoration. 11th-century.

E.C.M.W. 263; Arch. Camb., XCIV (1939), pp. 18–20; Radford, Margam, No. 13.
[1] For the site see p. 21 above. This stone is probably that seen in 1849 at 'Cwrt Uchaf Farm' but not otherwise recorded (Arch. Camb., 1857, p. 55).
[2] Arch. Camb., LXXVI (1921), p. 296.

Margam (E), Port Talbot (C).
    SS 78 N.E. (7670 8955)   13 xi 64   XXV S.W.

(907) MARGAM (The 'Conbelin Stone'). Slab-cross and quadrangular socketed base (Plates 8, 9) first noted as standing outside Margam churchyard,[1] subsequently moved into the ruins of the abbey, and in 1932 re-set in Margam Stones Museum. Both the cross and the base, of local Pennant sandstone, have carved decoration in low relief, slightly weathered; the slab-cross, which also has an inscription on the head, has almost certainly been reversed in relation to the base.

The head and shaft are formed of one stone 185 cm tall but lacking at least 18 cm broken off the foot of the shaft.[2] The disc-head is 107 cm in diameter and 15–18 cm in thickness; the shaft, 13 cm thick, is 57 cm wide but tapers slightly towards the foot. On the W. side (or front as re-set) a ringed cross potent almost fills the head symmetrically with the rim, which forms a plain edge-moulding continued down the angles of the shaft. The central square of the cross, the arms and the squared arm-ends, which project beyond the ring, are linked by a continuous edge-moulding, also continued down the shaft as a stem. The plaitwork or knotwork filling each panel is however quite discrete, consisting of successively down the vertical axis (i) plain twelve-cord plait with a single vertical break at the centre, (ii) plain eight-cord plait, (iii, central square) plain irregular knots and twists around a raised ring-and-boss slightly to the right of the centre of the panel and disc-head,

(iv) plain six-cord plait, (v) ten-cord plait (possibly double-beaded but too weathered for certainty) becoming (vi) figure-of-eight knots placed horizontally in vertical row down the shaft; on the horizontal axis (from the N. or left-hand) (vii) eight-cord double-beaded plait with breaks vertically and horizontally forming one free ring, (viii) two linked Stafford-knots, double-beaded, then (iii) as before, (ix) double-beaded knotwork based on six-cord plait, and (x) ten-cord double-beaded plait with irregular vertical and horizontal breaks forming one angular loop. Each arc of the ring is framed by plain edge-moulding and is filled with plain knotwork, of figure-of-eight pattern in the upper left and lower right arcs, and of Stafford-knots in double row in the other two arcs. The sunk inter-arm spaces and the surrounds of the ring are plain except for traces of inscriptions (see below). On the shaft the panels beside the stem of the cross contain in each a standing figure facing front, the space around the head being filled with a plain triquetra knot. The bearded figure on the left, holding a book before him, presumably represents St. John while that on the right (in three-quarter width only because of the narrowness of the panel) represents the Blessed Virgin Mary. Both figures (incomplete by fracture of the lower part of the shaft) have draped robes, open-necked in the former but gathered round a collar in the latter. The treatment of the hair in both figures (St. John's long, on the shoulder; St. Mary's, coiled at the end) as well as that of the garments (particularly the draping of folds over one arm for St. John) could be

modelled on such manuscript representations as are in the Book of Kells.[3]

The E. side (or back as now set) has lost much of the upper part of the disc-head by flaking, but retains the lower vertical member and lower arcs of a ringed cross potent similar in form to that on the opposite face. The panelled vertical arm is filled with two linked Stafford-knots, and the squared arm-end with diagonal key-pattern. The incomplete left-hand arc of the ring contains S-shaped frets terminating in square frets, while the other arc contains a plain two-cord twist. At the neck of the shaft is a horizontal band of plain figure-of-eight knotwork with one vertical break, each extreme end forming a stylised animal- or bird-head[4] with a prominent eye. Below, in a framed panel filling the width of the shaft, are pairs of linked squares of diagonal swastika key-pattern, two squares complete and part only of a lower pair. The narrow sides of the head and shaft are undecorated.

The rectangular base, 76 cm high (67 cm exposed), 102 cm wide and varying in thickness from 63 cm on the N. to 58 cm on the S., is decorated on all four sides and on the upper surface. The socket, 50 cm by 13 cm, and the panel around it have rectangular frames of single cable-twist, the panel itself being filled with plain four-cord figure-of-eight knotwork (with a complete break on the N.), merging on the wider E. side into plain six-cord plaitwork with irregular breaks. The vertical angle-mouldings are formed of beading and cable-twist (weathered and also partly fractured away at the N.E.)

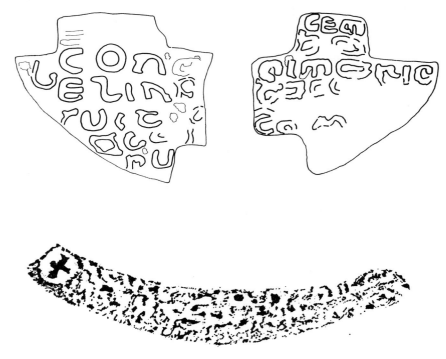

FIG. 12.

Margam, the 'Conbelin' stone (907). Above, inscription (i); below, inscription (ii). Scale ⅛.

carried over the top of the shorter faces, and the longer faces are both framed by a cable-twist also continued over the shorter faces to produce triple mouldings. The panel on the E. side (originally the front) presents a hunting scene with two horses and riders (right and centre) following three animals (on the left). The horses (one partly obscured by damage to the surface) are bridled and the riders are presented full-face, one of them having a buckler slung from his mount. The largest of the other three animals probably represents a stag, between two hounds. The space behind the head of the first rider is filled with a triquetra-knot, and that behind the other with a knot of two inter-twined oval loops.[5] On the S. side of the base a square panel of double-beaded (but weathered) eight-cord plaitwork is framed by a cable-twist and separated from the upper mouldings by a row of seven (originally eight) floral devices, each formed of a prominent bead surrounded by a ring of smaller beads. The W. side has a horizontal panel framed by cable-twist containing two linked double-beaded Stafford-knots in one third of it and two linked squares of plain diagonal swastika key-pattern in the remainder. A separate narrow vertical panel at the S. end is formed of plain figure-of-eight knotwork. The panel on the N. face, framed by a rectangle of cable-twist, contains a pattern of double-beaded (but weathered) six-cord plaitwork with doubled vertical break in the middle and other breaks.

A partly-eroded inscription (i, Fig. 12) fills the upper and lower left-hand inter-arm spaces of the W. side, incised in five and at least four lines respectively, reading downwards CON/BELIN P[O] / SUIT [.] / AC [C?] / RU / /CEM / ·P· [A] / NIMA RI[C?] / [T?]. . . / . . . ('Conbelin erected this cross for the soul of Ric . . .'). The lettering in rounded half-uncials has as manuscript features 'P' for *pro* (*cf.* No. 908) and, probably, a suprascript 'O' of *posuit* following the N of the first line; this 'O' is very faint, but is more likely to be explained thus than as part of the proper name *Conbelin* which occurs in that form in near-contemporary manuscripts (e.g. *Vita S. Cadoci*, chap. 66).

Another inscription (ii) fills the space between the arc of the ring and the outer edge in the same upper quadrant of the head, but is much eroded. The surviving traces, reproduced in Fig. 12 from a rubbing, are not clear enough for a reading, but are sufficient to establish that the inscription is incised[6] in half-uncials in two lines read from the outer edge downwards from the head; it is probably in Latin and roughly contemporary with the other inscription. A small cross in relief at the head of the panel is countersunk in relation to this and may have obliterated some letters.

This slab-cross, probably erected either to mark the bounds of the monastic enclosure or serve as a focus for public prayer,[7] is the most impressive of the monuments of this category in the county, if not in all Wales. It may be ascribed on stylistic grounds to the early 10th century or late in the preceding century.

E.C.M.W. 234; *C.I.I.C.* 1016; Radford, *Margam*, No. 7; *Arch. Camb.*, 1894, pp. 251–2; 1899, pp. 140–1; LXXXIII (1928), p. 392; *Y Cymmrodor*, XVIII (1905), pp. 28–9.

[1] In 1779, *Archaeologia*, VI, p. 25; R. Warner, *A Second Walk through Wales . . . in August and Sept., 1798* (Bath, 1799), p. 86, 'leaning against the wall of a cottage'.

[2] Possibly with shaft originally as tall as head. The uncompleted sketch in Stowe MS. 1024, fo. 25, shows that this fracture had occurred before *ca.* 1690; according to R. Allen in *Arch. Camb.*, 1899, pp. 15–16, the fractured end was re-fashioned to form a new tenon for the socketed base, which is unlikely to have been done after 1536.

[3] Henry, *Irish Art*, II, Plate D; *cf.* also Plates A and B.

[4] With a beak rather than 'biting jaws'.

[5] For the significance of the scene see p. 29 above.

[6] *Contra* R. A. S. Macalister, *Arch. Camb.*, XCIII (1938), p. 248 ('inscription in relief').

[7] *Cf.* Henry, *Irish Art*, I, pp. 118, 134–6. There was a tradition naming this as The Sanctuary Stone (Stowe MS. 1024).

Margam (E), Port Talbot (C).

SS 88 N.W. (8011 8632)   12 xi 64   XXXIII N.E.

(908) MARGAM (The 'Enniaun Stone'). (Plates 7, 12.) First recorded at Margam in 1874 as part of the lapidary collection,[1] and now in the Museum there. The slab of local Pennant sandstone, 1·88 m exposed height and 12·7 cm thick, has a circular head originally 71 cm in diameter but cut away roughly at the sides to the width of the neck of the shaft (61 cm) which splays out to 96 cm at the base. The main face is entirely decorated with ornament in low relief incorporating an inscription, but the sides and back are plain except for an outline cross on the latter.

The disc-head displays a ringed cross extending to the plain edge-moulding with square arm-ends and hollowed angles, outlined by a narrow moulding; the panelled arcs of the ring are similarly outlined. The inter-arm spaces and those between the ring and the edge-moulding are plain and sunk to emphasise the cross. Each arm-end is filled with plain six-cord plaitwork deriving from paired plaits twisted and linked diagonally at the hub where a lozenge-shaped panel is filled with a knot of two intertwined oval loops. The arcs of the ring contain differing patterns of triangular frets.

The shaft has plain rounded angle-mouldings continued below the disc-head by a narrow beading that merges into a horizontal beading returned at the ends as a triangular fret to fill the spandrels. The main panel forming the upper half of the shaft is filled with ten-cord triple-beaded plaitwork in five regular loops, framed by a plain inner moulding that is continued down the shaft parallel to the edge. The right-hand moulding is doubled back short of the foot to frame the lower panels which are divided by a vertical beading into one square panel (on the left) and a pair of smaller panels. Of the latter, the upper panel contains a diagonal swastika key-pattern and the lower a diagonal triangular key-pattern. In the square panel is a Latin inscription (Plate 12) in five horizontal lines reading CRUX · $\overline{\text{XPI}}$ · / + ENNIAUN · / ·P· ANIMA · / GUORGORET · FECIT · / ('The cross of Christ. Enniaun made it for the soul of Guorgoret'). The lettering is in regular half-uncials with dots separating the words. Manuscript influence may be seen in ·P· for *pro*, in the common abbreviated form of *et* used for the proper name ending, and in $\overline{\text{XPI}}$ for *Christi* the P having an open loop. In the second line the five minims here read as NNI are not linked, but the spelling of 'Enniaun' (later *Einion*) occurs in several early documents. In the Llancarfan charters 'Guoguoret' occurs as the name of a witness.[2] The small Latin cross before the name Enniaun has wedge-shaped arms. The narrow panel below these panels is plain except for an incised horizontal fret springing from each angle-moulding and doubly returned.

On the opposite face an incised outline Latin cross, 73 cm high, extends almost to the full width and height of the disc-head as well as below it.

The several features that this slab-cross has in common with No. 911 indicate a similar date in the late 9th century.

E.C.M.W. 231; C.I.I.C. 1014; Radford, Margam, No. 5.
[1] Arch. Camb., 1899, p. 139; Westwood, Lapid. Wall., pp. 28–9.
[2] Vita S. Cadoci, c. 55 in Vitae Sanct., p. 126.

Margam (E), Port Talbot (C).
ss 88 N.W. (8017 8633) 12 xi 64   XXXIII N.E.

(909) MARGAM. (Plate 7.) Reported to have been found in the Margam area and added to the lapidary collection about 1856,[1] where it remains in the Stones Museum. The slab of local Pennant sandstone, 1·34 m exposed height and 14 cm thick, has been roughly trimmed down on both narrow sides to 44 cm width; the disc-head was originally 1·0 m in diameter, but the shaft has traces of angle-mouldings that suggest it was straight-sided rather than splayed. The main face is decorated with carving in low relief, and there are traces of defaced or incomplete decoration on the other face.

The disc-head contains a ringed cross with widely splayed arms, rounded at the internal angles and extending to the plain edge-moulding. The cross is outlined by bold edge-moulding and further emphasised by deeply-sunk but plain inter-arm spaces. Each arm forms a splayed panel filled with irregular weathered knotwork, linked diagonally in the lowest three arms round the hub on which are traces of a former boss in relief. The arcs of the ring, in lower relief than the arms, are undecorated. On the shaft, in a moulded rectangular frame filling the space between the plain but damaged angle-mouldings, is a vertical panel of plain irregular beading, neither true plaitwork nor knotwork.

The opposite face has on the disc-head traces of an uncompleted cross formed of panels springing from a central boss, almost entirely removed by re-dressing or weathering.

The 'Anglian' form of the cross together with the debased carved decoration suggests that the slab should be dated to the late 10th or 11th century.

E.C.M.W. 235; Radford, Margam, No. 12.
[1] Westwood, Lapid. Wall., p. 30 and Pl. XIX.

Margam (E), Port Talbot (C).
ss 88 N.W. (8017 8633) 12 xi 64   XXXIII N.E.

(910) MARGAM (The 'Grutne' stone, Plate 12.) Formerly standing S. of the church,[1] and more recently re-set in Margam Stones Museum. The disc-shaped head and four-sided splayed shaft formed from one block of local sandstone stand 101 cm high, with a tenon at the base but lacking a socketed pedestal stone. The head is 44 cm in diameter and 17 cm thick; the shaft tapers in width from 48 cm at the base to 28 cm, and in thickness from 30 cm to 21 cm. Only one face is decorated, the other sides being dressed

smooth above a rounded base moulding. An equal-armed cross with 'fan-shaped' arms in relief and hollowed angles fills the head, outlined by rounded edge-moulding and containing a central ring and pellet. The shaft, framed by rounded angle-moulding, is filled with a Latin inscription in ten lines set horizontally reading INOMI / NE DI S / UMI · / CRUX / CRIZDI / PROP / ARABIT / GRUTNE / PRO ANMA / ANEST : · ('In the name of God Most High. The cross of Christ (which) Grutne prepared for the soul of Anest'). The lettering is in crude half-uncials with one square E (l. 8) and common manuscript abbreviations: 'inomine' for in nomine (cf. Nos. 928, 933), 'di' for dei and 'sumi' for summi (see p. 27 above). Though there is no spacing of words, two punctuation stops occur, one single and one triple. The form of the cross-head, resembling one variety of late Anglian cross in Northumberland[2] and more particularly some of the Whithorn (Galloway) cross-slabs, indicates a date in the 10th century.

E.C.M.W. 233; C.I.I.C. 1015; Radford, Margam, No. 6; Arch. Camb., 1851, p. 147; 1899, p. 142.
[1] Stowe MS. 1024, fo. 17; Arch. Camb., 1858, p. 345 (letter of E. Lhuyd, 1697).
[2] Collingwood, Northumbrian Crosses, p. 89.

Margam (E), Port Talbot (C).
ss 88 N.W. (8017 8633) 12 xi 64   XXXIII N.E.

(911) LLANTWIT MAJOR. (The 'Houelt' stone, Plates 10, 12.) First recorded as lying in the churchyard of St. Illtud's Church (possibly not its original location)[1] and, after standing in the porch, re-set upright within the W. nave of the church. The solid head and shaft though fractured and incomplete at the edges are formed of one slab of local gritstone, 1·9 m tall (with part of the concealed base butt extending a further 23 cm) and 15 cm thick; the disc-head is 81 cm in diameter, and the shaft is splayed in width from 43 cm at the neck to 66 cm (originally about 1·0 m) at the base. The main faces (E. and W.) and the rim of the head have carved decoration in low relief together with an inscription; the edges of the shaft have been trimmed away.

On the E. face the disc-head is filled with a ringed cross potent within a narrow edge-moulding, the ring being flush with the arm-ends. The squared arm-ends and central square are formed of diaper key-pattern, the connecting arms of paired T-shapes linked to the outer squares only. Each arc of the ring forms a panel within plain edge-moulding, filled with a plain twist in four lobes incorporating single and double pellets. In each sunk inter-arm space is a double-beaded triquetra-knot distorted to fill the panel and incorporating pellets. The face of the shaft consists almost entirely of one splayed panel originally framed by bold angle-mouldings (of which stumps remain) and filled with a triangular key-pattern in two paired bands, incorporating pellets at the base. A Latin inscription (Plate 12) in five horizontal lines completed the face below this, reading (I)]N INOMINE DI PATRIS ÉT S/PERETUS SANTDI ANC / [C (?)]RUCEM HOUELT PROPE[R]/ABIT PRO ANIMA RES PA[T]/RES EUS. ('In the name of God, the Father and the Holy Spirit, Houelt prepared this cross for the soul of Res his father'). The lettering is in fairly regular half-uncials without word-spacing or punctuation dots; the contracted *et* and the varied forms of 'S' (including majuscules, reversed in the last line) are common manuscript features. The intrusive 'I' before *nomine* is best interpreted as a blunder repeating the initial *in*, rather than as the abbreviation occurring on No. 910.

The more worn head and damaged shaft on the W. face are decorated much as the E. face. The disc-head has a similar ringed cross-potent differing only in that the diminutive arms between the squared centre and ends are formed of paired Greek frets. The shaft has two decorative panels, the upper one composed of a triangular key-pattern in double vertical band, looser than the similar design on the E. face; the lower panel, separated by a plain moulding, contains a pair of identical patterns of loose double-beaded knotwork, each consisting of a pair of Stafford knots joined by paired loops above and below.

The decoration of the narrow sides survives only on the rim of the disc-head where it is formed of a double band of triangular key-pattern.

Though not designated 'king' in this inscription, 'Houelt' is probably the Hywel ap Rhys, king of Glywysing, who in 884 was subject to Alfred of Wessex,[2] and whose death in 886 is recorded in the chronicles;[3] the names appear also in the genealogies of early rulers of S. Wales, though not certainly linked to earlier generations. The script and decorative style of the slab-cross accord with a date in the mid or late 9th century.

E.C.M.W. 220; *C.I.I.C.* 1011; *Arch. Camb.*, 1849, pp. 18–20; 1889, pp. 123–4; 1893, pp. 326–31; 1899, pp. 153–5.

[1] Correspondence to Strange 1770 (Bodleian Lib., MS. Gough, Wales 8, fo. 79ᵛ.), '. . . was said to be brought there from the great house' (i.e. Tŷ-mawr); *cf.* Iolo Morganwg (1798), found about 1730 'in an old ruinous place where tradition shows the places where seven churches are said to have been built' (quoted in *Arch. Camb.*, 1893, p. 328).
[2] W. H. Stevenson (ed.), *Asser's Life of King Alfred* (Oxford, new imp. 1959), c. 80.
[3] *Brut* (Peniarth), *s.a.* 885; *Ann. Camb.*, *s.a.* 885.

Llantwit Major.
    SS 96 N.E. (9659 6871)   10 ix 64   XLIX N.W.

(912) LLANTWIT MAJOR. (The 'Samson Cross'.) Shaft of composite cross, probably disc-headed (Plates 11, 12), originally standing in the churchyard N. of St. Illtud's Church, and re-erected in 1903 within the W. nave of the church. The exposed part of the stone (of local grit), with well-squared angles and splayed faces, stands 2·15 m high, the total length with the buried lower part being 3·10 m. The main faces taper upwards from 79 cm to 58 cm in width, and the thickness decreases from 29 cm to 24 cm. It has carved decoration on all faces, varyingly weathered, and both main faces carry inscriptions.

In the top of the shaft a rectangular mortice has been cut 11·4 cm deep, countersunk with wide shoulders 6·4 cm deep, for a separate cross-head now lacking. This most probably took the form of a disc-head, for which there is some evidence in the deliberate concavity of the upper surface[1] and in that the decorative patterns on the narrow sides need to be completed by being continued on the sides of a head of similar width (*cf.*

No. 911). Its size may be estimated by comparison with Nos. 903, 907 and 911 rather than from the degree of curvature of the surviving top surface.

On the E. face (as when *in situ* and as now re-set) the decoration forms three main panels in vertical order within plain continuous angle-mouldings. The uppermost panel has almost entirely flaked away, leaving weathered traces of diagonal swastika key-patterns probably arranged in six squares. A shorter panel below, framed and divided vertically by plain beading but not sunken, contains two horizontal inscriptions. That in the left-hand panel in five unequal lines (Plate 12) reads: ✠ SAM/SON / POSUIT / HANC C[R]/UCEM + ('Samson erected this cross'). That in the right-hand panel, possibly in four lines originally of which three survive, reads:]PRO A/NIMA EI/US : + ('for his soul'). The missing line might have read ORATE. The lettering is uniformly in rounded half-uncials, with variant forms of S. As first cut, the minims forming IM in *anima* were wrongly linked, with horizontal medial bar giving MI, but this was corrected by linking the tops of the last three minims. The initial incised Latin cross with serif-ends exceeds letter height, but the other incised crosses are of simple Latin form within the line. The lower part of the right-hand panel is cut back to leave in relief a four-lobed plain twist. The lowest main panel, partly defaced, is formed of four squares of diagonal swastika key-pattern with paired pellets in all the outer segments.

The narrow S. side of the shaft forms one vertical panel, its upper two-thirds containing seven knots of double-beaded intertwining oval loops, the remainder filled with three squares of swastika key-patterns.

The W. face has three main panels of carved ornament separated by two bands of demi-panels with inscriptions. The damaged topmost panel contains irregular double-beaded plaitwork incomplete in itself and formerly continued on the missing cross-head. A plain horizontal beading separates this from a pair of rectangular demi-panels below, each framed by similar beading but not sunken. In the left-hand one are an incised Latin cross with stepped base and a damaged inscription (Plate 12); the surviving letters read ILTU(?)[, but drawings made about 1693[2] and 1770[3] provide the original reading as ILTU/TI ('Of Illtud'). The inscription in the right-hand demi-panel (Plate 12) is in two lines divided medially by incised lines to read SAM/SON // RE/GIS ('Of Samson the king'), in half-uncials and with variant forms of S. The central main panel is a square containing ten-cord double-beaded loose plaitwork with unsymmetrical breaks. Below it in a horizontal row are four equal rectangular demi-panels, the two outer ones each filled with a knot of double-beaded intertwined oval loops. The inner demi-panels, framed by plain beading but not sunken, have inscriptions in two lines above an incised Greek cross, that on the left reading SAM/UEL and the other reading EBI/SAR, both in rounded half-uncials. The lower half of the face forms one large panel filled with regular plain sixteen-cord plait, in which there is one break at the top.

The narrow N. side forms one vertical panel filled with fourteen squares of diagonal key-pattern alternating in direction except that the five upper squares are identical. The top square is incomplete, suggesting that the pattern was continued on the head.

Of the personal names inscribed, 'Iltuti' may be taken as a dedication of the cross to St. Illtud, reputed founder of the religious establishment at Llantwit Major, but there can be no certainty in attempting to link the others thus commemorated with names in documentary sources. The 'Samson' who erected the cross was presumably head of the house and may even be identified with 'Samson abbas altari sancti Eltuti' in a Llancarfan charter,[4] though this charter in itself is no reliable guide for dating purposes.[5] The name 'Ebissar' occurs also on the Coychurch shaft (No. 935). The form of the shaft and in particular its decorative patterns are very similar to those on the 'Cross of Eiudon' (*E.C.M.W.* 159), and the two stones may have been carved by the same hand. It may be ascribed to the early 10th century.

E.C.M.W. 222; *C.I.I.C.* 1013.
[1] Cf. *E.C.M.W.* 159, 363.
[2] Stowe MS. 1024, fo. 15; Camden, *Britannia* (ed. Gibson, 1695), p. 618.
[3] Bodleian Lib. MS. Gough, Wales 8, fo. 79v.; *Arch. Camb.*, 1893, p. 327.
[4] *Vitae Sanct.*, p. 126 (*Vita S. Cadoci*, c. 55).
[5] C. Brooke in N. K. Chadwick (ed.), *Studies in the Early British Church* (Cambridge, 1958), pp. 220-1, 236-40.

Llantwit Major.
SS 96 N.E. (9662 6874)   10 ix 64   XLIX N.W.

(913) LLAN-GAN. (Plate 13.) Standing near the external W. wall of St. Canna's Church.[1] The head and diminutive shaft (probably incomplete) are formed of one block of local sandstone, 1·3 m high and 18 cm thick; the disc-head (partly fractured away) is 101 cm in diameter, and the shaft is slightly splayed, tapering from 56 cm at the base to 50 cm. Both main faces have crude carved decoration in low relief but with the plain edges are much affected by weathering.

On the W. face a sunk panel, framed by a weathered but probably plain border symmetrical with the disc-head, contains a Crucifixion scene. The figure of Christ is rendered naturalistically though crudely, facing front 66 cm high with arms extended to the frame and wearing a loin-cloth; the face may be bearded but is too poorly carved for certainty on this. Each quadrant below the arms is almost filled by a figure in profile facing inwards with bended legs, that on the right of Christ and wielding a lance represents Longinus and the other though less distinguishable must represent Stephaton the sponge-bearer. This rendering of the Crucifixion scene and in particular the treatment of the hair of both Christ and the attendant figures indicate the inspiration of Irish models, carved or in metalwork.[2] On the weathered shaft immediately below the figure of Christ is part of a smaller figure facing front with extended arms; the crude rendering of facial features makes it uncertain whether the figure is bearded or not. In the right hand is held a small cylindrical object, and in the left hand an inward-curving horn or short bow.[3] The E. side of the disc-head, extensively eroded, has a sunk panel framed by a raised border symmetrical with the edge and divided into quadrants by a plain linear cross in relief; in

6—3

each quadrant traces remain of a raised disc with central hole.

The cross may be dated to the late 9th or early 10th century.

E.C.M.W. 207; Westwood, *Lapid. Wall.*, p. 36, Pl. XXV.
[1] Re-set in a concrete base under a wooden shelter by the Department of the Environment; the original socket stone is lacking.
[2] Henry, *Irish Art*, II, pp. 159–62 and Pls. 53–4; J. R. Allen, *Early Christian Symbolism in Great Britain and Ireland before the Thirteenth Century* (London, 1887), Fig. 35. The upper quadrants may have contained figures of winged angels as in the Irish Crucifixion scenes, and there is some indication of this to the left of the head of Christ.
[3] For possible interpretations of the significance of this figure, see p. 29 above.

Llan-gan.
SS 97 N.E. (9574 7783)   8 ix 64   XLI S.W.

(c) 'Panelled-cross' Slabs (914–925)

(914) PORT TALBOT. (Plate 14.) Formed from a cross-incised pillar-stone (No. 868 above), first recorded in 1849 at Port Talbot[1] and later removed to Margam where it is re-set in Margam Stones Museum. It is of local Pennant sandstone, 1·32 m tall above the buried base, 63 cm wide and 30 cm thick, re-dressed to a slab-like form with rounded head. On the main face the head is filled with a panelled ring-cross derived from the *Chi-Rho* symbol, carved in low relief. Six double-beaded mouldings radiating from (but stopped short of) the central raised boss divide the head into four major and two minor segments, merging into the double-beaded ring; the vertical axis of the cross is slightly tilted. On the central boss are five 'dots' in cruciform pattern (*cf.* No. 906). The ring, slightly elongated vertically, is itself framed by a groove, and the head of the stone is shaped to this curvature. On each side of the head and on the top surface is a small boss with a central hole.[2]

The shaft narrows slightly below the head and is undecorated except for a device (Fig. 13) carved in relief and aligned on the axis of the cross. Its significance is obscure, but it is comparable with the symbols carved in Court Cave, East Wemyss (Fifeshire).[3] (*Cf.* also No. 918, n. 2.)

On the opposite face the re-dressing of the head is shaped around the earlier ring-cross on that face.

The stone as re-dressed is probably earlier than the fully developed panelled-crosses and attributable to the late 9th or 10th century.

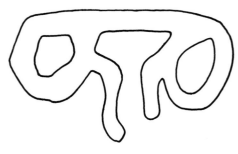

FIG. 13.

Port Talbot, carved device on panelled-cross slab (914). Scale ½.

E.C.M.W. 262; *Arch. Camb.*, XCIV (1939), pp. 17–18; Radford, *Margam*, No. 15.

[1] *Arch. Camb.*, 1857, pp. 57, 59.

[2] Similarly grouped bosses are found on the great cross-slab at Meigle (*E.C.M.S.*, 297; *Proc. Soc. Ant. Scot.*, LXXIV (1939–40), Pls. 30–1; and S. Cruden, *The Early Christian and Pictish Monuments of Scotland* (H.M.S.O., 1957), p. 16 and Pls. 26–7). Single bosses on the top edge of slabs occur at Kilberrihert, Co. Tipperary (P. Ó. ʜEailidhe in *North Munster Studies*). Their occurrence on cross-heads at Carlisle and Kirkburton (Collingwood, *Northumbrian Crosses*, pp. 87, 101) is more obviously derived from metalwork.

[3] *E.C.M.S.*, Fig. 388.

Margam (E), Port Talbot (C).

ss 78 N.E. (7670 8941)   12 xi 64   XXV S.W.

(915) NEATH. (Plate 14.) First noted about 1920 at Llantwit-juxta-Neath (at St. Illtud's Church),[1] and subsequently placed in St. Thomas' Church, Neath.[2] The weathered sandstone slab, 21 cm thick, has a shaped head 68 cm wide with chamfered angles possibly forming a pedimented head originally,[3] and tapering to 53 cm at the shaft; as now set in the floor, only the polygonal head is exposed, 84 cm high. The head is filled with a cross formy, the sunken arms springing from a rounded sunken hub, and is framed by a groove linking the arm-ends with rounded angles; part of the surface below the hub has flaked off. In each of the raised inter-arm spaces is a deeply incised linear cross, and in the sunken upper arm is an incised Latin linear cross that may be secondary. The other faces are plain. It is probably of late 9th- or early 10th-century date.

E.C.M.W. 251a.

[1] D. R. Phillips, *History of the Vale of Neath* (Swansea, 1925), p. 24: 'Till recent years . . . this stone stood in the boundary wall . . .'.

[2] Set against the W. wall of the nave at St. Thomas's Church at SS 7532 9767.

[3] Pedimented heads occur on slabs in Scotland (e.g. Glamis, Aberlemno and Nigg, *Proc. Soc. Ant. Scot.*, LXXIV (1939–40), Pls. XXVI, XXXII and XLII) and on the Fahan Mura slab, Donegal (Henry, *Irish Art*, I, Pls. 52, 54).

Llantwit-juxta-Neath (E), Tonna (C).

ss 79 N.E. (7619 9803)   9 x 64   XVI S.W.

(916) TYTHEGSTON. (Plate 14.) Standing in the churchyard of St. Tudwg's Church, where it was first recorded.[1] The weathered slab of local sandstone set in a modern socketed base is 84 cm high and 13 cm thick; the head is rounded at the top and has rounded projections at the sides (*cf.* No. 919), below which the shaft, 35 cm wide, is slightly flared towards the base.

The E. face is framed by plain angle-mouldings carried around the lateral projections. The head contains a ringed panelled cross formy, the sunken arms radiating from (but short of) a moulded hub consisting of a raised boss and ring in relief; in each of the inter-arm spaces is a ringed pellet in false relief (*cf.* No. 921), all much weathered. The shaft forms one squared panel framed by plain edge-moulding; it may have originally contained an inscription (possibly painted rather than incised) but is apparently plain.

The W. side is formed as one plain panel framed by the rounded angle-mouldings.

The slab is of 11th-century date.

E.C.M.W. 270a; *Arch. Camb.*, XCIV (1939), p. 20.

[1] Westwood, *Lapid. Wall.*, pp. 44–5 and Pl. XXIX (5).

Tythegston (E), T. Lower (C).

ss 87 N.E. (8576 7881)   5 vi 64   XL S.W.

(917) MERTHYR MAWR. (Plate 14.) Found in the churchyard of St. Teilo's Church,[1] and recently re-set upright in the lapidary collection there. The extensively weathered slab (probably Sutton stone) is regularly rectangular, 1·64 m tall, 66 cm wide and 20 cm thick except at the undressed base. Only one face shows traces of carved decoration in relief and of an inscription.

The upper half of the decorated face is filled by a ringed panelled cross formy, the splayed arms and equal inter-arm spaces all sunk; the moulded borders of these panels radiate from a moulded ring at the hub which seems to have enclosed a central bead surrounded by a ring of nine smaller beads (a device occurring on No. 907). The head, framed by angular grooving, was enclosed within moulded borders that continued down the face. The space between the ring and the upper framing is filled with indistinguishable ornament, probably degenerate plaitwork, but in the upper right-hand angle and outside the angular frame is an incised triquetra knot. The lower spandrels show traces of a pattern of frets.[2]

The lower half or shaft formerly contained an inscription in at least four lines tilted upwards to the right, but though some strokes of letters are detectable in rubbings no individual letters can be read with certainty.

The slab is of 11th-century date.

E.C.M.W. 241; *C.I.I.C.* 1021.

[1] *Trans. Cardiff Nat. Soc.*, XLI (1908), pp. 24–5.

[2] The representation of the decoration by Macalister in *Arch. Camb.*, LXXXIII (1928), p. 368, is largely imaginary.

Merthyr Mawr.

ss 87 N.E. (8828 7753)   9 ix 64   XL S.W.

(918) MERTHYR MAWR. Fragment of slab (Plate 17), found at St. Teilo's Church, Merthyr Mawr, and forming part of the lapidary collection there.[1] The stone, 18 cm thick and 81 cm in maximum width, constitutes most of the head (61 cm) of a slab similar to No. 916, with rounded top and lateral projections suggestive of the arms of a free-standing cross. It is decorated on both broad faces, the narrower sides being plain.

The more elaborately decorated face (or front) has all but the lowest members of a ringed panelled cross formy, the splayed arms and slightly larger inter-arm spaces all sunken; the hub from which the plain moulded borders radiate forms a double-moulded ring with sunken centre. Surrounding the outer ring is a much-weathered pattern of irregular frets incorporating a ringed bead in each of the upper angles,[2] all framed by plain angle-moulding that extends round the lateral projections.

The opposite face (or back) retains the three upper members of an equal-armed cross formy with narrow sunken arms radiating from (but short of) a hub consisting of a moulded ring with sunken centre; there is some indication that this hub originally had a raised boss since lost by fracture. The face is otherwise plain.

The fragment is of 11th-century date.

E.C.M.W. 242.
[1] *Trans. Cardiff Nat. Soc.*, XLI (1908), pp. 24–5.
[2] Incorporated also on the right-hand is a device similar to that carved in isolation on No. 914 above.

Merthyr Mawr.

ss 87 N.E. (8828 7753)   9 ix 64   XL S.W.

(919) MARGAM. (The 'Ilquici' stone, Plate 16.) First noted about 1693 at Cwrt-y-defaid,[1] and later added to the Margam lapidary collection; it is now re-set in Margam Stones Museum. The large squared slab of Pennant sandstone standing 1·93 m above the buried base and 25 cm thick has slight lateral projections as though indicating the arms of a standing cross, 93 cm maximum width, and is tapered slightly towards the top and the foot. All faces have carved ornament, together with traces of an inscription on one face.

The N. face as re-set is framed by plain angle mouldings continued round the head and indented at the springing of the lateral projections. The upper half (or 'head') in which the angle-moulding is doubled contains a ringed panelled cross formy, the splayed arms and larger inter-arm spaces all sunk and radiating from a central boss with triple mouldings; the plain ribs (or 'spokes') connect the outer moulding with the surrounding moulded ring. The space between the ring and the edge-mouldings is filled with a debased and irregular pattern of frets forming spirals in the upper spandrels and including a ringed boss in one lower spandrel. In the undecorated lower half (or 'shaft') part of a Latin inscription survives on the surface worn smooth by former use of the stone as a footbridge. It is incised in at least six horizontal lines, of which the first (a half-line) and second are tilted upwards to the right. The lettering, in regular half-uncials, gives H[E(?)..] / [.]PETRI ILQUICI / [.]E[...]ACER / [....]C(?)E[.]C HANC / [....]U[.]T / with traces of letters below; the final letter of *hanc* is cut on the angle-moulding. The opening words may originally have read *hec (est) petri* (for *haec est petra*, 'This is the stone of'), while the spelling *Ilquici* (a proper name) is possibly a blunder for *Ilgwici*.[2]

The opposite S. face has similar angle-mouldings with corresponding indentations, and the upper half contains a ringed panelled cross formy similar to that on the N. face except that the ring has double mouldings. Only the upper spandrels are filled with debased fret-patterns forming spirals. The lower half is plain (and partly flaked) with an incised outline cross 48 cm tall, placed centrally.

On both narrow faces (E. and W.) the projecting 'arm' is framed by bold edge-mouldings as a plain panel, and the panel above is similarly framed and plain. The rest of each side below the 'arm' is filled with debased fret-patterns, differing as between E. and W., the latter including a pair of ringed pellets. The slab is of 10th- or 11th-century date.

E.C.M.W. 236; *C.I.I.C.* 1018; *Arch. Camb.*, 1899, pp. 136–8; Radford, *Margam*, No. 10.
[1] By E. Lhuyd, Stowe MS. 1024, p. 14: 'A Foot-bridge at Margam consisting of two stones of this fform, which seem to have been Crosses.'
[2] *Trans. Anglesey Antiq. Soc.*, 1939, p. 29 (Sir Ifor Williams), referring to the name *Iluic* occurring in the Book of Llandaf; but as is noted there (*Lib. Land.*, pp. 74, 75) the manuscript leaves it uncertain whether the spelling was 'iu' or 'ui'.

Margam (E), Port Talbot (C).

ss 88 N.W. (8009 8555)   12 xi 64   XXXIII S.E.

(920) MARGAM. (The 'Ilci' stone, Plate 17.) Recorded about 1693 with No. 919 near Margam,[1] and re-set in Margam Stones Museum. The slab of Pennant sandstone is 1·65 m high above the buried base and 25 cm thick. The upper half forms a squared head 79 cm wide and tapering slightly in thickness at the top, while the narrower lower half or shaft tapers in width to 63 cm at the foot (one angle fractured off). Each face has carved or incised decoration, one face also having an inscription.

On both the main faces (N. and S.) the head is framed by rounded angle-mouldings, continued down the shaft, and is filled with a ringed panelled cross formy; the splayed arms and larger inter-arm spaces are all sunken, the plain ribs (or 'spokes') radiating from a central ringed boss (that on the S. face lost by fracture). Incorporated in the outer moulded ring on the S. face and also in the upper spandrels of both faces are single incised rings.

The shaft on the S. face forms a panel framed by edge-moulding in false relief that incorporates a pair of incised rings towards the foot of one side, and in each upper angle is another incised ring (the W. one worn away). In the panel is an inscription in four horizontal lines, partly worn away and reading   ]ILCI · [FE]CIT / H[ANC] · CRUCE/M · I[N]N[O]MIN/E · DI · SUMMI ('Ilci made this cross in the name of God Most High'). The lettering is mostly in regular half-uncials with E-s of a rounded Roman form; the words are separated by single dots. *Di* for *Dei* is a common form. It remains uncertain (because of wear on the surface) whether the proper name *Ilci* is complete in itself or lacks an initial letter.[2] It is also possible that one or more additional lines have been lost by obliteration. The opposite face has a panel on the shaft similarly framed but plain.

On the narrow E. side the head is decorated with two unequal incised rings at the top joined by an incised serpentine line to a larger double ring, the weathered shaft below showing traces of a serpentine line. The W. side has at the top a single incised ring from which depends an incised serpentine line, and another similar but discontinuous line fills the shaft.

The slab is of late 10th- to 11th-century date.

E.C.M.W. 237; *C.I.I.C.* 1019; *Arch. Camb.*, 1899, pp. 138–9; Radford, *Margam*, No. 9.
[1] Stowe MS. 1024, pp. 14 and 62 (E. Lhuyd).
[2] *Cf.* 'Elci' and similar forms cited by Rhys in *Arch. Camb.*, 1899, pp. 138–9.

Margam (E), Port Talbot (C).

ss 88 N.W. (8009 8555)   12 xi 64   XXXIII S.E.

(921) EGLWYS NYNNID near Margam. (Plate 15.) First noted at this site in 1869[1] and subsequently moved to Margam where it is re-set in Margam Stones Museum. The roughly rectangular slab of local Pennant sandstone, 1·16 m high above the buried base and 61 cm wide, is 25 cm at its thickest, narrowing slightly towards head and base; part of the head and one side are damaged by fracture. One main face and the narrow sides are decorated, retaining also traces of an inscription.

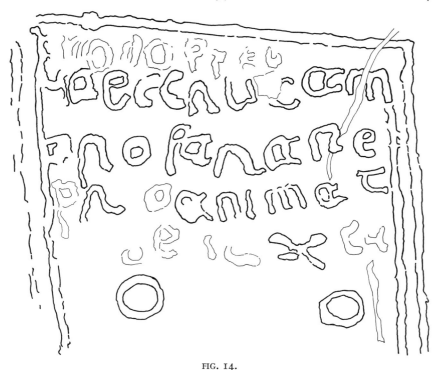

FIG. 14.

Eglwys Nynnid, inscription on panelled-cross slab (921). Scale ⅕.

The main face, framed by plain rounded angle-mouldings, is divided into two equal square panels. The upper panel or head is filled with a panelled cross formy, the sunken arms radiating from (but short of) a moulded hub formed of a raised boss and ring. In each of the inter-arm spaces is an incised ring, the upper right-hand one almost obliterated by fracture. The lower panel is separated from the upper by a double incised border and is similarly framed within the angle-mouldings. It is almost filled with a mutilated inscription set out in irregular horizontal lines (discussed further below), with two incised rings in the space below the lettering.

The narrow face to the right, damaged by fracture of the head and base, retains a central panel outlined by a rectangular groove and filled with an incised pattern of debased scrolls or spirals (cf. Nos. 906, 956). The other narrow face to the left forms one vertical rectangular panel outlined by grooves and containing an incised wavy line between ring-and-boss devices in relief at top and bottom (cf. No. 920). The angle-mouldings make a panel of the remaining face which is dressed and apparently plain but is weathered.

Sufficient letters and strokes remain of the mutilated inscription (Fig. 14) to establish that it is in five horizontal lines tilted upwards towards the right, formed in fully developed half-uncials. The only certain letters in the first half-line are O..O (or A) P.., but the strokes do not sustain 'in nomine' (C.I.I.C. 1020), and a proper name seems to have been intended. The second line would seem to read HAEC CRUCAM, of which

only EC, CR and AM are quite certain. The third line reads PROPARARET, only its initial letter being blurred and the final T placed below the line. In the fourth line the second half reads ANIMA, preceded by the R of PRO with faint traces of other letters. The fifth line includes the letters E (or C), U (or I), presumably part of a proper name. For other variant forms of proparavit, see Nos. 910–11, 923 and 933.

The slab is probably of 10th-century date.

E.C.M.W. 200; Arch. Camb., 1899, p. 144; XCIV (1939), pp. 15–17; Radford, Margam, No. 8.

[1] Arch. Camb., 1869, p. 445. Westwood, Lapid. Wall., pp. 32–3 and Pl. XXII (3).

Margam (E), Port Talbot (C).
  SS 88 S.W. (8029 8472)   12 xi 64   XXXIII S.E.

(922) PEN-Y-FAI, Bridgend (Plate 14). Found in 1968 just over half a mile S.W. of Pen-y-fai near Bridgend,[1] and subsequently deposited in the National Museum of Wales. The shaped but weathered slab of coarse sandstone is 1·27 m tall including the undressed foot (38 cm) and 18–20 cm thick, with rounded head 59 cm wide and narrower shaft tapering from 48 cm to 40 cm. On the one decorated face the head is filled by a ringed panelled cross formy, the arms more deeply sunken than the smaller inter-arm spaces, all within an angular moulded frame. The squared hub has an incised ring somewhat off-centre, and each of the lower spandrels contains a ringed

pellet. The shaft is treated as one rectangular panel framed by the angle-mouldings and is apparently plain, but faint traces of letters indicate a former pecked inscription in four lines which was presumably deliberately effaced at an early date.

The slab is of 10th-century date.

[1] Turned up by ploughing a field, and possibly re-used as a boundary mark of lands belonging to Margam Abbey, *Arch. Camb.*, CXIX (1970), pp. 71–4.

Newcastle (E), N. Higher (C).

SS 88 S.E. (8873 8115)　　11 xii 68　　　　　XL N.E.

(923) CWM GWENFFRWD. (Plate 15.) First recorded in 1846 as 'having been removed from a small holy-well' near 'Bryn Cefneithan'[1] (more correctly Bryncyneithwyn,[2] formerly a farm N. of Blaenavon in Cwm Gwenffrwd, which lies 3 miles E. of Neath); it was subsequently moved to Neath, but is now in the National Museum of Wales.

The sandstone slab is incomplete, about half of its surviving height of 86 cm lost by fracture off the base; it is 66 cm in maximum width, tapering down to 45 cm, and 20 cm thick. The rounded head on the one decorated face 57 cm wide is filled by an equal-armed ringed cross in which the inter-arm spaces form panels outlined by the raised edges of the arms and arcs of the ring, all framed by a double edge-moulding. At the intersection is a small moulded ringed pellet, and the moulded edges of the cross incorporate paired pellets in false relief, one pair at the top and two at the lower edge.

The shaft forms a single panel framed by a continuation of the outer angle-mouldings of the head doubled by an inner moulding and is filled with an inscription of which three horizontal lines survive complete with traces of a fourth line. The inscription, in rounded half-uncials, reads PROP / ARAUI/T GAI C/ [. . . ('Gai[. . .] prepared . . .'). The stone is of 10th-century date.

E.C.M.W. 265; *C.I.I.C.* 1027.
[1] *Arch. Camb.*, 1865, pp. 65–6 (Westwood).
[2] The site of Bryncyneithwyn as shown and named on the Tithe Award for Baglan parish, 1841 ('Bryncanaithwen' in the schedule and 'Bryncaenithwen' on the MS. O.S. map of 1813), is that occupied by Abergwenffrwd Row. The site of the holy well cannot be identified from several springs in the vicinity but Cae Cwmffynnon is named to the S.E. of the farm site (at SS 8045 9696).

Baglan (E), B. Higher (C).

SS 89 N.W. (8014 9726 approx.)　　8 xii 64　　XVI S.E.

(924) EWENNI. (Plate 14.) Incomplete slab from the Priory Church;[1] the top and much of the lowest part of the original slab are lacking. The surviving portion, 91 cm long and 20 cm thick, is broken in two pieces and its edges have been trimmed (maximum width 49 cm). The upper part (or head) contains a cross formy with sunken inter-arm spaces, within a double-beaded angular frame which embodies a ringed bead in the lower left-hand angle; the arms, outlined by double-beaded moulding, may have contained knots or frets, and at the centre is a ringed pellet in relief. The lower part (or shaft) retains traces of debased patterns of frets around an incomplete and indistinguishable central design. In the upper left-hand angle

is a small equal-armed cross with moulded edges set in false relief within a circle.

The slab fragment is of late 10th- or 11th-century date.

E.C.M.W. 196; Radford *Ewenny*, p. 16 (No. 1).
[1] Probably recovered from building material in the demolition of the 16th-century N. Aisle in 1895–6, *Arch. Camb.*, 1913, pp. 25–6.

Ewenni.

SS 97 N.W. (9125 7781)　　9 ix 64　　　　　XL S.E.

(925) LLAN-GAN. (Plate 18.) Incomplete broken slab found in 1909 (in the garden of the rectory immediately W. of the churchyard) and preserved at St. Canna's Church there.[1] Three pieces survive, of local Rhaetic sandstone, forming most of the head with part of the shaft of a cross-slab with rounded head and squared sides, 79 cm wide and 18 cm thick; they represent 107 cm of the original height. Except for one defaced narrow side, the slab has carved decoration on each face with rounded angle-mouldings.

The head of the main face shows a ringed cross formy with sunken inter-arm spaces; the arms, outlined by continuous double-beaded moulding, contain traces of knots in false relief with a double-beaded ring at the hub probably enclosing formerly a central boss or pellet. The ring linking the arm-ends is doubled by an outer moulding which is distorted into a spiral device in the lower right-hand angle of the ring. The left-hand spandrel formed below the angular frame is filled with a ringed pellet. Immediately below the cross and frame is a panelled horizontal band of square frets in a vertical row, conjoined to another decorative pattern lost by fracture.

The opposite face is much weathered but has traces of a cross formy with sunken arms (*cf.* the 'back' of No. 918), enclosed by a distorted ring of double incised lines.

The narrow side to the right of the main face forms part of a series of narrow vertical panels within the rounded angle-mouldings, the surviving panel filled with wide-beaded two-cord twist.

The slab fragments are of 11th-century date.

E.C.M.W. 208.
[1] *Arch. Camb.*, 1909, p. 373 (illustrated with fragments wrongly grouped).

Llan-gan.

SS 97 N.E. (9575 7783)　　8 ix 64　　　　　XLI S.W.

(d) Slab-crosses (926–928)

(926) OGMORE. (Plate 15.) Incomplete shaft of composite slab-cross, of which the cross-head and base are lacking. It was discovered at Ogmore Castle in 1929 built into the base of a 19th-century limekiln, and was transferred to the National Museum of Wales. The rectangular block of local sandstone with a rough tenon at the foot is 86 cm high, varying from 70 cm by 20 cm at the top to 58 cm by 23 cm at the base of the shaft. The main faces, each carrying an incomplete inscription within triple-moulded borders, were probably framed originally by angle-mouldings which have weathered away and have been trimmed down.

An inscription on side (i) surviving as seven lines somewhat

tilted from the horizontal reads] / EST [ ] / QUOD ·
DED[IT] / ARTHMAIL / AGRUM DO / ET GLIGUIS · /
ET NERTAT ET FILIE : SU[A] (' Be it [known to all men]
that Arthmail gave (this) field to God and Glywys and Nertat
and his daughter'). The words *sciendum* before and *omnibus*
(OMIB;?) after the first surviving word would complete the
sense, giving a formula found in early land grants.[1] The lettering
is chiefly in half-uncials with square forms of E and F, the usual
symbol for *et* and manuscript abbreviation 'DO' for *Deo*; the
final T of the penultimate line is inserted below the A, utilising a
surface fracture. Abrasion of the surface has obscured part of
the last line: after the clear E are punctuation dots, and the
succeeding letter is more probably minuscule S than P or F
(the lower stroke or loop is part of the abrasion), followed by
two vertical strokes and faint traces of a final letter; the
reading EPI (for *episcopi*)[2] would not account for all the visible
strokes. The proper names are discussed above (p. 27).

Side (ii) to the left of (i) has traces of two panels within
moulded borders, the upper one with a vertical fret-pattern,
the lower one possibly with horizontal frets, all much
weathered.

The inscription on side (iii) survives in four lines with traces
of at least one other line, in lay-out and script similar to that on
side (i), increasingly eroded towards the base. It may be read:
] / DI SUMI CRO/SI [R?] HGERTH / BRANTUI / [P]
RUS [/ ('[In the name] of God Most High, the cross of . . .').
The final letter of the first line is O rather than U, giving a
variant form of *Crux*, while the final letter of the next line,
H rather than I, partly coincides with the incised frame. The
complete inscription presumably began with *In Nomine* (*cf.*
No. 928) and concluded with a conventional phrase (as on
Nos. 910–12).

Side (iv) shows two panels divided horizontally by grooves
(remnant of the moulded borders), the upper panel containing
an incised cross with looped arm-ends set between incised
rings, the lower with a single T-fret.

The stone is of 11th-century date.

E.C.M.W. 255; C.I.I.C. 1024; *Arch. Camb.*, LXXXV (1930), pp.
396–402; LXXXVII (1932), pp. 232–8.
[1] *Arch. Camb.*, LXXXVII (1932), p. 233.
[2] *Ibid.*, p. 238 (Sir Ifor Williams), and *E.C.M.W.*

St. Brides Major and Wick (E), St. Brides Major (C).
ss 87 N.E. (8817 7698)   8 xii 64   XL S.W.

(927) MERTHYR MAWR. (Plate 18.) First recorded by Lhuyd
in 1697 as standing on the river bank at Merthyr Mawr,[1] subsequently preserved in the grounds of the mansion and recently
re-set within the remains of St. Roque's Chapel there.[2] It
lacks the cross-head sketched in 1697, of expanded flat-topped
form with a cross patée on one face and (probably) sunk inter-
arm spaces on the other (Fig. 15). The sandstone four-sided
block surviving is 1·22 m above the buried base, 56 cm wide
and 34 cm in thickness at the base, tapering to 29 cm.
Plain angle-mouldings frame the faces, much eroded in part.
The N. panel (originally facing E.) is almost filled by an
inscription in eleven lines, framed by a plain roll-mould
between deep chaces and divided (five and six) by a horizontal

FIG. 15.
Merthyr Mawr, drawing by Lhuyd of damaged slab (927).

chace. The Latin inscription, cut in irregular half-uncials, reads [CO]NBELANI / [P]OSSUIT HANC / CRUCEM PRO / ANIMA EIUS / SCI (G)LIUSSI / NERTTA(N) ET / FRATRIS EIU/S ET PATER / EIU(S) A ME / PREPARA/TUS + SCILOC ('Conbelan(i) erected this cross for his soul, for Saint Glywys, Nertta(n) and his brother and his father. Prepared by me, + Sciloc'). The missing initial letters of the first two lines are provided by Lhuyd's drawing, and though some letters in lines 5–6 are uncertain the forms of the names given here are suggested by their occurrence on the Ogmore stone (No. 926); *et* is given as a manuscript abbreviation. The E. panel contains six-cord plaitwork merging into irregular knotwork towards the base with pellets at the edges. On the S. face a row of pellets (partly fractured away) marks the neck border; the panel below, framed by a single-beaded moulding, is filled with tight interlace beginning as knotwork but continued as a ten-cord plait with pellets at the edges. The W. panel contains a nearly symmetrical pattern of loose interlace, twisted twice and plaited at the foot, with pellets interspersed singly and clustered. 11th-century.

E.C.M.W. 239; *C.I.I.C.* 1023; *Arch. Camb.*, 1899, pp. 158–63; LXXXVII (1932), p. 237.
[1] Stowe MS. 1024, fo. 41 (456–7 of original numbering); *Arch. Camb.*, 1861, p. 231.
[2] At SS 8886 7808.

Merthyr Mawr.
    ss 87 N.E. (8850 7751)   10 xi 64   XL S.W.

(928) MERTHYR MAWR. (Plate 19.) Monolithic shaft and ringed cross-head, originally standing to the N. of Merthyr Mawr,[1] and subsequently moved (with No. 927) to the grounds of Merthyr Mawr House where it has been re-set inside St. Roque's Chapel. The shaft and head are formed from one block of coarse sandstone, standing 2·2 m above ground, much weathered and lacking part of the head and a section out of one side. The shaft, tapering slightly towards the base, is 91 cm at its widest and 26 cm thick. The original diameter of the cross-head was 96 cm, its width at the neck being 84 cm, and it is 21 cm thick. On both main faces (E. and W.) of the cross-head the decorated splayed arms with hollowed angles are linked by a ring of plain square section recessed below them; the lowest member spreads out to the full width of the shaft, with a narrow band representing the neck. The arm-ends were probably all originally decorated with the pattern of straight frets surviving only on part of the N. arm-end. The carved faces of the shaft are framed by upper and lower edge-moulding and by bulbous angle-mouldings with much-weathered traces of carved decoration (? plaitwork) between roll-mouldings of three bands at the head and base.

On the E. face or 'front', the decoration of the cross-head consists of double-beaded triquetra knots in the upper arms which in the lower member resolve into plain beading incorporating a single pellet, all linked around the central plain raised hub and double-beaded ring; the edge-moulding is also double-beaded. Below the straight lower edge the brief neck band is ribbed vertically. The face of the shaft forms a panel framed by double-beaded moulding and is entirely filled with

a much-weathered Latin inscription, apparently in sixteen lines divided (six and ten) by a horizontal chace. The inscription in rounded half-uncials with squared E-s and abbreviated 'et' may be read INOMINE DI PAT/RIS ET FILI SPERI/TUS SANTI[ ]A /]FI[ ] /]MA[/]IN[// (5 lines not readable) / / I · PA[ ]E · [ ] / COISTO · IN · GRE/FIUM · INPRO/PRIUM · USQ · / IN DIEM · IUDICI ('In the name of God, Father and Son (and) Holy Spirit . . . in writing, in perpetuity unto the Judgement Day'). The stone would thus seem to have recorded the transfer of land to a religious body, as No. 926.[2]

The narrow vertical panel on the S. side of the shaft is much weathered but has traces of a pattern of twists and frets, the lowest section forming a square of diagonal swastika key-pattern.

The W. side of the cross-head has double-beaded edge-moulding, within which the arm-ends contain double-beaded triquetra-knots linked around the central damaged hub without ring. The neck-band has centrally a plain two-cord twist of four lobes set between vertical ribbing. The upper edge-moulding of the shaft has alternate bands of vertical and horizontal ribbing in contrast to the plain double-moulding on the E. side. Eight irregular panels of diagonal swastika key-patterns, framed and divided vertically by a double-beaded moulding, fill the face on the shaft. On the N. side, the arm-end of the cross shows traces of straight fretwork, while the neck is boldly ribbed vertically. The incomplete panel of the shaft has above the missing section a double-beaded loop and twist, and below it a similar loop separated by horizontal ribbing from triangular fretwork at the foot. 11th-century.

E.C.M.W. 240; *C.I.I.C.* 1022; *Arch. Camb.*, 1899, pp. 156–8; LXXXIII (1928), p. 370.
[1] *Trans. Cardiff Nat. Soc.*, XLI (1908), p. 25; Stowe MS. 1024, fols. 20–1, 'in a field called Kaer Groes'; drawing shows cross-head complete.
[2] *Cf.* similar phrases in charters to Llancarfan, *Vitae Sanct.*, pp. 126, 128, 132.

Merthyr Mawr.
    ss 87 N.E. (8801 7867)   10 xi 64   XL S.W.

(929) PORT TALBOT. Fragment of a large slab found in 1972 at Llanmihangel near Pyle where it remains, having lain in the bed of a stream N. of the house. The weathered and water-worn block of Pennant sandstone forms the upper half of a cross-slab of the 'panelled-cross' type (more particularly No. 924), 82 cms high and 95 cms wide at the fracture line (corresponding to the waist) tapering to 60 cms at the top; it is 25 cms thick. One main face and one narrow side have traces of carved decoration in low relief; the other faces are much worn but were probably plain.

The decoration on the main face consists of a cross formy with widely splayed arms and elongated sunken hollows between the arms (as on one Merthyr Mawr slab, No. 928), which has at the centre a boss and moulded ring. Much of the top arm and all of the right-hand arm are eroded away. The arms of the cross have a bold edge-moulding and were filled with key-pattern of which only slight traces remain. At the lower left hand (on a detached fragment) is part of a ringed hollow.

On the left-hand side of the stone is a vertical sunken rectangular panel containing traces of indeterminable decoration. Below it is a narrow horizontal sunken chace.

Another large rectangular block of similar stone, which may be the lower part (or 'shaft') of this monument or another like it, lies 150 m E. of the house (at ss 8170 8286). One edge is a fracture and the faces are dressed, making a squared plain panel over most of one broad face, but without any clear butt to be set in the ground.

The major fragment may be ascribed to the late 10th or early 11th century.

Margam (E), Port Talbot (C).

ss 88 s.w. (8155 8295)   20 ix 73   XXXIII S.E.

Rejected Monument

At LLANRHIDIAN, a slab-like stone cemented into an outcrop of rock on the village green has sometimes been regarded as an incomplete cross.[1] The upper part of the slab, which is 2·0 m high, 1·05 m wide and 25 cm thick, shows traces of some dressing, as if to form the lower 'arm' and parts of the ring (or wheel) of a 'Celtic' cross-head; the upper angles of this 'arm' are hollowed like the armpits of such a cross. But though these features are reminiscent of, for example, Irish high-crosses, the design is unlike any known monument, and the springing of the arcs of the ring from the sides of the slab is uncharacteristic of such crosses. The material of the stone, moreover, is a local coarse conglomerate, quite unsuitable for the usual surface decoration.

From an entry in parochial records it has been established that the stone was erected at this spot in 1821.[2]

[1] *Arch. Camb.*, 1920, pp. 310–11. It is not included in *E.C.M.W.*
[2] *Gower*, XXII (1971), pp. 10–13.

Llanrhidian (E), Ll. Lower (C).

ss 49 s.e. (4975 9223)   9 xi 64   XXII S.W.

931–941. *CLASS E: PILLAR-CROSSES*

(931) LLANGYFELACH. (Plate 25.) Socketed base of pillar-cross standing in the churchyard at Llangyfelach, S. of the tower of the former church, and since 1926 raised out of its original setting in the ground. The roughly rectangular gritstone block, with three sides very slightly splayed and one face (the W.) more widely splayed, is 76 cm tall at maximum (half of this dimension being originally below the ground surface); its lateral dimensions, 104 cm by 58 cm at the top, increase to 114 cm by 68 cm at the base. A rectangular socket, 48 cm by 30 cm in the upper surface and 33 cm deep, provided seating for a pillar-cross probably some 3 m tall but has a modern stone covering. A simple stepped moulding, symmetrical with the socket but doubled at the elongated W. end, defines the edges of the upper surface but its S.W. angle is lost by fracture.

On each face is a narrow horizontal panel of decoration carved in low relief and slightly distorted to fit the irregularity of the block; a fracture line on the N. face has been filled with cement. The E. panel with bead-moulding only on its upper edge contains double-beaded knotwork of six cords forming

four Stafford-knots and a pair of loops at the N. edge. On the S. side the main panel of triangular key-pattern in a double band is abutted on the W. by a small square panel of diaper key-pattern, a modification enforced by the shape of the block even before the fracture of the S.W. upper angle. The W. panel contains a triangular key-pattern in a double band compressed at the S. edge for the same reason. The N. side is filled by a panel of plain loose five-cord plaitwork with pellets of varying sizes filling the spaces. The stylistic features suggest a date early in the 10th century or possibly late in the preceding century.

E.C.M.W. 212; *Arch. Camb.*, 1903, pp. 181–8.

Llangyfelach.

ss 69 n.w. (6463 9893)   9 x 64   XIV N.E.

(932) LLANTWIT MAJOR. (Plate 22.) Shaft of pillar-cross at St. Illtud's Church, re-set in modern plinth at the W. end of the western church but presumably originally standing in the churchyard. It is a single four-sided block of local sandstone (fractured near the top) with plain squared angles and of uniform thickness (24 cm), but the main faces (E. and W.) are splayed in width from 30 cm at the top to 40 cm towards the base. The visible height (1·44 m) includes both the narrower, tapering base butt and, at the top, the lower part of the necking which is set back slightly from the faces of the shaft.

Each face has a single vertical recessed panel containing decoration carved in relief, those on the main face splayed out towards the base. The E. panel has eight-cord double-beaded plaitwork with four cruciform breaks regularly placed to right and left alternately. In the S. panel is a four-cord double-beaded plait with four breaks, Z-shaped but up-ended. The W. panel contains six-cord double-beaded plaitwork incorporating three Z-shaped breaks, and the more weathered N. panel a regular four-cord plait, double-beaded at the top merging possibly into plain plaits.

The resemblance to No. 933 suggests that it is of late 9th-century date.

E.C.M.W. 221; *Arch. Camb.*, 1889, pp. 119, 325.

Llantwit Major.

ss 96 n.e. (9659 6871)   10 ix 64   XLIX N.W.

(933) LLANTWIT MAJOR. (Plate 23.) Shaft of pillar-cross originally standing in the churchyard of St. Illtud's Church just E. of the porch, and having fallen was re-erected near that spot in 1793; in 1900 it was re-set within the W. nave of the church.[1] The block of local sandstone, four-sided with rounded angles and tapered towards the head, is 2·75 m tall (visible height 2·36 m) and 72 cm wide at the base, tapering to 40 cm); its thickness, 40 cm, is uniform but reduced by partial fracturing of the upper third. There is trace of a socket for a cross-head in the upper surface, but the shaft was set in the ground without a pedestal.

The part of the main face that was originally exposed (the S. face as now re-set) is entirely filled by a panel containing an inscription, the panel being defined by a plain roll-moulding within the rounded angle-mouldings. The Latin inscription

(Plate 23) set horizontally in twenty-one lines (with an over-spill letter) reads: IN NOM/INE DI SU/MMI INCI/PIT : CRU/X · SAL/UATO/RIS · QUA/E PREPA/RAUIT_/ SAMSO/NIS APA/TI PRO / ANIMA / ̲SUA : E͡T [P]/RO ANI/MA IU / THAHE / LO RE͡X :· / E͡T ART/MALI :· [E͡T]/TEC[A]/N, with a small cross placed centrally at the base ('In the name of God Most High begins the cross of the Saviour which Samson the abbot prepared for his soul, and for the soul of Iuthahelo the king, and (of) Artma(i)l (and) Tec(a)n'). The lettering is crude half-uncials with such common manuscript features as ligatured forms of *et* and *-ex*, punctuation dots (single, double or triple), and the use of both majuscule and minuscule forms in a word in which the letter is repeated (M in *summi*, and S in *Samsonis*).

The E. (or right-hand) side has a narrow vertical panel framed by a rounded moulding and filled with double-beaded plaitwork formed of an eight-lobe open twist incorporating six (or possibly seven) rings.[2] At the base, and probably concealed when the stone was erected, is a weathered square panel containing traces of plaitwork within a moulded frame.

The king named in the inscription can plausibly be identified with Iudhail (Ithel), king of Gwent, whose death in A.D. 848 is recorded in the native chronicles, and who is probably the Ithel ab Athrwys of the early genealogies.[3] For the other names, see p. 31 above. Both the style of the shaft and the lettering of the inscription are consistent with a late 9th-century date.[4]

E.C.M.W. 223; C.I.I.C. 1012; Arch. Camb., 1899, pp. 147–50.
[1] Arch. Camb., 1893, pp. 328–9; 1900, p. 148.
[2] An identical panel occurs on the North Cross, Castledermot (Co. Kildare), of 9th-century date (A. K. Porter, The Crosses and Culture of Ireland (Newhaven, 1931), pp. 59–60; Henry, Irish Art, II, pp. 147–8). Cf. No. 941 below.
[3] Brut (Peniarth), s.a.; Ann. Camb., s.a.; Bartrum, Tracts, p. 12.
[4] Cf. E.C.M.W. 301. For the 'free-ring' interlacement, v. E.C.M.W. 364 (n. 4); N. Åberg, The Occident and the Orient in the Art of the Seventh Century. I: the British Isles (Stockholm, 1943), p. 98; and no. 2 above.

Llantwit Major.
ss 96 N.E. (9661 6870)   10 ix 64   XLIX N.W.

(934) COYCHURCH. (Plates 20, 25.) Consists of a cross-head (with ringed cross) on a quadrangular neck and squared shaft with a secondary splayed square base, originally standing close to the S. wall of St. Crallo's Church. It was fractured by the collapse of the central tower in 1877 and has been re-assembled inside the church.[1]

The cross-head and neck are formed of a single block (the arm-ends fractured off but restored), 91 cm high and 15 cm thick. The ringed cross with expanded arm-ends is 70 cm in diameter, and the neck tapers in width from 33 cm at the base to 28 cm; only the stumps of the ring between the arms are original, the remainder restoration. The shaft, surmounted by a moulded but much eroded collar, is 1·78 m tall and 43 cm by 35 cm in width, the angles now broadly chamfered but probably originally showing bulbous angle-mouldings. A fracture 28 cm above the base is indicated in a late-17th-century drawing[2] and represents earlier damage than that recorded in 1877; immediately above this fracture on the N. and W. faces are traces of an incised horizontal edge-moulding

and butt which may indicate the original length of the shaft. The portion of the shaft below the fracture does not closely conform to the main shaft in dimensions and is probably secondary. The base itself, 43 cm high, is of medieval type with moulded octagonal socket and plain faces splayed out from 61 cm to 89 cm.

The faces of the cross-head and shaft are decorated with carving in low relief, extensively weathered and (on the shaft) possibly re-dressed. The arms of the cross-head (Plate 25) on both E. and W. faces (the upper arm-end much eroded) have plain edge-mouldings forming panels filled with double-beaded triquetra-knots, all linked on the hub around a central bead; on the sides each panelled arm-end contains a four-lobe twist. The surviving stump of the ring has traces of edge-moulding framing possibly a row of pellets. Both E. and W. faces of the neck have a panel framed by plain edge-moulding containing double-beaded six-cord plaitwork in three regular loops; the N. and S. panels each have a three-lobe twist.

The enlarged collar at the head of the shaft, chamfered on its upper surface around the mortice, is much weathered and lacks most of its N. edge. On each face upper and lower mouldings frame a row of boldly moulded pellets or balls, one at each angle and three between them. The decoration of the shaft has been largely obliterated by weathering and by possible re-dressing of the face. On the E. face are four vertical panels framed by plain edge-moulding (the side mouldings removed by the cutting of the chamfered angles) with a blank space below them; the upper three panels show traces of diagonal key-patterns and the lowest slightly larger panel shows possible knotwork. The S. face has four panels similarly spaced containing traces of straight fret-patterns including T-frets;[3] below the panels the shaft is plain. The W. face has traces of vertical panels not aligned to the other faces but the patterns are indecipherable. The N. face has one continuous band of six-cord plaitwork with possible horizontal breaks. The remainder of the shaft below the fracture is plain, as is also the whole of the base.

In its original form the cross is of 10th- to early-11th-century date, but it has been modified to conform to that of the usual late medieval churchyard cross. The lowest portion of the shaft and the pedestal base are of the 14th or 15th century.

E.C.M.W. 194; C.I.I.C. 1008.
[1] Original position just W. of S. Transept (Arch. Camb., 1888, p. 402); present position at W. end of N. Aisle of Nave.
[2] Stowe MS. 1024, fo. 13.
[3] The reading of an inscription in two horizontal lines in the top panel (Arch. Camb., 1899, p. 164) cannot be reconciled with the evidence for the decorative pattern of frets, and was no doubt influenced by the name 'Ebissar' appearing on the cross-shaft at Coychurch (No. 935).

Coychurch (E), C. Lower (C).
ss 97 N.W. (9397 7968)   8 ix 64   XLI N.W.

(935) COYCHURCH. (Plate 22.) Shaft formerly in the church-yard of St. Crallo's Church, E. of the chancel, and recently placed inside the church. The four-sided block of local Rhaetic sandstone stands 1·62 m above floor level. Despite its slab-like dimensions, 66 cm by 38 cm, it resembles composite

moulded pillar-crosses (particularly No. 936), though lacking the cross-head for which there is a weathered socket in the top.

Each face has a vertical panel recessed between bulbous angle-mouldings and the rounded upper edge, all very much weathered. The angle-mouldings were originally decorated with plain plaitwork, though only one retains any trace of this; the upper edges have traces of ring-and-pellet decoration. The panel on the E. face has a defaced inscription at the head (see below), separated by a narrow band of irregular plain knotwork from a distorted triangular key-pattern forming two pairs of crosses (much weathered, but hardly a swastika key-pattern); the lower border is formed of a double plain moulding. On the S. side in a vertical panel is a double looped knot separated by a moulded border from the pattern of irregular knotwork, the lower half much decayed. On the W. side the panel and angle-mouldings are so weathered as to leave only traces of irregular knotwork at the top of the panel. In the narrow vertical panel on the N. side a looped knot and a pattern of irregular knotwork below a moulded border fill the upper half, the remainder of the panel being weathered.

The inscription on the E. face (Fig. 16), in four or possibly five horizontal lines, is so much weathered that only parts of the first and last lines in half-uncials can be read, giving EBISSA[R?] / [P?]... / ... / QUE[SCIT?]. It is uncertain whether the final letter of the first line is R, giving *Ebissar* (*cf. Ebisar* on the 'Samson' Cross (No. 912) at Llantwit Major), or S, giving *Ebissas*. The stone is of 10th- to 11th-century date.

E.C.M.W. 193; *C.I.I.C.* 1009; *Arch. Camb.*, 1899, p. 164; LXXXIII (1928), p. 388.

Coychurch (E), C. Lower (C).
ss 97 N.W. (9399 7970)   8 ix 64   XLI N.W.

FIG. 16.
Coychurch, inscription on shaft of pillar-cross (935). Scale ⅛.

(936) 'CARREG FEDYDDIOL', BRIDGEND. Shaft (Plate 24) of composite pillar-cross standing until 1969 near Pen-yr-allt on the E. bank of the R. Ogmore, one mile N. of Bridgend, and subsequently moved to Margam Stones Museum.[1] The site of the stone is near a spring, and the question of their association is considered further below.

The much-weathered four-sided block of sandstone is 1·2 m tall and tapers slightly towards the base (from 56 cm by 45 cm at the upper edges to 46 cm by 40 cm). In the top surface is a rectangular socket 20 cm deep for the tenon of a missing upper stone. Each of the faces has a vertical panel recessed between bulbous angle-mouldings linking the upper and lower frames. The rounded upper edges, deformed by weathering, have traces of ring-and-pellet mouldings in single rows, while the angle-mouldings are carved with plain plaitwork bordered by roll-mouldings of four bands at the top and two at the base. In the panel on the S.W. face (as positioned before transfer to Margam) a single moulding frames two patterns of irregular plain knotwork incorporating pellets and separated by a row of pellets; further decoration or lettering is faintly indicated in the panel below these. The N.W. panel contains two patterns of plain knotwork incorporating pellets, the lowest third being blank, and each separated by a single pellet. The N.E. face is extremely weathered but seems to have had some decoration in relief between the angle-mouldings. The panel on the S.E. side is filled with an irregular diagonal key-pattern merging into irregular plain knotwork with a separate pattern of irregular plain knotwork below it; a band of ringed pellets defines the bottom of the panel. The decorative features common to this and Nos. 937–8 indicate a late 10th- or early 11th-century date.

The severe weathering of the N.E. face of the stone as it recently stood (an effect to be expected on a S.W. face) suggests that it had been moved from an earlier position probably to serve as a cattle rubbing post. This earlier position might have been at the spring 20 m to the N., although there is no long-standing tradition recorded of this being regarded as a holy well.[2] The well itself was described in 1877 as 'a rudely and massively walled enclosure domed over with large, flat, overlying stones',[3] but it is now partly ruinous and much overgrown. The squared well-chamber is 1·2 m high with one covering slab remaining, and except for the open W. side is completely incorporated in a field bank; a modern brick water-channel has been added. The structure is not likely to be more than two or three centuries old.

E.C.M.W. 252.
[1] The only authority for the name 'Carreg Fedyddiol' (the Baptismal Stone) is the older edition of the O.S. Six-inch map.
[2] The identification of the well as the 'finnaun Liss' named in an early charter to Llandaf (*Arch. Camb.*, 1877, pp. 63–4; Clark, *Cartae*, II, p. 29) cannot be maintained; *cf.* F. Jones, *The Holy Wells of Wales* Cardiff, 1954), p. 189, placing it in St. Brides-super-Ely.
[3] *Arch. Camb.*, 1877, p. 64.

Coety (E), C. Higher (C).
ss 98 S.W. (9053 8199)   8 ix 64   XL N.E.

(937) LLANDAF. (Plate 24.) Upper section of a composite pillar-cross of which the main shaft and base are lacking;

discovered in 1870 built into part of the fabric of the Bishop's Palace, Llandaf, and after standing outside for many years was moved into the cathedral in 1939. It is described as now placed in the S. chancel aisle.

The single block of Sutton stone is 86 cm tall, the shaft 30 cm wide and 20 cm thick, and the ringed head 33 cm in diameter. On both main faces the equal-armed cross has splayed arms and rounded deep interspaces, framed by a simple roll edge-moulding that merges into the bulbous angle-mouldings of the shaft; the ring joining the arms is similarly roll-moulded, but the damaged central raised boss seems to have been plain. The arms of the cross-head (the upper arm on the E. side missing) are filled with linked plain knotwork in relief, continued down the shaft as plain plait-work, on the E. face in irregular six-cord with below it four-cord, on the W. face in eight-cord surmounting six-cord. On the sides, the arm-end of the cross-head has a roll-moulded panel filled with plain knotwork; the shaft, framed by the angle-mouldings and by narrower moulding at the neck and base, has a vertical panel of plain knotwork, three S-shaped knots on the S., and paired knots on the N. developing into loose four-cord plaitwork below.

The features which link the stone with the more complete cross at Llandough (No. 938) point to the period late 10th- to early 11th-century.

E.C.M.W. 205.

Llandaf (E), Cardiff (C).
 ST 17 N.E. (1569 7791); 11 ix 64 XLIII S.W.

(938) LLANDOUGH. (Frontispiece and Plates 21, 22.) Composite pillar-cross consisting of two-part squared shaft with massive central collar or knop and splayed base but lacking the cross-head, standing in the churchyard of St. Dochdwy's Church. It is formed of four moulded blocks of Sutton stone, of which the base and collar are mortised for tenons on the two shaft stones. Though the upper shaft is square in section, the main part of the cross is rectangular with wider faces to E. and W., 2·97 m in overall height.[1] Both the upper and lower shafts have bulbous angle-mouldings framing narrow panels decorated in relief. The moulded collar is stepped like an inverted capital but the plain necking on which it rests is the head of the lower shaft. The base, roughly pyramidal with the narrow faces more splayed than the main faces, has edge-mouldings framing carved panels. All the carved detail is varyingly eroded by weathering.

The upper shaft, 89 cm tall and 33 cm square, has plain rounded angle-mouldings fractured off at the lowest N.E. and S.E. angles; a fragment formerly broken off the top of the E. face and restored in position shows traces of the single band moulding at the top similar to that at the surviving lowest angles. Part of the original cross-head was *in situ* in the 1690s when the monument was sketched by or for E. Lhuyd (Fig. 17).[2] The decoration of the E. panel shows a double-beaded figure-of-eight knot (probably terminating the decoration of the missing cross-head) linked to five pairs of plain Stafford-knots in double vertical row. The S. panel has a double-beaded diagonal key-pattern, the W. panel double-beaded figure-of-eight knotwork terminating in a Stafford-knot, and the N. panel double-beaded knotwork forming four S-shaped knots.

The collar or knop, 40 cm high, is formed of five horizontal bands of decoration each stepped in above the fourth band which is widest, 68 cm by 58 cm and has beading immediately above and below it. The bands are decorated with (top to bottom) a twist, a three-cord plait, a twist, a twist, and the lowest band is formed by a cable-moulding.

The lower shaft, 1·2 m high, is asymmetrical in its dimensions which average 50 cm by 40 cm at the base, swelling to a maximum width of 58 cm by 45 cm, and tapers to 50 cm by 33 cm below the necking. The squared-off necking, 50 cm by 40 cm is plain, with rounded angles (the S.E. angle fractured off); a single-line inscription in half-uncials cut on the W. face reads IRBICI (presumably a personal name); faint indications of lettering on the E. side (?]NUR[ ) are suggested but the surface is much eroded. The angle-mouldings of the shaft, more massive than those of the upper shaft but tapering towards

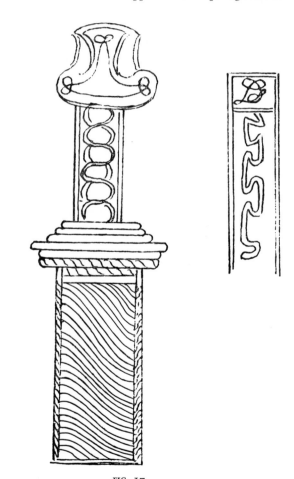

FIG. 17.
Llandough, drawing by Lluyd of pillar-cross (938).

the head, have irregular plaitwork (? double-beaded) in broad loose cords, but the N.E. angle-moulding has close plaitwork of narrower cords and some knotwork. Each angle-moulding has at the top a roll with a twist on it, and at the base a broad band of knotwork set between an upper and a lower horizontal twist. Of the panels framed by the angle-mouldings, only the wider faces are decorated, the E. panel showing five pairs of plain Stafford-knots in double vertical row, and the W. panel showing figure-of-eight knotwork terminating top and bottom in Stafford-knots.

The edge-mouldings of the base show traces of plain plait-work and, on the upper edge of the W. side, figure-of-eight knots, but are badly eroded. The E. panel (Plate 22) contains in relief five human figures in a row, seated (?) facing front, each with vestments showing a high collar (amice?) and holding a cross-headed staff or sceptre (one lacking); the northernmost figure is probably crowned. The S. panel has the bust of a man in relief set between two patterns of simple plaitwork ending in twists. The W. panel (Plate 22) shows centrally a man on horseback and, between the legs of the horse, a pattern of interlinked oval rings; the space before the horse is filled with broad irregular plaitwork incorporating a ring, and that behind has possibly a standing figure. In the N. panel is the bust of a man in relief between two patterns of plaitwork, four-cord (left) and irregular (right).

Late 10th- to early 11th-century.

E.C.M.W. 206; *C.I.I.C.* 1007; *Arch. Camb.*, 1899, p. 15; 1904, pp. 247–52; LXXXVIII (1933), pp. 392–5.
[1] The cross has been restored to an upright position during the present century.
[2] Stowe MS. 1024, fo. 19.

Llandough, Cogan and Leckwith (E), Penarth (C).
　　ST 17 S.E. (1679 7325)　　11 ix 64　　　　XLVII N.W.

(939) COETY. Fragment of cross-head (Plate 25), recorded first at Ty-newydd, Coety,[1] and removed in 1894 to St. Roque's Chapel, Merthyr Mawr, where it remains. The fragment, of Sutton stone *ca.* 10 cm thick, consists of part of the rounded hub with two of the three expanded upper arms set free-armed, 50 cm in overall length; its original diameter would have been about 72 cm. On one face the hub has carved in low relief a central bead or pellet within a double moulded ring, the arms being plain (though pitted by weathering). The other face has traces of a moulded ring-and-pellet in the upper arm, and on the hub are six (originally nine?) small square sockets, with a small rectangular socket in the centre of each cross-arm, all much weathered. Such sockets may have served as settings for enamelled, glass or jewelled studs or to affix metallic ornament. In the upper surface of the top arm is a rounded hole, 5 cm deep, to secure an ornamental finial. Probably 11th-century.

E.C.M.W. 192.
Trans. Cardiff Nat. Soc., XLI (1908), p. 28.

Coety (E), C. Higher (C).
　　SS 98 S.W. (9240 8134);
　　now at SS 8886 7808　　10 xi 64　　　　XL N.E.

(940) LLANCARFAN. Fragment of shaft of probable pillar-cross (Plate 24) in St. Cadoc's Church. The squared block of Sutton stone, 81 cm long and 33 cm by 29 cm tapering to 29 cm by 24 cm, represents the upper part of a shaft similar to Nos. 932 and 933 at Llantwit Major. On one face a narrow sunk panel (incomplete through severing of the shaft) contains triple-looped knotwork ('figure of eight') in three lobes and part of another, the other faces being plain; the surface is mutilated through re-use as building material. The shaft is of late 9th- or 10th-century date.

Letters of a partly obliterated inscription down one side of the panelled face may be read as]MSCEP[I?...] P...SES·C[, cut as squared capitals and probably of 11th- or 12th-century date. Other strokes, more deeply cut, on this face are probably modern.

E.C.M.W. 204; Westwood, *Lapid. Wall.*, p. 236–7, Pl. CI (3, 4).

Llancarfan.
　　ST 07 S.E. (0513 7020)　　11 xi 64　　　　XLVI S.W.

(941) ST. GEORGE. Fragment of cross-head (Plate 25), first recorded about 1900 at Coedarhyd-y-glyn, St. George parish,[1] and subsequently transferred to the National Museum of Wales. The fragment, of oolitic limestone from the area immediately N. of St. Fagans,[2] consists of the hub and two adjacent expanded arms linked by one arc of a ring, and was originally 50 cm in diameter and 11 cm thick; the squared arms, 16·5 cm wide with hollowed angles, project beyond the narrower ring. Carved decoration in low relief is confined to one face, the rest being plain. The arms, edged with plain bead-moulding, are filled with double-beaded six-cord plaitwork devolving between the hollows into two-cord twists which are linked around the central plain boss. The arc of the ring has a cable-twist moulding between plain inner and outer edge-mould-ing.[3] It is of early 10th-century date.

E.C.M.W. 267; *Arch. Camb.*, XCII (1937), pp. 7–9.
[1] *Arch. Camb.*, XCII (1937), p. 7, quoting former owner.
[2] *Ibid.*, quoting examination by Dr. F. J. North.
[3] For similar decorative design on a slab, *cf.* No. 907.

St. George.
　　ST 17 N.W. (1045 7515)　　8 xii 64　　　　XLVI N.E.

951–956. CLASS F: OTHER DECORATED STONES

(951) LLANRHIDIAN. Slab (Plates 26, 27) discovered shortly before 1888 in the churchyard, and subsequently set in the porch of St. Illtud's Church.[1] The stone, 2·05 m long and tapering in thickness from 50 cm at one end to 30 cm, is decorated only on the widest face, with levelled upper edge but damaged by fracture of the lower edge (63 cm at its widest). The other surfaces are undressed, and the ends are tapered as if to form tenons, one partly fractured off. The stone probably served as a lintel over a doorway or some other architectural function.[2]

The decorated face has carved ornament in low relief and also incised decoration. Two human figures occupy the centre (Plate 27), facing front with pyriform heads and squared bodies.[3] In the right-hand figure the outline mouldings ter–

minate in a pair of spirals, possibly representing feet,[4] the body or garment indicated by diagonal frets.[5] The left-hand figure apparently has a pair of disc-brooches at the shoulders,[6] the folds of the garment represented by irregular plaits. Between the two heads are two incised patterns, one of diagonal frets with paired rings below, the other cruciform with radiants between the arms and similarly resting on a pair of rings; they may be stylised representations of human or angelic figures. Two other stylised figures (Plate 27), presumably animals, flank the central group, the right-hand one up against the human figure but the other separated by a slight surface depression. Both creatures stand rampant, with the body ornamented internally by wavy lines.[7] The right-hand figure has spirals representing the head and fore-legs, with a knot for the hind-legs; the head of the other beast is represented by a three-lobed knot.[8]

The scene represented may be the meeting of SS Paul and Anthony in the desert (cf. No. 902), a theme which is common in Irish art of the pre-Norman period, and the stylistic features of the stone suggest Irish influence in its execution. It is probably of 9th- or 10th-century date.

E.C.M.W. 218; Arch. Camb., 1888, pp. 173–6.
[1] Arch. Camb., 1888, p. 174.
[2] For decorated lintels in Ireland cf. Henry, Irish Art, I, Pls. 22–3; II, Pl. 6 and pp. 188–9; H. G. Leask, Irish Churches and Monastic Buildings, I (Dundalk, 1955), pp. 56–9, 86 and Figs. 30–1, 94 and Pl. III.
[3] A conventional rendering occurring notably on the high cross at Moone, Kildare (Henry, Irish Art, I, pp. 139, 141–2 and Pl. 68) and in manuscript decoration in 'The Book of Deer' (Cambridge Univ. Lib.), reproduced in H. James, Facsimiles of National Manuscripts of Scotland, pt. I (ed. C. Innes, Southampton, 1867) and in J. O. Westwood, Facsimiles of the Miniatures and Ornaments of Anglo-Saxon and Irish Manuscripts (London, 1868), Pl. 51; the drawing in Arch. Camb., 1888, p. 174 is slightly inaccurate.
[4] This device occurs as a termination of the trunk of the body in addition to the legs on the Duvillaun slab, Co. Mayo (Henry, Irish Art, I, Pl. 51).
[5] As on the 'Corp Naomh' shrine cover (Henry, Irish Art, II, Pl. 55, also illustrated in Proc. Soc. Ant. Scot., LXXIV (1939–40), Pl. L), and also on figures in 'The Book of Deer' (n. 3 above).
[6] As on roughly similar figures on the Invergaurie slab, Angus (Proc. Soc. Ant. Scot., LXXIV (1939–40), Pl. XLIX).
[7] As on animal (and human) figures in the Southampton Psalter scene of David and the lion (Henry, Irish Art, II, Pl. M).
[8] Cf. heads of beasts in the Psalter of Ricemarch (Henry, Irish Art, II, Pl. 46).

Llanrhidian (E), Ll. Lower (C).
SS 49 S.E. (4967 9224)   9 xi 64   XXII S.W.

(952) MERTHYR MAWR. Fragment of slab (Plate 26) in the lapidary collection at St. Teilo's Church, where it was presumably found.[1] The surviving portion, which has been re-shaped for secondary architectural use, is of Sutton stone, 39 cm by 35 cm and 15 cm thick. One face is decorated with an incomplete pattern of loose double-beaded plaitwork in low relief formed of a square with looped angles[2] entwined with a similar square set diagonally, incorporating five pellets in the inner spaces. It is of 11th- or early 12th-century date.

E.C.M.W. 243.
[1] Trans. Cardiff Nat. Soc., XLI (1908), pp. 24–5. Possibly the fragment recorded by Westwood at Eglwys Nynnid (Westwood, Lapid. Wall., p. 32) and listed as E.C.M.W. 201.

[2] A device occurring also on Nos. 955 and 984; it is found on later gravestones at Llantwit Major, at Fishguard (Pembs.), and at Llangarren (Inv. Herefs., I, Pl. 9).

Merthyr Mawr.
SS 87 N.E. (8828 7753)   9 ix 64   XL S.W.

(953) LLANTWIT MAJOR. Shaft or pillar (Plate 26) first noted in 1695 as standing against the external N. wall of St. Illtud's Church (W. nave),[1] and more recently re-set within that part of the church. The stone, of local sandstone, is cylindrical in form, tapering from a flared base towards the head which has fractured off and is lacking. Its visible height is almost 2 m (with about 45 cm buried), and the diameter decreases from 45 cm to roughly 33 cm. The whole surface is decorated with carved ornament in low relief formed in four horizontal panels and divided vertically for its full height by a heavily incised V-shaped groove, 7 cm deep. The edges of the groove have a plain bead-moulding which is continued horizontally to divide the panels, each of which is framed within similar moulding (thus forming triple-mouldings). In the incomplete upper panel are traces of regular double-beaded plaitwork, while the panel below has irregular eight-cord double-beaded plaitwork with horizontal and vertical breaks. The taller panel below this contains twelve-cord double-beaded plaitwork with mostly regular breaks but incorporating a free ring in one corner. In the lowest panel an irregular pattern of double chevrons forms a base border.

While the original function of the pillar remains obscure, it may have formed, with No. 954, a pair of identical pillars in which the vertical grooves supported a slab or upright board. 10th- or 11th-century.

E.C.M.W. 224; Arch. Camb., 1889, pp. 125, 317–26.
[1] Camden, Britannia (ed. Gibson), p. 618 (E. Lhuyd); Bodleian Lib., MS. Gough, Wales 8, fo. 79v. (1770).

Llantwit Major.
SS 96 N.E. (9659 6871)   10 ix 64   XLIX N.W.

(954) LLANTWIT MAJOR. Fragment of pillar (Plate 26), found in 1899 at St. Illtud's Church, being the damaged base of a cylindrical pillar similar to No. 953 and set beside it there. The block of local sandstone is 53 cm tall and is 48 cm in diameter at its widest. Its base retains part of a horizontal bead-moulding with traces of a base splay as occur on No. 953, and there is also some indication of a similar V-shaped groove. The remainder of the surface has been chipped off. Presumably of 10th- or 11th-century date as No. 953.

E.C.M.W. 226; Arch. Camb., 1900, p. 149.

Llantwit Major.
SS 96 N.E. (9659 6871)   10 ix 64   XLIX N.W.

(955) EWENNI. Fragment of slab (Plate 26) at the Priory Church,[1] of Sutton stone 18 cm thick and 36 cm in maximum length, representing part of a slab similar to No. 952; it has been re-used for part of a trefoiled window head with glazing groove. The original decoration survives on one face with an

original edge, and consists of loose double-beaded plaitwork in false relief forming two entwined squares and incorporating pellets.[2] It is of 11th- or early 12th-century date.

E.C.M.W. 244.
[1] Probably recovered from the rubble of the N. Aisle rebuilt in 1895-6, and noted in *Arch. Camb.*, 1913, p. 26.
[2] *Vide* No. 952, n. 2.

Ewenni.
     SS 97 N.W. (9125 7781)   9 ix 64   XL S.E.

(956) LLYSWYRNY. Fragment (Plate 27) of slab or possibly of pillar-stone, built into the external S. wall of the nave of St. Tudful's Church. The stone, probably of Sutton stone, is 71 cm long and 35 cm wide, with one rounded angle but fractured across the width. The exposed surface is almost entirely filled with carved ornament in false relief. Along one edge is a band of small diaper squares,[1] and parallel to it is a row of chevrons terminating in a loop. A pattern of debased spirals similarly aligned ends at the middle of the fragment in an indeterminate lobed device, while another shorter pattern of debased spirals set at right angles occupies the remaining space at one end.[2] The original function of the complete stone, possibly a lintel, and the significance of its ornament remain indeterminate. It is of 11th- or 12th-century date.

[1] A common feature of Romanesque architectural decoration (e.g. the S. doorway of Kilpeck Church, Herefordshire).
[2] *Cf.* the debased scrolls on crosses at Beckermet, Haile and St. Bees Collingwood, *Northumbrian Crosses*, p. 147).

Llyswyrny.
     SS 97 S.E. (9619 7410)   7 ix 64   XLV N.W.

Lost Stones

Other fragmentary stones with carved decoration that have been recorded but are no longer traceable include:
(i) stone at Eglwys Nynnid (SS 802 847), described but not illustrated in Westwood, *Lapid. Wall.*, p. 33; *E.C.M.W.* 201 (*cf.* No. 952).
(ii) Two stones at St. Illtud's Church, Llantwit Major (SS 965 687); *E.C.M.W.* 225.
(iii) 'An ancient stone cross' at Cardiff; *Arch. Camb.*, 1897, p. 167.
(iv) 'Part of a cross, with an interlaced pattern' at Port Talbot (*cf.* No. 906), *Arch. Camb.*, 1857, p. 55; *E.C.M.W.* 264.

961-988. CLASS G: HEADSTONES AND GRAVE-SLABS OF THE LATE PERIOD

(961) BAGLAN (Plate 29). In churchyard on the S. side of the former parish church. It is a shaped rectangular slab (headstone?) of local sandstone, 61 cm high above ground, 40 cm wide and 13 cm thick. On the E. face is an equal-armed incised outline cross (Fig. 8, r) with slightly expanded arms, 40 cm by 37 cm. It probably dates from the 11th or 12th century.
Baglan (E), Port Talbot (C).
     SS 79 S.E. (7535 9228)   7 x 64   XXV N.W.

(962) TYTHEGSTON. Slab with ring-cross, serving as the head of a window in the N. wall of the chancel of St. Tudwg's Church. The sandstone block, 66 cm long and at least 15 cm thick, tapers slightly from 45 cm wide at the head to 42 cm at the waist. The 14th-century re-use of the stone as a cusped trefoil window-head with deeply cut spandrels has destroyed most of the original design, leaving traces of a lightly picked cross within a single lightly incised ring with outline stem (*cf.* No. 969). It is of 12th-century date.
Tythegston (E), T. Lower (C).
     SS 87 N.E. (8578 7883)   2 vii 66   XL S.W.

(963) LALESTON. Cross-head (Plate 29) of headstone or possibly of slab-cross, found about 1885 built into a barn at Laleston and subsequently transferred to the National Museum of Wales.[1] The rounded block of local sandstone has a maximum diameter of 52 cm, and varies in thickness up to 15 cm, with traces of a broken-off shaft or tenon about 27 cm wide. The one dressed face is defined by a plain double-beaded ring (partly fractured away), within which is a ring-cross carved in high relief with slightly expanded arms and sunk inter-arm spaces. The rounded hub consists of a ring-and-pellet device.[2] It is of 11th- or 12th-century date.

E.C.M.W. 202; *Arch. Camb.*, XCII (1937), p. 9.
[1] *Arch. Camb.*, XCII (1937), p. 9, in which a supposed association with Llangewydd church (SS 8754 8091) is discounted as conjectural.
[2] The whole design is similar to that on at least one slab at Clonmacnois (*C.I.I.C.* 715; R. A. S. Macalister, *The Memorial Slabs of Clonmacnois* (Dublin, 1909), No. 159).

Laleston.
     SS 87 N.E. (875 798 approx.)   8 xii 64   XL N.W.

(964-70) MERTHYR MAWR. The following group of seven stones in the lapidary collection at the parish church is temporarily under shelter on the N. side of the churchyard (*see also* Nos. 847, 917-18, 952 also in the collection). All have been found on the site of the church (rebuilt in 1848-52) or in its immediate vicinity.

(964) SLAB with outline cross (Plate 29). The weathered rectangular block of limestone, with rounded upper corners, 35 cm tall, 30 cm wide and 15 cm thick, forms the upper half of a probable headstone. One face has an incised outline Latin cross (Fig. 8, l) edge to edge, with intersecting arms and open arm-ends, possibly splayed at the head. The stone has been re-used for building, a mortice with broad chamfer being cut in the back. It is probably of 10th- to 12th-century date.

(965) SLAB with two outline crosses (Plate 28). The rectangular stone, 58 cm tall, 49 cm wide and 13 cm thick, is fractured into three pieces and is less than its original length. Each main face bears an incised outline cross potent (Fig. 8, p), somewhat irregular, one being slightly smaller and incomplete by trimming of the stone. It is of early 12th-century date.

E.C.M.W. 245-6.

(966) SLAB with two crosses (Plate 28). The damaged rectangular slab of limestone, shaped as a headstone 60 cm tall, 33 cm wide and 13 cm thick, is set in a concrete base. One face (the south face as re-set) has a cross formy (Fig. 8, g) set off in low relief by an incised ring 25 cm in diameter with sunk inter-arm spaces. On the opposite (N.) face is an incised outline cross potent. It dates from the 12th century.

E.C.M.W. 247.

(967) SLAB, headstone, with two incised crosses (Plate 28, Fig. 8, d, e). The stone, of Sutton stone, is fractured in three or more pieces, of which two survive forming the rounded head,[1] 38 cm long (maximum), 34 cm wide and 10 cm thick; the edge is rounded. One face has an incised ring-cross of six-leaf marigold pattern[2] within a double incised ring the outer member of which has been cut away over the head. The opposite face has an incised outline Latin cross with trefoil terminals, lacking the foot of the stem.

While the latter device is post-Norman, possibly 13th century, it represents a re-use of an earlier stone of 11th- or 12th-century date by trimming down the original squared head to the arc of the ring-cross, resulting in the loss of the outer incised ring around the head of the stone.

[1] One found N. of the churchyard at the time of investigation.
[2] Marigold patterns, while rare on the Welsh monuments (*cf.* the font in Llanover parish church, Monmouthshire), are usual on Irish slabs and pillar-stones. *Proc. Roy. Irish Acad.*, Vol. 61 (C, 1961), pp. 110–12.

(968) PART OF HEADSTONE with ring-crosses (Plate 29). The re-used squared block, 35 cm by 26 cm and 16 cm thick, has on each main face the major part of a cross of arcs within an incised ring and with sunk inter-arm spaces; both identical. Early 12th century.

Trans. Cardiff Nat. Soc., XLI (1908), Fig. 37.

(969) SLAB with ring-cross (Plate 28). The square-headed fragment of Pennant sandstone, 35 cm long, 32 cm wide tapering to 29 cm and 7·5 cm thick, forms the upper half of a recumbent slab. The face has a shallow incised cross of arcs framed by an incised ring 23 cm in diameter with common stem below in outline (Fig. 8, a; *cf. E.C.M.W.* 90). It is probably of 11th- or 12th-century date. Found N. of churchyard in course of investigation, 1964.

(970) FRAGMENT OF SLAB, 29 cm by 25 cm and 7·5 cm thick. Both faces have traces of an inscribed cross, one a plain Latin cross, possibly the crossletted arm of a larger cross. The other face is much weathered and has had letters (18th-century?) and other markings incised, but shows one arm of a cross potent. Originally the complete stone may have resembled one at Castlemartin, Pembs. (*E.C.M.W.* 304), tentatively given a 7th- to 9th-century date, and was probably re-used as a headstone.

Merthyr Mawr.
  SS 87 N.E. (8829 7747)   8 x 64   XL S.W.

(971) PYLE. Slab with incised cross (Plate 29), originally recorded 'between Kenfig and Pyle' on the roadside,[1] standing in the garden of 65 Marlas Road, Pyle. The stone, 1·06 m high, tapering in width from 50 cm to 38 cm and in thickness from 20 cm to 15 cm is roughly dressed with rounded head but is badly weathered. The base is shouldered. The plain linear cross (Fig. 8, k), 25 cm by 21 cm is cut as a V-shaped groove, with slightly splayed arms. In recent years the stone was re-set in a concrete base with the cross on its west face, the opposite face having an O.S. bench mark and modern initials. It is probably of 11th or 12th-century date.

E.C.M.W. 199.
[1] *Arch. Camb.*, 1894, p. 327; T. Gray, *The Buried City of Kenfig* (London, 1909), p. 189.

Pyle and Kenfig (E), Pyle/Kenfig (C).
  SS 88 S.W. (8224 8232)   9 x 64   XXXIX N.E.

(972) LALESTON. Headstone with ring-cross (Plate 29, Fig. 8, i, j), first noted 'embedded in the wall of a field at Cae yr Hen Eglwys, near Bridgend'[1]. The squared rectangular block of weathered Sutton stone is 66 cm tall (lacking part of the head), 44 cm wide tapering to 35 cm at base, and 14 cm thick. On one face is an incised cross of arcs with central disc, framed by a double incised ring. The opposite face has another cross delineated by four smaller incised rings as inter-arm spaces. The stone has been re-set in Margam Stones Museum. It dates from the 12th century.

E.C.M.W. 203; Radford, *Margam*, No. 14.
[1] *Arch. Camb.*, 1894, p. 327.

Laleston.
  SS 88 S.E. (8754 8091)   12 xi 64   XL N.W.

(973) PORT TALBOT. Rounded cross-head of headstone or possibly of pillar-cross, discovered at Penhydd Waelod in 1933[1] but subsequently lost; it is described from a cast in the National Museum of Wales. The stone, 34 cm by 29 cm and probably 11 cm thick, has on its dressed face an incised outline cross of arcs of intersecting lines, the arm-ends forming disconnected segments of a ring-cross. Traces remain of the enclosing incised double ring framing regularly spaced incised dots. This may represent a debased form of the pelleted border occurring on sculptured crosses of the late Saxon period.[2] Probably 11th- or 12th-century in date.

E.C.M.W. 230.
[1] *Arch. Camb.*, XCI (1936), pp. 139–40. Field names at Penhydd-fawr (25 N.E.) suggest the former existence of a grange and chapel there rather than at the recorded find-spot of the stone.
[2] *Cf. Arch. Camb.*, 1891, p. 114.

Margam (E), Port Talbot (C).
  SS 89 S.W. (8018 9201)   8 xii 64   XXV S.E.

(974) LLANTWIT MAJOR. Fragment of slab with ring-cross in St. Illtud's Church. The sandstone slab, originally a grave-marker but reduced for building material, is 32 cm by 20 cm and 8 cm thick. The cross (Fig. 8, c) is formed by equal arms contiguous with the framing ring of rounded section, separated

from the flat inter-arm spaces by incised grooves. It is probably of 11th- or 12th-century date.

Llantwit Major.

SS 96 N.E. (9659 6871)   10 ix 64   XLIX N.W.

(975–81) EWENNI. The following group of stones at the Priory Church was recovered during restoration of the eastern parts of the fabric by the Ministry of Works (now the Department of the Environment) in 1950–52. All had been re-used as building material and are placed in the S. transept, together with Nos. 924 and 955 (above).

(975) FRAGMENT OF SLAB of Sutton stone, 23 cm high, 20 cm wide and 15 cm thick. One face has part of an incised outline Latin cross (Fig. 8, n). Probably 10th to 12th century.

(976) FRAGMENT OF HEADSTONE (Plate 29) with traces of an elaborated linear cross (Fig. 8, o). It is of Sutton stone, weathered and re-dressed for secondary use, 52 cm tall, 37 cm wide and 20 cm thick. The upper terminals of the cross were apparently bifurcated. 8th to 10th century.

(977) HEADSTONE with outline cross (Plate 28), of Sutton stone, 47 cm high, 23 cm wide and 12 cm thick. Though dressed to a regular rectangular shape, it probably lacks part of the head through re-use as building material. The outline cross potent (Fig. 8, m) is set off by deeply incised bevelled grooves, the foot forming a spike, possibly in imitation of wooden standing crosses (*cf. E.C.M.W.* p. 23 and numbers there cited). 11th to 12th century.

Radford, *Ewenny*, pp. 16–17.

(978) PART OF HEADSTONE with outline cross (Fig. 8, q), of Sutton stone, 50 cm by 44 cm and 21 cm thick. Though slightly less than its original width through re-use as building material, it retains one chamfered edge. The dressed face bears an incised outline cross potent, part of the foot being lost with the missing base of the stone. The original squared head and chamfered edges point to a 12th-century date.

Radford, *Ewenny*, p. 16.

(979) PART OF HEADSTONE with ring-cross, 86 cm high, 20 cm wide and 15 cm thick, representing one lateral half of the original stone. The cross, indicated by one arm surviving with slightly expanded arm-end (*cf.* No. 982), is set in low relief by an incised groove. It is probably of 10th- or 11th-century date.

(980) PART OF HEADSTONE with incised crosses. The surviving fragment, 24 cm in diameter and 7 cm thick, probably formed the rounded head of a rectangular upright stone at the head or foot of a grave rather than simply a disc-like stone.[1] One face has an incised cross of arcs from edge to edge (rounded) without an incised ring (Fig. 8, b).

The other face has a simple linear Latin cross with slightly expanded terminals. It is probably of 12th-century date.

[1] *Cf. E.C.M.W.* 202, 230; a similar stone, apparently now lost, is recorded in *Arch. Camb.*, 1894, p. 338, as 'found in a stable yard' near (?) Bridgend.

(981) FRAGMENT OF HEADSTONE, of Sutton stone, with incomplete ring-cross (Plate 28, Fig. 8, f). Its maximum dimensions are 48 cm in length by 40 cm and it is 17 cm thick. The cross of arcs is in low relief, framed by an incised double ring. 10th to early 12th century.

Radford, *Ewenny*, p. 16.

Ewenni.

SS 97 N.W. (9125 7781)   9 ix 64   XL S.E.

(982) LLAN-GAN. Two fragments of probable headstones with ring-cross, built into the external chancel walls of St. Canna's Church, Llan-gan. Stone (i) in the east wall, 20 cm by 23 cm, a Rhaetic sandstone squared off on two edges, has one splayed arm of an incised cross within part of a double incised ring *ca.* 28 cm in diameter.[1] Stone (ii) in the south wall near the S.E. corner is of similar material, 25 cm by 19 cm, retaining half of a cross with expanded terminals set in relief by sunk inter-arm spaces, within a double incised ring *ca.* 25 cm in diameter (Fig. 8, h). The fragments, both of 11th- or 12th-century date, are from two distinct headstones.

[1] *Cf.* H. S. Crawford, *Handbook of Carved Ornament from Irish Monuments of the Christian Period* (Dublin, 1926), Fig. 4F; *C.I.I.C.* 715.

Llan-gan.

SS 97 N.E. (9574 7783)   8 ix 64   XLI S.W.

(983) NEWCASTLE, Bridgend. Slab with incised outline crosses (Plate 28), found with No. 984 at St. Leonard's Church. The large rectangular slab of local sandstone, originally recumbent, is 1·75 m long, 61 cm wide (one end very slightly narrower), and 15 cm thick. It has fractured at the waist, and the central surface is mostly worn away through former use as a step. At each end is a large ring-cross formed of four separated quadrants,[1] 47 cm in diameter. In the less worn half of the central space is a smaller cross with outline stem and foot, the ring head formed of four sunk quadrants; a similar cross may have been placed symmetrically in the other half but is entirely without trace. The slab is set upright within the church against the N. wall of the tower. Probably 11th or 12th century.

E.C.M.W. 254.

[1] There is no common stem as stated in *E.C.M.W.*, the line being formed by mortar that bonded another stone lying on top of it.

Newcastle (E), Bridgend (C).

SS 98 S.W. (9024 8003)   7 x 64   XL N.E.

(984) NEWCASTLE, Bridgend. Coped grave-slab (Plate 28) at St. Leonard's Church, discovered in 1853 serving as a step (with No. 983) to the S. door of the chancel[1] and subsequently set upright against the internal N. wall of the W. tower. The weathered slab of Sutton stone is 1·9 m long and 56 cm wide at the slightly convex head tapering to 38 cm at the squared foot; at the ridge it is 30 cm thick, the surface sloping to vertical sides of 20 cm. It has carved and incised ornament as well as inscriptions.

The upper half of the coped surface contains an equal-armed cross in low relief, its arms formed of double-beaded cable-twist around a central boss which has traces of plain knotwork. The upper arm abuts a convex edge-moulding at the top, the slightly expanded cross arms extend to the edges of the slab, and the lower arm rests against the expanded terminal of a stem of single-beaded cable-twist forming the ridge; the whole thus takes the form of a processional cross. The upper panels of the head each contain an incised pattern of plain six-cord plaitwork (that to the right almost obliterated), with an inscription (see below). In each of the lower panels is a single-beaded square with large loops at the angles, and near the base to the right of the stem is a similar device set diagonally, all in low relief. A second inscription fills the face between the two looped squares on the right.

One vertical side of the slab, to the left of the coped face, is decorated with a series of twelve double-beaded half-loops in low relief imitating arcading, but is much defaced by weathering of the stone.

The inscription above the horizontal arms of the cross is incised in two horizontal lines each side of the stem reading HIC·I[AC]E[T] / GVLGVE //N·F[IL]IV / S·EIV[S], and presumably continued by the second inscription incised in two lines down the face reading AERERN FECIT· LAPIDEM / EMIT·HU[TR]VM·LAPIDEM ('Here lies Gulguen. His son Aerern made the stone. Hu[tr]um bought the stone.') The lettering (Fig. 18) combines debased

half-uncials (H, E, G, M) with revived Roman capitals (V, R, N, T) of which the V-s have prominent serifs; the first G in the second line is partly defaced by a fracture but its tail can be traced; and the form of the M-s with the first two minims closed as a loop is a late feature, though also occurring on an early inscription (No. 850). Punctuation dots separate the words. For the name *Gulguen* cf. *Gelugui(n)* on No. 884, and for *Hutrum* cf. *Heutren* on a stone from Llanllwni, Carmarthenshire (*E.C.M.W.* 164).

The form of the stone with a processional cross in relief, recalls some late Saxon coped slabs,[2] but the decoration and lettering point to an 11th-century or early 12th-century date.

E.C.M.W. 253; *Arch. Camb.*, 1873, pp. 192–5; LXXXIII (1928), pp. 310–11.
[1] *Arch. Camb.*, 1852, p. 156; 1873, p. 192.
[2] At Crosscanonby (Cumberland) and Hickling (Notts.), T. D. Kendrick, *Late Saxon and Viking Art* (London, 1949), Pls. 45, 53.

Newcastle (E), Bridgend (C).
        SS 98 S.W. (9024 8003)   7 x 64   XL N.E.

(985) LLANDAF. Two fragments of headstones with incised ring-cross, incorporated into the fabric of the Cathedral internally, over the west door. Stone (i) is approximately 61 cm by 25 cm with lightly incised radii springing from a central raised disc and framed by an incised ring 14 cm in diameter, forming a cross formy of equal segments. Stone (ii) is similar, with cross formy framed by double incised ring 15 cm in diameter, but without central disc. Both stones are of 11th- or 12th-century date.
Llandaf (E), Cardiff (C).
        ST 17 N.E. (1569 7791)   3 ix 64   XLIII S.W.

FIG. 18.
Newcastle, Bridgend, inscription on grave slab (984). Scale ⅕.

(986) LLANGUICKE. Socketed stone for small standing slab, in the churchyard of St. Ciwg's Church, S. of the nave. The roughly rectangular stone, about 1·0 m long and 30 cm high, has a levelled upper surface in the centre of which is a shallow socket 38 cm by 8 cm with rounded ends.[1] The upright slab which would face E.–W. is lacking. 9th to 12th century.

[1] For socket stone with slab *in situ*, *cf. Proc. Roy. Irish Acad.*, Vol. 61 (C, 1961), Pl. XXVI (2).

Llanguicke.

SN 70 N.W. (7238 0557)   7 xii 64   VIII N.E.

(987) MERTHYR MAWR. Socketed stone (Plate 29) in the churchyard of St. Teilo's Church, on the S. side of the nave.[1] The shaped rectangular stone of local conglomerate is 1·07 m long by 63 cm and is 35 cm high; the upper angles seem to have been chamfered but the stone is somewhat weathered. Central to the upper surface is a socket 40 cm by 15 cm with rounded ends, and it is 30 cm deep. The stone, which may not be *in situ*, is probably of 11th- or 12th-century date.

[1] Said by local informant to have been found on Merthyr Mawr Warren together with fragments of an upright cross.

Merthyr Mawr.

SS 87 N.E. (8830 7748)   13 xi 64   XL S.W.

(988) LLANGYNWYD. Part of socketed stone, preserved in the porch of St. Cynwyd's Church, where it was discovered in the rubble of the chancel wall about 1850.[1] The present dimensions of the stone, 71 cm by 33 cm and 14 cm thick, are almost certainly less than its original size, but the socket itself remains with rounded ends, 33 cm long by 7 cm and 13 cm deep. The upper surface is much abraded by grooves formed by secondary use. 9th to 12th century.

[1] Westwood, *Lapid. Wall.*, p. 45 and Pl. 29 (6).

Llangynwyd (E), Ll. Middle (C).

SS 88 N.E. (8573 8882)   17 iii 65   XXVI S.W.

Lost Stone

A roughly-shaped headstone or slab was recorded by Lhuyd 'at Llandaff in the Middle of the street being Supposed to be Conveyed out of the Cathedral', with the inscription EPISCOPI / IOSEPH, preceded by a line of uncertain letters.[1] This might seem to refer to the bishop of that name whose death in 1045 was noted in the chronicles,[2] but he is stated to have died in Rome. The lettering as sketched may not be very reliable but it shows a squared form of the letter C which is characteristic of inscriptions of the 11th and 12th centuries (*cf.* No. 940).

[1] Stowe MS. 1024, fo. 35.
[2] *Brut* (Peniarth), *s.a.* 1043; *Ann. Camb.*, *s.a.* 1046; *Epis. Acts*, I, p. 67.

Llandaf (E), Cardiff (C).

ST 17 N.E. (156 779)   XLIII S.W.

PAGAN SCULPTURE

(991) PAGAN CULT HEAD (Plate 27), formerly built into a road-side wall at Port Talbot[1] and in 1953 transferred to the National Museum of Wales. The roughly squared pillar-stone of Pennant sandstone, 65 cm tall and 23 cm square, has on one side a human face carved in low relief, its pyriform outline marked by a deep groove; the top of the stone is rounded to the curvature of the upper part of the human face which is partly affected by flaking. The form of the stone, the rendering of facial detail (in particular the lentoid eyes, the flattened nose and straight mouth), together with the oval cowl-like surround all belong to a native pagan Celtic tradition of cult figures, more especially the cult of the head.[2] The resemblance to another cult pillar-stone from Maryport, Cumberland,[3] strengthens the supposition that the form of the stone has a phallic significance. Comparable cult figures with Romano-British associations suggest it should be dated to the period 1st to 4th centuries A.D.

Arch. Camb., CXV (1966), pp. 94–8 (J. V. S. Megaw).
[1] At Gwarycaeau on the N.E. edge of the town, *Trans. Port Talbot Hist. Soc.*, I, No. 1 (1963), p. 65 (A. L. Evans); its original location cannot be known, but may be presumed to have been in the vicinity, possibly in association with a spring.
[2] A. Ross, *Pagan Celtic Britain* (London, 1967), chap. 2 ('The Cult of the Head'), espec. pp. 92–3).
[3] *Ibid.* and refs. cited in *Arch. Camb.*, CXV (1966), pp. 94–5.

Margam (E), Port Talbot (C).

SS 78 N.E. (773 898 approx.)   8 xii 64   XXV S.W.

(992) PAGAN CULT SITE. A natural spring at the foot of a rock face on the W. side of Nantcastellau, N. of Llantrisant, has associated carvings which suggest it was a site of pagan Celtic veneration. Its name 'Tarren Deusant', was recorded in 1696 together with a note that there were 'two persons engraved'.[1] The rock face above a natural ledge S. of the spring features a lightly-coloured boulder of phallic appearance surrounded by a band of dark and relatively soft mudstone; the surface of this band of softer rock is almost entirely decorated with various designs incised or in relief, including at least eight stylised human faces with socketed eyes (Plate 30).

The association of human heads (actual or representational) with sacred waters is a characteristic of pagan Celtic beliefs,[2] and the primitive stylised rendering of these faces accords with the iconography of such beliefs elsewhere.[3] Two heads in low relief to the left of the boulder show incised 'eye-brows' as well as the 'slit' mouth characteristic of some Celtic cult heads,[4] but in this case of multiple imitation there is no certain criterion for establishing which if any of those now visible are authentically of pre-Christian age.

[1] Lhuyd, *Parochialia*, III, p. 9.
[2] A. Ross, *Pagan Celtic Britain* (London, 1967), pp. 104–13.
[3] *Ibid.*, Pls. 50–3, 60, 63 and 94; *Antiquity*, XLII (1968), pp. 314–15.
[4] *Ibid.*, Pls. 20–1, 29.

Llantrisant.

ST 08 N.E. (0520 8720)   13 vii 68   XXXVI N.W.

UNCLASSIFIED STRUCTURES

THERE are three enclosures which appear to be ancient, but which do not fall into any defined class; they may be medieval or later, and one (No. 1002) may be of natural origin.

(1001) ENCLOSURE, Clyne Common, at about 80 m above O.D. on the sloping E. side of a small stream. It consists of a bank enclosing a circular area 9 m in diameter; the interior is lower than the exterior ground level, the bank having an effective height of up to 1·3 m from the inside, and a width of up to 6 m. There are two entrances, opposing each other at N.W. and S.E., both about 2 m wide. The purpose of the enclosure is uncertain; its situation by a stream may indicate an agricultural use connected with livestock; or the effectiveness of the bank from the inside may suggest its use for a rural sport such as cock-fighting.

Oystermouth.

SS 58 N.E. (5981 8901)   29 ix 59   XXXII N.E.

(1002) RING, W. of Southerndown. On the cliff-top, close to the blow-hole Pwll y Gwynt, at about 50 m above O.D., a well-defined ring is indicated by several aerial photographs.[1] It is almost truly circular, 65 m in diameter, bisected by a field-wall. At the date of inspection nothing was visible on the ground within the field, but on the unenclosed ground to the south the mark was visible as a band about 0·8 m wide of turf in which the grass was browner and sparser than elsewhere. There is no change in surface relief.

These characteristics suggest that the feature may be a fungus-ring;[2] against this must be set its unusual size, its regularity (which is not distorted where it crosses the field-wall) and the absence of any comparable rings on the cliff-top. If it is in fact artificial, the accuracy of its setting-out suggests a ritual rather than a domestic function.

[1] O.S. 1/2500 AP, set 67–001, No. 063.
[2] Cf. O. G. S. Crawford and A. Keiller, *Wessex from the Air* (Oxford, 1928), Pls. XXVII, XXXII, L and pp. 187, 254.

St. Brides Major and Wick (E), St. Brides Major (C).

SS 87 S.W. (8777 7378)   25 i 72   XLIV N.W.

(1003) RING W. of Heol-y-llan, at about 100 m above O.D., on a flat marshy valley-bottom. A slight bank and external ditch, 5·5 m wide by 0·3 m high overall, forms an enclosure of total diameter 43 m overall, almost circular but slightly flattened on the S.W. quarter. A concentric ditch, about 3 m wide and 0·1 m deep, 26 m in diameter overall, is visible on the E. of a modern field-boundary which bisects the site.

Coety (E), C. Higher (C).

SS 98 S.W. (9346 8332)   21 iv 67   XXXV S.W.

NAMES OF PLACES IN GLAMORGAN

THE written forms of place-names in Glamorgan may be grouped as follows:
  (i) Welsh forms spelt according to established orthographical rules as recommended by the Board of Celtic Studies of the University of Wales.
  (ii) Welsh forms commonly mis-spelt: e.g. Bettws *for* Betws, Coity *for* Coety, Merthyr Tydfil *for* Merthur Tudful, Porthcawl *for* Porth-cawl, Rhossily *for* Rhosili.
  (iii) Anglicised spellings of Welsh forms: e.g. Aberthaw *for* Aberddawan, Kilvey *for* Cilfái, Lisvane *for* Llys-faen, Llantwit *for* Llanilltud, Loughor *for* Llwchwr.
  (iv) Non-Welsh forms, almost entirely of English origin: e.g. Cheriton, Oxwich, Reynoldston.
  (v) Alternative Welsh and English forms for the same place: e.g. Abertawe/Swansea, Llandeilo Ferwallt/Bishopston, Llanilltud Gŵyr/Ilston, Tresimwn/Bonvilston.

In recent years, following the recommendations of the Board of Celtic Studies (see *Rhestr o Enwau Lleoedd: A Gazetteer of Welsh Place-names*, Cardiff, 1958), the Welsh spelling of forms in groups (ii), (iii) and (v) has become more generally adopted in official publications and notices. In this Inventory the correct Welsh forms of groups (ii) and (iii) are used where the differences are not likely to cause confusion in, for instance, the use of O.S. maps. The alternatives of group (v) are not normally used in the descriptive entries.

The two lists of place-names below are intended mainly to assist the reader, rather than to provide a comprehensive index. The first gives the English and anglicised forms alphabetically, with their correct Welsh equivalents, but only includes names which do not appear in the lists of Ecclesiastical and Civil Parishes (pp. xvii–xxiv), to which it is supplementary. The second list gives the correct spelling of Welsh names alphabetically, including the alternatives of group (v), and is more complete in order to serve as a cross-index both to the parish lists and to the Inventory text. No entries are included for the names of natural features which differ mainly in the choice between Welsh and English for a descriptive term, such as Mynydd or Mountain, Afon or River. The final column indicates that the form given in the second column is that used in the Ecclesiastical (E) or Civil (C) parish list, where the incidence of monuments in parishes is indexed.

English or anglicised form	Correct Welsh form	English or anglicised form	Correct Welsh form
Aberthaw	Aberddawan	Kenfig Hill	Mynyddcynffig
Bargoed	Bargod	Killay	Cilâ
Boverton	Trebefered	Kilvey	Cilfái
Candleston	Tregantllo	Loughor (river)	Llwchwr
Crynant	Y Creunant	Miskin	Meisgyn
Cwmavon	Cwmafan	Mountain Ash	Aberpennar
Dunraven	Dwnrhefn	Ogmore	Ogwr
Ely (place)	Trelái	Taff's Well	Ffynnon Taf
Ely (river)	Elái	Van	Y Fan
Glyn-neath	Glyn-nedd	Worm's Head	Pen Pyrod
Gower	Gŵyr		

71

Correct Welsh form	English or anglicised form	E	C	Correct Welsh form	English or anglicised form	E	C
Aberafan	Aberavon	E		Llangynydd	Llangennith	E	C
Aberddawan	Aberthaw			Llanilltud Faerdref	Llantwit Fardre	E	C
Aberpennar	Mountain Ash			Llanilltud Fawr	Llantwit Major	E	C
Abertawe	Swansea	E	C	Llanilltud Gŵyr	Ilston	E	C
Yr As Fach	Nash		C	Llanilltud Nedd	Llantwit-juxta-Neath	E	
Yr As Fawr	Monknash	E	C	Llansanffraid-ar-Elái	St. Brides-super-Ely	E	C
Bargod	Bargoed			Llansanffraid-ar-Ogwr	St. Brides Minor	E	C
Y Barri	Barry	E	C	Llansawel	Briton Ferry	E	
Y Bont-faen	Cowbridge		C	Llantriddyd	Llantrithyd	E	C
Caerdydd	Cardiff	E	C	Llan-y-tair-mair	Knelston	E	C
Casllwchwr	Loughor (place)	E	C	Llwchwr	Loughor (river)		
Castell-nedd	Neath	E	C	Llwyneliddon	St. Lythans	E	C
Y Castellnewydd	Newcastle	E	C	Llys-faen	Lisvane	E	C
Cilâ	Killay			Meisgyn	Miskin		
Cilfái	Kilvey			Mynyddcynffig	Kenfig Hill		
Y Clun	Clyne		C	Ogwr	Ogmore		
Y Creunant	Crynant			Pen Pyrod	Worm's Head		
Cwmafan	Cwmavon			Pen-rhys	Penrice	E	C
Cynffig	Kenfig		C	Pen-y-bont ar Ogwr	Bridgend		C
Drenewydd yn Notais	Newton Nottage	E	C	Y Pîl	Pyle	E	C
Dwnrhefn	Dunraven			Porthceri	Porthkerry	E	C
Eglwys Fair y Mynydd	St. Mary Hill	E	C	Rugos	Rhigos		C
Yr Eglwys Newydd	Whitchurch	E		Y Rhath	Roath	E	
Elái	Ely (river)			Rhydri	Rudry	E	C
Y Fan	Van		C	Sain Dunwyd	St. Donats	E	C
Ffynnon Taf	Taff's Well			Sain Ffagan	St. Fagans	E	C
Glyn-nedd	Glyn-neath			Sain Nicolas	St. Nicholas	E	C
Gwenfô	Wenvoe	E	C	Sain Siorys	St. George	E	C
Gŵyr	Gower			Saint Andras	St. Andrews	E	C
Larnog	Lavernock	E	C	Sain Tathan	St. Athan	E	C
Lecwydd	Leckwith		C	Saint Hilari	St. Hilary	E	C
Llanbedr-ar-fynydd	Peterston-super-montem		C	Saint-y-brid	St. Brides Major	E	C
Llanbedr-y-fro	Peterston-super-Ely	E	C	Y Sgêr	Sker	E	
Llandeilo Ferwallt	Bishopston	E	C	Sili	Sully	E	C
Llandochau	Llandough	E		Silstwn	Gileston	E	C
Llandudwg	Tythegston	E	C	Trebefered	Boverton		
Llanddunwyd	Welsh St. Donats	E	C	Tredelerch	Rumney	E	
Llan-faes	Llanmaes	E	C	Trefflemin	Flemingston	E	C
Llan-fair	St. Mary Church	E		Tregantllo	Candleston		
Llanfeuthin	Llanvithyn		C	Tregatwg	Cadoxton-juxta-Barry	E	
Llanfihangel-ar-Elái	Michaelston-super-Ely	E		Tregolwyn	Colwinston	E	C
Llanfihangel y Bont-faen	Llanmihangel	E	C	Tre-gŵyr	Gowerton		C
Llanfihangel-y-fedw	Michaelston-y-Vedw	E		Trelái	Ely (place)		
Llanfihangel-ynys-Afan	Michaelston Higher		C	Trelales	Laleston	E	C
Llanfihangel-y-pwll	Michaelston-le-Pit	E	C	Tresimwn	Bonvilston	E	C
Llanfleiddan	Llanblethian	E	C	Uchelolau	Highlight	E	
Llangatwg Nedd	Cadoxton-juxta-Neath	E		Y Wig	Wick	E	C
Llan-giwg	Llanguicke	E	C	Ystumllwynarth	Oystermouth	E	C
Llangrallo	Coychurch	E	C				

GLOSSARY

Words adequately defined in the Shorter Oxford Dictionary are not included unless they have been used in a more specialised sense than is given there. The list is further limited by the exclusion of proper names and terms of cultural significance, as well as typological definitions of artifacts, which can be determined from standard works. Definitions are only given in the list when reference to an appropriate section of the Inventory will not suffice. Welsh words are indicated by (W).

CLAS (W).—See p. 13.

CROSSES.—See general discussion, pp. 18–34.

DISC-HEADED SLAB.—See p. 20.

FALSE RELIEF.—Relief achieved by excision of the field, leaving the design at the original surface.

FORFID.—A symbol supplementary to the basic Ogam alphabet.

FORMY.—Of crosses, with arms widening uniformly from the centre to squared ends.

HALF-UNCIAL.—A style of lettering involving both majuscule and minuscule forms, of rounded shape suitable for pen-work.

ORTHOSTAT.—An upright, earthfast stone.

PANELLED CROSS.—See p. 20.

PATÉE.—Of crosses, as formy, but with the arms notched in two places at the ends.

PILLAR-CROSS.—See p. 30.

QUILLON.—A short cross-piece between the blade and the handle of a sword.

RING-CAIRN.—A circular bank of stone surrounding a burial-place.

INDEX OF NATIONAL GRID REFERENCES

This index gives the six-figure reference and corresponding monument number or page for every surviving structure mentioned in the Inventory, apart from roads and trackways for which the arrangement would be unsuitable. Its purpose is to simplify direct reference to the entry corresponding to a site located according to the National Grid, for which the proper name may be unknown or difficult to determine.

The references are classified according to the main categories of the Inventory, and lead not only to the descriptive entries of authentic sites, but to alternative categories where doubtful character has occasioned cross-reference in the text. Many rejected sites have been included under categories to which field archaeologists might be inclined to refer them on their own assessment.

The index for each of the three parts of Volume I contains no direct reference to the other two parts, which should be separately consulted when necessary.

DYKES

G.R.	INV.	G.R.	INV.	G.R.	INV.
SN 666 062–673 063	801	SS 790 980–786 981	806	SS 939 944–940 945	811
SN 918 091–917 030	802	SS 833 881–831 880	p. 8b	SS 958 936–958 937	p. 6
SN 946 033	803	SS 889 773–888 775	807	SS 970 996–972 996	810
SO 110 012	804	SS 894 948–895 947	808	ST 098 901–102 912	812
SO 117 002	805	SS 919 951–921 951	809		

EARLY MONASTIC SITES

G.R.	INV.	G.R.	INV.	G.R.	INV.
SS 400 925	821	SS 882 775	824	ST 156 779	829
SS 577 893	822	SS 966 687	826	ST 167 732	828
SS 646 989	823	ST 051 702	827	ST 220 650	830
SS 801 863	825				

CHRISTIAN MONUMENTS

G.R.	INV.	G.R.	INV.	G.R.	INV.
SN 702 042	903	SS 765 895	867	SS 887 811	922
SN 723 055	986	SS 767 894	868; 914	SS 902 800	983; 984
SN 826 006	861	SS 767 895	885; 906	SS 905 819	936
SN 84 11	904	SS 783 873	846	SS 912 778	924; 955; 975–981
SN 851 085	841	SS 800 855	919; 920	SS 924 813	939
SN 95 05	p. 39a, i	SS 801 863	901; 907–910	SS 939 796	934
SO 050 015	863	SS 801 920	973	SS 939 797	935
SO 103 034	842	SS 801 972	923	SS 957 778	913; 925; 982
SO 137 026	843; 881	SS 802 847	921; p. 64a	SS 961 741	956
SS 428 914	905	SS 803 844	849	SS 962 729	902
SS 438 934	865; 866	SS 806 931	870	SS 965 687	911; 932; 953; 954; 974; p. 64a
SS 439 934	844	SS 815 829	929	SS 966 687	912; 933
SS 478 892	864	SS 822 823	971	ST 030 956	889; 890
SS 496 922	951; p. 39b, ii	SS 830 887	848	ST 046 834	888
SS 497 922	p. 58b	SS 857 788	916; 962	ST 051 702	940
SS 575 981	845	SS 875 798	963	ST 095 799	850
SS 646 989	882; 883; 931	SS 875 809	972	ST 104 751	941
SS 738 973	871	SS 880 786	928	ST 106 890	891
SS 740 976	869	SS 881 769	926	ST 124 992	892
SS 753 922	886; 961	SS 882 774	964–970	ST 156 779	937; 985; p. 68a
SS 761 980	915	SS 882 775	847; 917; 918; 952	ST 167 732	938
SS 762 901	887	SS 883 774	987	ST 219 649	893
SS 763 899	884	SS 885 775	927		

PAGAN SCULPTURE

G.R.	INV.	G.R.	INV.
SS 773 898	991	ST 052 872	992

UNCLASSIFIED STRUCTURES

G.R.	INV.	G.R.	INV.	G.R.	INV.
SS 598 890	1001	SS 877 737	1002	SS 934 833	1003

INDEX

Figures in brackets denote the serial numbers of monuments; the page number follows, with 'a' or 'b' indicating the left-hand or right-hand column respectively. References to the main site entries are printed in bold type.

Printed in England for Her Majesty's Stationery Office by
Ebenezer Baylis and Son Limited, The Trinity Press, Worcester, and London

Dd. 503868 K 12

PLATES

PLATE I

Inscribed stones of Class A: *a.* Clwydi Banwen (841), early 6th century; *b.* Mynydd Margam (848), 6th century; *c.* Capel Llanill-tern (850), late 6th–early 7th century; *d.* Port Talbot (846), 6th century; *e, f.* Merthyr Mawr (847), late 5th century; *g.* Llanmadog (844), late 5th–early 6th century. (Scale 1:10).

Plate 2

Inscribed stones of Class A: *a.* Eglwys Nynnid near Margam (849), mid 6th century; *b.* ibid., showing ogams; *c.* Capel Brithdir, Bargoed (843), early 7th century; *d.* Loughor, re-used Roman altar (845), 5th or early 6th century; *e.* ibid., showing ogams; *f.* Cefn Gelli-gaer (842), late 6th–early 7th century. (Scales *a, b,* 1:12.5; *c,* 1:18; *d,* 1:11.5).

Plate 3

Pillar stones of Class B: *a*. Carn Caca (861), 7th–9th century; *b*. Merthyr Tudful (862), 8th–9th century; *c, d*. Port Talbot (867), crosses (b) and (c), 8th–9th century; *e*. Pont-rhyd-y-fen (870), 9th or 10th century; *f, g*. Reynoldston (864), S.E. and N.W. sides, 9th century; *h*. Neath (869), N. side, 7th–8th century; *i*. Mynydd Merthyr (863), 7th–9th century; *j*. Llanmadog (865), 7th–9th century. (Scale approximately 1:13).

PLATE 4

Recumbent slabs of Class C: *a*. Llantrisant (888), 7th–9th century; *b*. Capel Brithdir, Bargoed (881), 7th–9th century; *c*. (Class B) Llanmadog (866), 9th century; *d, e*. Port Talbot (887), 9th–11th century; *f*. Gelli-gaer (892), 8th–9th century; *g*. Flatholm (893), 7th–9th century; *h*. Llanwynno (889), possibly 7th–9th century. (Scale 1:10).

PLATE 5

Slabs of Class C: *a.* Baglan (886), late 9th or early 10th century; *b.* Port Talbot (885), late 9th or early 10th century; *c.* Llangy-felach (882), 9th century; *d.* Port Talbot (884), 8th–9th century; *e.* Eglwysilan (891), 8th–10th century; *f, g.* (Class D) Port Talbot (906), 11th century. (Scale 1:10).

Plate 6

'Disc-headed' slabs of Class D: *a, b.* Mynydd Gellionnen, Pontardawe (903), 9th century; *c.* Cefn Hirfynydd, Coelbren (904), 10th century; *d.* (Plain slab of Class D) Margam (901), 10th century. (Scale 1:10).

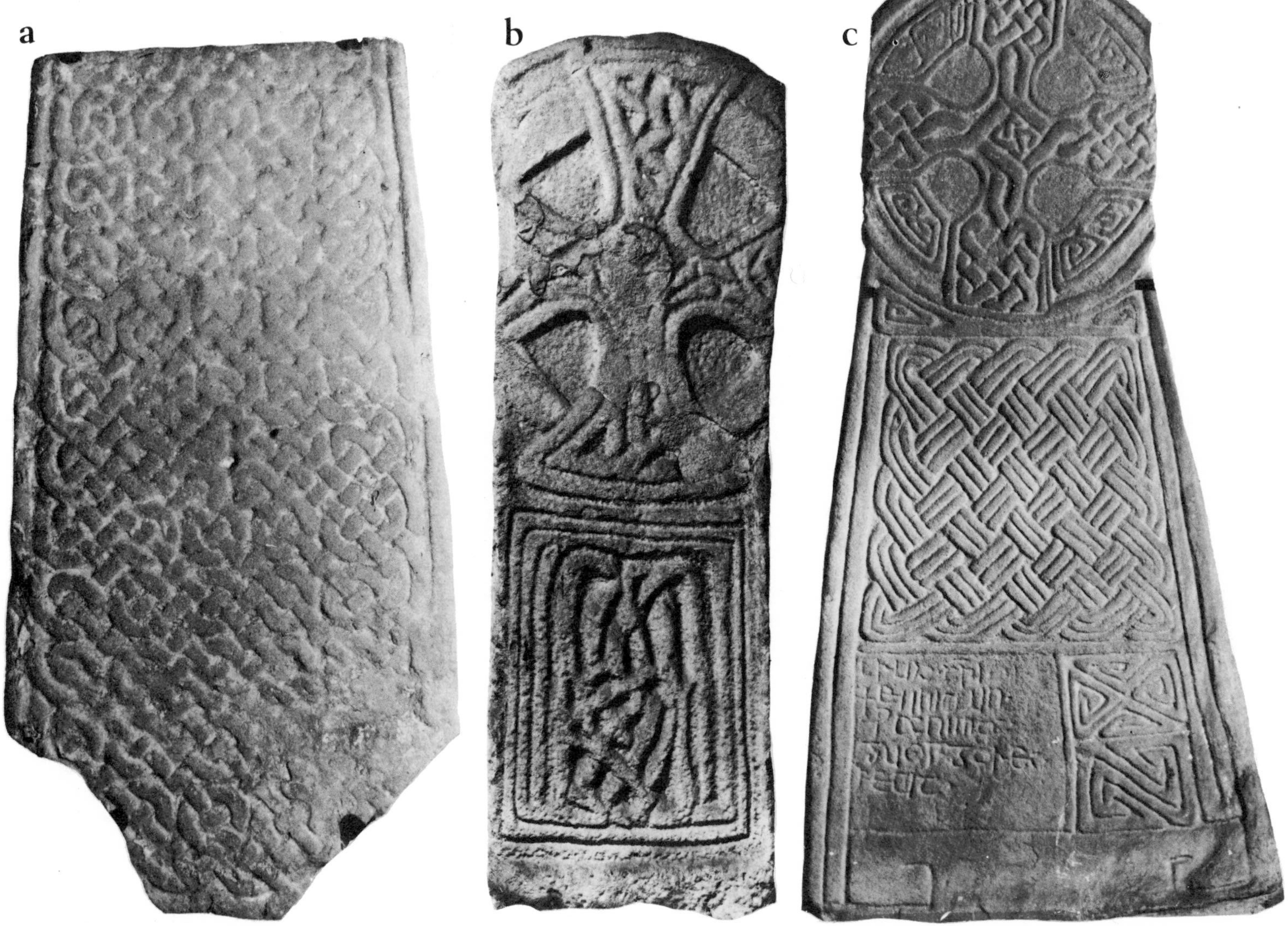

PLATE 7

'Disc-headed' slabs of Class D: *a.* Llangennith (905), 9th century; *b.* Margam (909), late 10th or 11th century; *c.* Margam, the 'Enniaun' stone (908), late 9th century. (Scale 1:10).

PLATE 8

Margam, the 'Conbelin' stone, **W**. side (907), late 9th or early 10th century. (Scale approximately 1:10).

PLATE 9

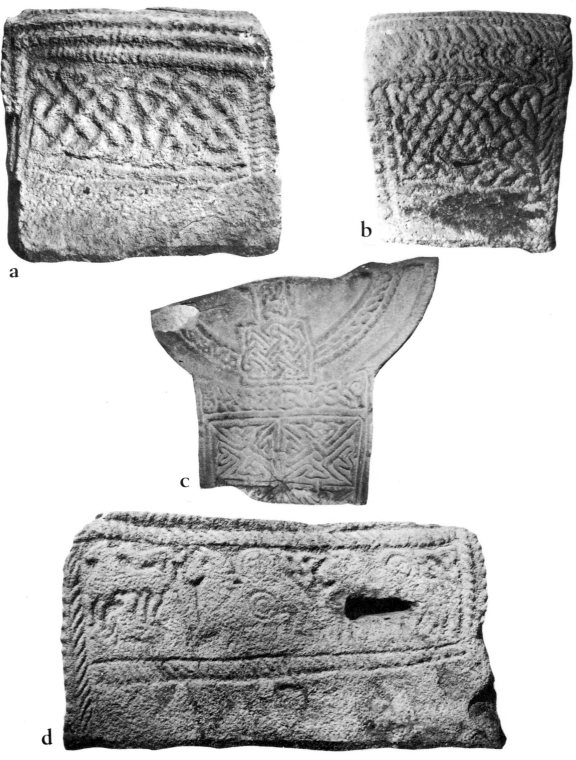

Margam, the 'Conbelin' stone (907): *a*. base, N. side; *b*. base, S. side; *c*. shaft, E. side; *d*. base, E. side; late 9th or early 10th century. (Scale approximately 1:10).

PLATE 10

Llantwit Major, the 'Houelt' stone (911): *left*, E. side; *right*, W. side; late 9th century. (Scale approximately 1:10).

PLATE 11

Llantwit Major, the 'Samson' stone (912): *left,* E. side; *right,* N. and W. sides; early 10th century. (Scale approximately 1:10.5).

PLATE 12

Inscriptions on 'disc-headed' slabs of Class D: *a*. Margam, the 'Grutne' stone (910), 10th century; *b*. Margam, the 'Enniaun' stone (908); *c*. Llantwit Major, the 'Samson' stone (912), E. side; *d*. ibid., W. side, lower inscription; *e*. ibid., W. side, upper inscription; *f*. Llantwit Major, the 'Houelt' stone (911).

PLATE 13

Llan-gan, 'disc-headed' slab (913): *left*, W. side; *right*, E. side; late 9th–early 10th century. (Scale approximately 1:10).

PLATE 14

'Panelled-cross' slabs of Class D: *a*. Port Talbot (914), late 9th or 10th century; *b*. Merthyr Mawr (917), 11th century; *c*. Pen-y-fai, Bridgend (922), 10th century; *d*. Tythegston (916), 11th century; *e*. Neath (915), late 9th or early 10th century; *f*. Ewenni (924), late 10th–11th century. (Scales *a, c* 1:12.5; *b*, 1:13; *d, f*, 1:10; *e*, 1:11).

PLATE 15

Slab-cross of Class D: Ogmore (926): *a.* side (i), *b.* side (iii), *c.* side (iv), 11th century. 'Panelled-cross' slabs of Class D: *d.* Eglwys Nynnid (921), probably 10th century; *e.* Cwm Gwenffrwd, Neath (923), 10th century. (Scales *a–c,* 1:11; *d, e,* 1:10).

PLATE 16

Margam, the 'Ilquici' stone (919): *left*, N. and W. sides; *right*, S. and E. sides; 10th–11th century. (Scale 1:11).

PLATE 17

'Panelled-cross' slabs of Class D: *a*. Margam, the 'Ilci' stone (920), S. side, late 10th–11th century; *b*. ibid., N. and W. sides; *c, d*. Merthyr Mawr, fragment of head (918), 11th century. (Scales *a, b*, 1:11.4; *c, d*. approximately 1:10).

PLATE 18

Slab-cross of Class D: Merthyr Mawr (927): *a.* N. side, *b.* W. and S. sides,   *c.* S. and E. sides, 11th century.   'Panelled-cross' slab of Class D: *d, e.* Llan-gan, broken slab (925), 11th century. (Scales *a–c* approximately 1:10;   *d, e* 1:13).

PLATE 19

Merthyr Mawr, slab-cross (928): *a*. E. side, *b*. W. side, *c*. N. arm-end, *d*. N. side, top, *e*. N. side, bottom, *f*. S. side, bottom; 11th century. (Scale *a, b* 1:14.3).

PLATE 20

Left: Standing slab of Class D: (Nash 902), probably 10th century. *Right:* Pillar-cross of Class E: Coychurch (934), originally 10th–early 11th century with later modification. (Scales *a* 1:13; *b* 1:14.24).

Llandough, pillar-cross (938): *left,* N. side; *centre,* E. side; *right,* S. side; late 10th–early 11th century. (Scale 1:14.5).

PLATE 21

PLATE 22

Pillar-crosses of Class E: *a*. Llandough (938), base, E. side; *b*. ibid., W. side; *c*. Llantwit Major (932), E. side, late 9th century; *d*. ibid., W. and S. sides; *e*. Coychurch (935), E. side, 10th–11th century; *f*. ibid., N. side. (Scale of *c* and *e* 1:12.5).

PLATE 23

Llantwit Major, pillar-cross (933): *left,* S. and E. sides; *right,* inscription; late 9th century. (Scale of *a* 1:12.5).

PLATE 24

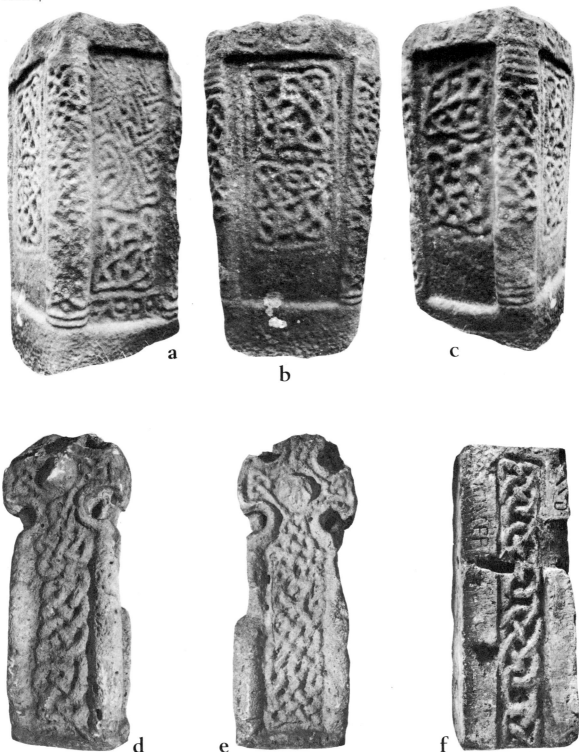

Pillar-crosses of Class E: *a*. 'Carreg Fedyddiol', Bridgend (936), S.E. side; *b*. ibid., S.W. side; *c*. ibid., N.W. side, late 10th–early 11th century; *d*. Llandaf (937), E. side; *e*. ibid., W. side, late 10th–early 11th century; *f*. Llancarfan (940), late 9th or 10th century. (Scales *a–c* 1:12.5, *d–f* 1:10).

Plate 25

Pillar-crosses of Class E: *a*. Llangyfelach, base (931), S. side; *b*. ibid., W. side; *c*. ibid., N. side; *d*. ibid., E. side, early 10th century; *e*. Coychurch, head of cross (934), 10th–early 11th century; *f, g*. Coety, fragment of cross-head (939), probably 11th century; *h*. St. George, fragment of cross-head (941), early 10th century. (Scale of *a–d* 1:12.5).

PLATE 26

Decorated stones of Class F: *a*. Llanrhidian, slab (951), 9th or 10th century; *b*. Llantwit Major, pillar (953), 10th or 11th century; *c*. Merthyr Mawr, fragment of slab (952), 11th or early 12th century; *d*. Ewenni, fragment of slab (955), 11th or early 12th century; *e*. Llantwit Major, fragment of pillar (954), 10th–11th century. (Scale 1:13, except *c–d* 1:8.5).

PLATE 27

Decorated stones of Class F: *a–c.* Llanrhidian, slab (951), details; *d.* Llyswyrny (956), 11th or 12th century. Pagan cult head: *e.* Port Talbot (991), 1st–4th centuries. (Scales *d* 1:8; *e* 1:6).

PLATE 28

Headstones and slabs of Class G: *a*. Merthyr Mawr (969), 11th–12th century; *b*. Ewenni (981), 10th–early 12th century; *c*. Merthyr Mawr (967), 11th–12th century; *d*. Ewenni (977), 11th–12th century; *e*. Newcastle, Bridgend (984), 11th–early 12th century; *f*. Newcastle, Bridgend (983), 11th–12th century; *g*, *h*. Merthyr Mawr (966), 12th century; *i*. Merthyr Mawr (965), early 12th century. (Scales *a–d*, *g–i* 1:10; *e*, *f* 1:12.5).

PLATE 29

Headstones and slabs of Class G: *a*. Laleston (972), 12th century; *b*. Baglan (961), 11th–12th century; *c*. Ewenni (976), 8th–10th century; *d*. Merthyr Mawr (964), 10th–12th century; *e*. Laleston (963), 11th or 12th century; *f*. Merthyr Mawr (968), early 12th century; *g*. Merthyr Mawr, socketed stone (987), 11th–12th century; *h*. Pyle (971), 11th–12th century. (Scale 1:10).

PLATE 30

Pagan cult site, Tarrendeusant (992): *left*, view of rock face; *right*, detail of carved faces.